Also by Roger Welsch:

CATHER'S KITCHENS: FOODWAYS IN
  LITERATURE AND LIFE
CATFISH AT THE PUMP: HUMOR AND THE
  FRONTIER
MISTER, YOU GOT YOURSELF A HORSE:
  TALES OF OLD-TIME HORSE TRADING
SHINGLING THE FOG AND OTHER PLAINS
  LIES
TREASURY OF NEBRASKA PIONEER
  FOLKLORE
OMAHA TRIBAL MYTHS AND TRICKSTER
  TALES

IT'S NOT THE END OF THE EARTH, BUT YOU CAN SEE IT FROM HERE

TALES OF THE GREAT PLAINS

Roger Welsch

FAWCETT BOOKS • NEW YORK

FOR ANTONIA

CONTENTS

ACKNOWLEDGMENTS

I owe an enormous debt of gratitude to my wife, not only for her unwavering support but also for her careful reading of my manuscript and for her helpful suggestions and criticism. I must also acknowledge the guidance and encouragement of my literary representative Freya Manston; she is a good friend as well as a valuable business associate.

INTRODUCTION

A FEW YEARS ago I walked away from about as cushy a life as you can imagine—full professor, with tenure, in the departments of English and Anthropology at the University of Nebraska, but the fact of the matter is, I came out here to the hinterland for an education.

I had owned this small farm we now live on (actually a useless piece of overgrazed sand waste) for fifteen years and used it mostly as a retreat, a place to do some fishing, some walking, some loafing. I came to love the land and its river so much that it became obvious to me that sooner or later I would have to figure out some way to live out here full-time. It's not so much that I hated the city and academic life as that I was drawn inexorably to this rural countryside.

But the land was the least of it. The real attraction of Centralia and Bleaker County is the people. I love the people.

I wonder if I should be reluctant to tell you all this; it may very well be that this is one of those little gems of truth that disappears once it is shared with too many people. You see, the people in the city and at the university think that they are simply the most marvelous folks in the world. They believe all too often that their conversations are witty and scintillating, they believe that oh, so much *happens* in the city (and by implication that *nothing* ever happens in a small town), they believe that they are in the midst of the cauldron from which comes the stew of culture.

Well, they're wrong. The bigger the city, the more they think that way and the further they are from the truth. In the floor of the Town Tavern here, there is a plaque reading "GEOGRAPHIC CENTER OF WESTERN CIVILIZATION." Visitors to town laugh because they think that's supposed to be a joke; I only smile, because I know it's not.

The American small town seethes with ideas and humor, with friendship and contention, with wit and warmth, with silliness and depravity, with calm and violence. The education I sought when I left the city for this farm has been far richer than I hoped.

My academic training and most of my teaching experience was in folklore, so I learned quite early in my intellectual history to appreciate, to appreciate *profoundly* the importance, the charm, the beauty, and the value of the typical. That's what folklore is. While the university art departments dwell on the exceptional and unique, the history departments focus on the significant and singular, the English departments examine the best, we in folklore are interested in what represents the typical, the ordinary, the everyday.

The ballet is not typical; the small-town wedding dance is. The events of a Harlequin romance or a soap opera are anything but everyday; the gossip and anecdotes told over the breakfast table in the café in Centralia are *precisely* everyday; they are indeed the very definition of "everyday." Is the everyday of less value or attraction than the exceptional? That has most certainly not been my experience. Nor, probably, yours. Virtually every homemade quilt you have ever seen, for example, is superior by many times to 90 percent of the art that currently insults the walls of the galleries. We have all at one time or another, perhaps on a regular basis, eaten roast beef, mash potatoes, and gravy in a humble kitchen that put to shame the finest gourmet meal we have ever enjoyed. Medical science still sorts through folk medicine for the truths it may yet have in its pharmacopoeia.

I, like so many writers of far greater skills, have come to appreciate the power of what seems at first blush to be some pretty ordinary folks doing some pretty ordinary things.

I write about America's Great Plains and the people of the Great Plains. I suppose I could have encountered and written about pretty much the same sort of people as Woodrow, Slick, and CeCe in another geography—Baltimore perhaps, the Ozarks, or Cannery Row. But the Great Plains is the geography I know and the geography I love, and the geography where I am—no small consideration after all.

There is a widespread perception that small-town life moves without color, without variety, without *interest*, but that certainly has not been my experience. My little town is like an extended family: there are my favorite "uncles," a mean cousin or two, some kin I rarely see and do not miss, and some I can never get enough of. It was in the city during my academic career that I complained about grinding sameness. The houses in my city neighborhood were worth about the same amount of money and so they were owned and occupied by very much the same sort of people. I worked in a university building surrounded by other English teachers. While there were minor differences in our interests—she studies eighteenth-century English novels, he writes poetry, and she knows more about Willa Cather than any other living human being—it was in the small town that I found the variety I love so much.

I was once interviewed by Dick Cavett on his television show and I told him that what attracted me about rural life is that when I sit down for coffee up at the Chew 'n' Chat Cafe in town, I converse with the banker, the town drunk, the most honest man in town, a carpenter, a farmer, and my best friend.

I smiled inwardly when I said that because I knew that the citizens of my little town who were watching that show knew what I was *really* saying. I was talking about my friend Eric. During the decade I've known him, he has been all those things. That private joke aside, the spirit of what I said on Cavett's show is the truth. On America's rural landscape associating only with those in your own image would be difficult because chances are you are one of a kind where there are so few images to begin with.

My long history as a teacher impels me to pass along to you the rich curriculum I have followed here in the country, away from the city. It's just too good to keep to myself.

That's why I wrote this book. The stories and the ideas I write about are good. That's not a matter of personal vanity, because the material is not really mine. I'm only passing along a folk literature that has been generated among and belongs ultimately to the people it is about. My only real concern and my real task is that I pass it along with something close to the same eloquence, narrative skill, character delineation, and cultural impact with which the stories came to me. I hope I can overcome my academic training and urban experience enough to imitate the consummate and inherent rhetorical skills I find on a daily basis among my new circle of rural, uneducated colleagues.

Some of the pieces in this collection are like short stories—narratives, with at least some hint of plot. Some are simply descriptions of characters I have encountered here on the Plains. Some of the pieces are essays, exploring ideas—again mostly ideas I have encountered during my tenure in the rural countryside. Some of the sections are humorous—not the kind that make you laugh but the sort that make you smile—and some are serious.

I realize that this is an unusual mixture: if you write a book, it's supposed to be a book of inspirational essays or a book of short stories. You're supposed to be consistently hilarious or purely serious. Otherwise, the reasoning seems to go, how can readers trust you? Can anyone take seriously a person who laughs? How can someone who is funny possibly say anything serious?

That's the way life is in America's rural landscape. Here you'll find that it is precisely the man or woman with the sharpest wit who is the best source for serious advice. It *is* the best storyteller who offers the most profound philosophical statements over morning coffee. Often it is the funniest that is also the most inspirational, the silliest experience that carries the most powerful lesson, the most trivial that strips away pretense and bares the starkest framework of wisdom.

I came here to the heart of America's rural landscape for an education, and I found it. In these pages I want to share with you what I have learned from Lunchbox, Woodrow, Slick, CeCe, and Goose. I want to share with you the perspectives I have found in the great spaces in the American Great Plains. Believe me, they are worth paying some attention to. For once, writing outside the academic confines that have characterized my previous work, I haven't had to concern myself with the classification of the materials before me. It doesn't matter in this case whether I am dealing with literature, oral history, folklore, local color, gossip, truth, or fiction. Here I have had the heady liberty of writing without worrying about what name to affix to what I am writing.

Moreover, that's really the way things happen in Bleaker County. In daily conversation, ideas are mixed with anecdotes and jokes, humor stands cheek-by-jowl with tragedy, business with nonsense, anger with love. Increasingly I see life here as these word-snapshots strung together in an ill-kept photo album. Sometimes there are three or four powerful images on one page of that album—several memorable vignettes I encounter in one day, even in one afternoon. And then there are many empty pages in this album, weeks when there is little of note.

The fabric of the rural community is not the empty spaces in the album, but rather the photographs wherever we find them scattered throughout the pages. During the quiet times in Bleaker County when it probably seems to the outsider that nothing is going on, there is for the people here a continuing appreciation for the last vignette, an anticipation of the next. Indeed, the echoes and resonances are often even more satisfying than the events themselves. I sometimes find myself more eager to hear Slick's or Woodrow's report of what went on in town last night than to make sure I am there when I know that something is coming up.

What's impressive, in my mind, is that every single event in this book really *did* happen. I didn't make this up, mostly because my imagination isn't that good. As a matter of fact, I don't think anyone's imagination is that good. I think everyone who writes "fiction," including Shakespeare, Steinbeck, and Walt Kelly, uses events they have witnessed, heard about, or been involved in themselves—that is to say, *non*fiction.

That's because nothing is more unlikely than reality. If the name Roger Welsch is remembered for anything, I suspect it will be immortalized in Welsch's law: "The function of the creative writer is to mitigate reality so that it becomes believable." That's all I've done in these pages. I have tried to mellow and dilute the preposterousness of reality to a point where you can believe it. You wouldn't believe the truth, believe me.

But the truth is here. The events of these tales did not happen precisely as I have described them, it's true; there are no such people, precisely, as CeCe, Slick, Woodrow, or Lunchbox, I confess. I have combined and collated the people, places, and events of Bleaker County to focus events, to compact narrative, to protect the innocent—and the guilty. In some characters I have combined four or five people, sometimes many more, into one character.

No, the inventions and characters in these pages are not precisely factual; they are *truer* than factual. There is no CeCe, no Slick, no Woodrow, no Lunchbox, and yet I hope you will recognize them because they are not only people I have known, they are people you have known. In fact, if you are at all like me, they are people you have *been*.

About once a week my daughter Antonia comes running into the house saying, "Dad, guess what I learned in school today!" It is not enough for her to have stored away new gems of information; she wants me to feel the same excitement and surprise that she feels in her discovery. That's what's exciting about learning.

And that's what this book is about. This is a celebration of the rural education of Roger Welsch. "Hey, you guys, guess what I learned up in town today!"

HISTORY

I NEVER LIKED history. I was one of those guys who avoided history classes at every step during junior high school, high school, and college. All those important names and important dates taught in conventional history classes meant nothing to me and my life. I guess I've always agreed with a statement attributed to Harry Truman: "The problem with history is that it's just one damned thing after another."

And so I found folklore—or maybe folklore found me. Folklore, the common songs and common stories of the common people. And I found that there is also a folk history, the common lives of the common people and their common vision of how the course of human events runs through time.

I can remember almost precisely the moment I encountered that idea. I was teaching at Dana College, a small school, in Blair, a small town in eastern Nebraska. I was collecting Danish folk tales for my folklore research and I visited a nice old Danish lady in the Good Shepherd Home there in Blair. Before she would tell me the folk tales she knew from the Old Country, she wanted to tell me a little about her life and how she came to be in America. She told me a story I've never forgotten, a story that changed my perception of what history is.

She said she grew up to be a young woman in Copenhagen, Denmark, before the turn of the century. She said that she lived a life very much like a young single woman lives in America today. I preface her statement with "she said" because the fact of the matter is, she led a life *nicer* than most young single women in America today.

She said that she had a very nice apartment and in the morning her landlady would waken her by knocking at her door, leaving a cup of coffee and the morning paper outside her door so she could scan the headlines and enjoy a cup of coffee as she prepared for the day.

Not many landladies will do *that* for you today!

She would dress and go downstairs where her landlady had prepared a nice breakfast. She stepped outside and caught the trolley that took her to the department store where she sold linen goods. After work she would catch a trolley home and share a pleasant supper with her landlady. Then they might read a good book or perhaps go to the theater and after a pleasant day she would go to bed in a warm, clean, dry bed.

One day her brother came by, excited about an advertisement in the Copenhagen newspaper in which two brothers from Ord, Nebraska, were advertising for a hired hand and a housekeeper for their ranch in Nebraska's Sandhills, an enormous region that wasn't even opened for homesteading until 1904. He thought it would be a great adventure to come to America, and to Nebraska, and to the frontier. It didn't take much, she admitted to me that day, for him to convince her too.

They answered the ad and the brothers sent them the money to sail across the ocean and take the train to Grand Island, where the brothers met them in a flatbed farm wagon. They started off up the North Loup valley toward Ord, at the edge of the Nebraska Sandhills, the largest sand-dune area in the Western Hemisphere, the largest sand-dune area in this half of the world. She said she could see at once the terrible mistake they had made, leaving their sophisticated life in Copenhagen for this desolate hell at the rim of the earth.

She told me that the brothers finally stopped the wagon and announced, "Well, here we are." She said there was nothing. Nothing in any direction. Not a tree, not a house, not a fence post, nothing. Nothing but grass and sand and hills and sky.

"Where is this house that I'm supposed to be house-keeper in?" she asked, and the brothers pointed down; their "house," it turned out, was a cave dug back into the hill under that wagon. She told me that she wept for months at the prospect of keeping house in a dirt cave.

"After all," she smiled at me, "how do you know where the dirt ends and the house begins?"

And then she began to cry. As I watched her tears and waited helplessly, she tried to pull herself together. I thought to myself, "This is what history is all about. History has nothing to do with generals and presidents, governors and senators. They are the dullest, most ineffectual people on the face of the earth. This woman, *she* is what moves mankind and shapes destiny. This is what history is about, agonies so profound that even after seventy-five years they reduce this strong person to sobs as she remembers what it was like to be that young woman so far from home, so far from anywhere. In her pain she represents the pain experienced by hundreds of thousands of other women on the frontier."

After a few moments the old lady regained her composure and apologized. I was so moved by the power of her story I couldn't even find the words to tell her that apologies were unnecessary.

Then she smiled, leaned forward, and told me that she had eventually had her revenge: she married one of those brothers and *never let him forget for a single moment what he had taken her away from!*

While I was still laughing at her gentle revenge, she added, "And when he died, I married the *other* brother and *never let him forget for a moment what* he *took me away from!*"

Her laughter had us both laughing on that occasion, as perhaps it has you laughing now, and I realized that the West was won not with a gun or with barbed wire, but with laughter, the remarkable capacity of a lady like this to face a hell we cannot imagine today, a pain that could bring her to tears generations later, and through all this she could *laugh.*

Laugh. Laugh not at another religion, or race, or ethnic group, or sex, but at herself. I don't know if it was the laughers on the frontier who survived or the survivors of the frontier who laughed, but there is a correlation there that we cannot, and should not, deny for a moment.

UNCLE VIC'S MULE

WHENEVER UNCLE VIC pushed back his chair from the card table in the Town Tavern, everyone used to run for the door. This explosive reaction always surprised tourists. It would happen just like that: Vic would push back his chair and say something like "Whelp," and suddenly everyone was throwing on coats and hats and gloves as if the fire siren had gone off. Vic never seemed to notice or to change his own pace but all around him there was this flurry of activity and then all these people trying to get out the tavern door all at once.

Out in the street five or six car engines would spring into full power and cars would be shuffling from one side of the main street to the other in a ballet, looking like a bunch of Shriners driving those little cars in the Fourth of July parade.

See, Vic had this great big old Buick, and what he would do when he was leaving for home, just a couple of blocks from the main street, was to start the car, get the engine moving at a pretty good speed, pop the clutch, and back up until he hit something. Then he would go forward all the way home. He didn't very often hit anything going forward, which always surprised me, since he had to look out through the steering wheel over that great expanse of sheet metal in front of him, but he *always* hit something when he was going backward because he never stopped going backward until he did hit something.

Well, everyone hoped it wouldn't be his car that signaled the end of Vic's backward movement. Even if you only drove a junker, you were concerned because that monstrous Buick could reduce it to scrap metal. Vic once drove right over the top of six bicycles and never so much as slowed down even though two of the bikes were jammed up underneath that Buick and the next day Herb had to use a cutting torch to get them free of the automobile.

All of that made good conversation, but Vic's driving finally got so bad it was dangerous. He scolded Hat for almost three weeks after they ran into each other with their cars at the highway intersection. "You damned fool," Vic shouted in Hat's face, "why did you run into me like that?"

"Well, you old idiot, you didn't even slow down for that stop sign," Hat responded, smiling. He smiled, I think, because it was one of the two or three accidents he had ever participated in that wasn't a result of his being drunk. Hat once got two drunk-driving tickets in one day, setting a state record that has never been broken. "I thought you'd at least slow down."

"Hat, how long have you known me?"

"Well, probably forty years, Vic."

"And haven't I left the tavern and gone through that

intersection at precisely nine-thirty p and goddamn m every day of my life?"

"Well, I suppose so, but . . ."

"And have you ever seen me stop at that stop sign, Hat?"

"Well, no, Vic, but . . ."

"Then, you damned fool, what made you think I was going to stop *this* time?"

Hat didn't have an answer for that, and neither did the rest of us, but eventually the sheriff did. He finally asked the State Patrol to pull Old Vic's driver's license, and they did. The argument went that Uncle Vic was too old to drive, that he had become a danger to the community, and, most convincing of all, a real threat to his own safety and life. He was just too old, too blind, too deaf, too weak, and too stubborn to drive anymore, everyone pretty much agreed.

Except of course for Uncle Vic. He and Em lived about three blocks away from the tavern, and he could have walked over there for his daily card game with no trouble at all. In fact, the exercise probably would have done him some good, everyone agreed, but precisely because everyone agreed, Vic insisted on driving.

For a while after he lost his license to drive the Buick, he drove his 1937 Allis-Chalmers tractor, but then one day the crank kicked back and broke his wrist so Em sold the tractor to Slick for "parts." Vic warned Slick that if he so much as loosened a lug nut on that tractor he would tell everyone in town, especially Connie, about the time he got so drunk at a volunteer Fire Department meeting that one of the CPR instructors, a nurse from Rising City, had to take him out and help him take a leak. Slick said he wasn't sure Vic would ever tell that story to a woman anyway, or if he did whether Connie would believe it, or even if she did believe it that it would make any difference, since she seemed to think he was sleeping with every woman in town anyway, but I did notice that he never so much as loosened a lug nut on that Allis.

Anyway, next Vic took to driving his riding lawn mower to the tavern, but then one night when it was cloudy and there wasn't much of a moon he drove over Em's deaf cat while he was still in the garage. The only thing that bothered Vic about the accident, he insisted, was cleaning out the canvas bag that catches the grass clippings—or in this case cat clippings, but Em took it all a good deal more seriously, just as she always seemed to take everything a good deal more seriously than Uncle Vic.

Well, it got to be a bit of a game over at the tavern to see how Vic was going to travel those three blocks from his house to the tavern next. When the Buick had been sold, the Allis-Chalmers given away, and the lawn mower locked up in the garden shed, there didn't seem to be much left for Vic except walking.

Now, no one would think it at all unreasonable for Uncle Vic to ask Woodrow and Lunchbox for a ride over to the Thursday evening community auction in Rising City, and so no one did. But if anyone had considered for a moment the time that Woodrow and Lunchbox took me over there, fed me beers, and then prodded me and encouraged me into buying sixty-seven baby ducks, they might have also wondered about the wisdom of letting Uncle Vic go to that sale with Woodrow and Lunchbox and no responsible supervision.

Any normal-thinking person might have raised some objection when Uncle Vic started bidding on the grizzled white mule toward the end of the evening, but that is not the style of Woodrow and Lunchbox. Far from exercising any sort of responsibility on their own part, they did whatever they could to relieve Uncle Vic of whatever self-control he might have had had he been enjoying more favorable company.

"You got the bid now, Vic," they goaded. "Don't let that Rising City square-head take that mule away from you now, Vic. Keep bidding, Vic. Show 'em how, Vic. Don't let 'em push you around," and when the auctioneer hammered a "Sold!" Vic had bought that mule for a price that even brought a smile to the mule's face.

Normal people might have wondered how they were going to get that mule led to the truck, yet home, but not Woodrow and Lunchbox. They "helped" Uncle Vic buy a saddle, reins, and a kiddie carriage, all for only $422. "We'll hitch him to the carriage, throw the saddle and tack into the carriage, and then Vic can sit on top of all the stuff and drive him home. It's only a few miles," reasoned Woodrow, while Lunchbox smiled and nodded in agreement.

To show you just how wrong a fellow can be, I thought that an eight-mile ride at night on gravel roads in a kiddie cart behind that mule would kill Uncle Vic, but I was wrong. The carriage had been brought up to the mule, but not a single piece of harness had touched his quivering hide before he unleashed four kicks with both of his spring-loaded rear hoofs that reduced that carriage to a pile of dusty wood and antique hardware.

And you would think that any reasoning human being would then just walk away from the kind of potential disaster that obviously headstrong mule represented. I've done that. You just pretend that whatever you've bought and paid for isn't yours, leave it lying right where it is, and the auctioneer will just sell it again, if he can find someone about as dumb as you.

Not Vic. He actually smiled at the pile of wire, scrap metal, and kindling that had been his kiddie carriage. Believe it or not, even before the dust settled, Vic liked this mule even more because of what he had just done. Vic liked the way all of us bystanders stepped back about ten yards from that mule because Vic had seen us do the same thing with him. Vic and that mule had, as the phrase goes these days, begun "to bond." Not a half-hour after they met, they were as close as kin.

Woodrow called Lloyd, who was looking for a reason to get out of the house and away from LaVerne for a while anyway, and he came over to Rising City with his stock trailer. The mule was no dummy and could see that the trailer was not something that would be as easily reduced to its elements as the kiddie carriage was, so he just stepped up into that wagon as if there was nothing in this world he would rather have done than cooperate with his new friends and owner.

Woodrow, Lloyd, and Lunchbox got the trailer to Centralia in fine condition, helped Vic get the mule into the old shed behind Vic and Em's place, taking great care not to wake Em up. They had the mule in the shed when the yard light came on and suddenly Woodrow, Lloyd, and Lunchbox remembered that they had lots of things to do at home, and they jumped in their trucks and took off, leaving it up to Vic to explain to Em just what the hell was going on with this mule and saddle and tack and the three cardboard boxes of carriage hardware.

It was several days before any of us saw Uncle Vic again. But when we did, it was a moment of glory. "Sweet

Jesus," Slick exploded from behind the bar, "will you look at that?!" and we did, and there was Uncle Vic riding into town on that mule. We all went out onto the street to watch this marvel, and it was worth the effort. The mule was walking along just as if he was proud of being a mule. Vic had soaped up that saddle until it looked new. The mule was brushed and curried up nice. All in all, there was not a soul who would have argued that Uncle Vic's arrival was anything but a triumph.

We helped Vic tie the mule to the Allis out in back of the tavern, and Vic played cards that night with a renewed enthusiasm. What had seemed to be an impossible situation now seemed to have been resolved more easily than any of us could have guessed.

At nine thirty p and goddamn m, as Vic put it, he folded his cards, smiled, finished his orange juice, and said, "Well, I guess Silver and I will be heading home."

Silver. He had named the mule "Silver." We all went to the back door of the tavern to wave Vic and Silver goodby. Vic untied the reins, put his left foot in the stirrup, and prepared to swing his right leg up into the saddle. But the mule took a couple steps while Vic hopped along beside him, his left foot in the stirrup and his right foot still on the ground. "Hold still, you miserable oat-burner," Vic said. "Whoa, Silver, whoa!" He waved to us sort of, still hanging on to the saddle horn and reins, still hopping alongside Silver, as they went out of sight around the corner of the tavern.

"Hold still, you obnoxious beast," we heard Vic yell, and then, "See you guys in the morning," and we all laughed our farewells and went inside to congratulate ourselves on how well things seemed to work in our little town of Centralia.

We buried Vic Monday. Herb said he was just closing up the service station when Uncle Vic came by, waving and laughing and hopping alongside that mule, still trying to get his right leg over the saddle. "See you tomorrow," Herb said Vic yelled to him.

Herb said that Vic then hollered something like, "Silver, you no-good, lop-eared fool, whoa, will you? *Whoa.*"

Hat said that Vic went by his place north of town about nine-forty, still hopping, still trying to get up into the saddle.

"Need some help, Vic?" Hat said he hollered.

"What the hell kind of help would you be with a mule if you can't even drive a car?" Vic yelled, and then something like, "Silver, whoa, you miserable, spavined devil."

The sheriff followed the trail down the gravel the next day—a set of mule tracks and about ten thousand right shoe prints alongside, all the way to the Rising City community auction barn. It was there they found the mule helping himself to a pickup load of corn someone had brought for the sale, and Uncle Vic, lying not far away, dead but looking as if he could sit up and cuss any time.

Silver was sold again at the auction house the next Thursday to a city fellow looking for a gentle mount for his wife, who had refused him a divorce only the week before. He said he'd read about Uncle Vic's unusual death and his faithful mule, Silver, in the Omaha newspaper.

FINGERWAVES

ALL AMERICANS BELIEVE in pretty much the same sort of things, but we are different enough from region to region that occasionally a story in the news means very different things to us, depending on our regional experiences. In the Midwest there are some of us who have a hard time understanding the recent shootings on the freeways around Los Angeles and other urban areas of the United States.

I've been wondering, for example, where the folks doing the shooting were going that they were in such a hurry. Now, I can imagine shooting at someone in my way while I was trying to get *out* of Los Angeles, but I cannot for the life of me imagine plugging someone slowing me down while going *into* Los Angeles. It just doesn't strike me as being the sort of place I'd kill to get into.

It's not as if we are without traffic troubles in Centralia. The last time I went to an American Legion fish fry up in town, I had to park clear over by the Baptist Church, nearly a block away. Sometimes when Bob Gans pulls a load of hay through town, some of it falls off and you have to drive around it until Ralph Barker's boy Bernard salvages it for his rabbits. Most mornings Carl Pete parks his pickup truck halfway onto the sidewalk in front of Slick's tavern; nobody knows exactly why.

From my own experience I know that the rush hour in Indianapolis is not the rush hour in New York. I understand that the rush hour in Yankton, South Dakota, is not the rush hour in Indianapolis. But the rush hour in Centralia is not even the rush hour in Yankton. The only rush hour in Centralia is Sunday morning, right after the Lutheran Church lets out.

In Centralia, if you are driving down Main Street and you meet someone you want to talk to, you just stop window to window and talk, right there in the middle of Main Street. No one will shoot you, even though it is standard practice to carry hunting rifles and shotguns in vehicles on a day-to-day basis. You see, in the Midwest we consider it impolite to honk and downright rude to shoot. After all, everyone can see you're busy talking, so they just turn a block early and go to the next street over, or work their way around you if there's room, or stop and join in the conversation.

When I leave the interstate highway that crosses Nebraska I automatically move my hands from the sides of the steering wheel to a position where at least one of my hands, usually the right, is at the top of the steering wheel, where it can be seen by oncoming drivers.

As if by the rules in some unwritten book of driving etiquette, most rural drivers in the western reaches of the Midwest raise a finger of greeting to other drivers, just as was the habit when America's farmers met each other while driving their teams and wagons to and from town. It was considered the courteous thing to do to acknowledge other drivers, and that custom prevails still today, even at fifty-five miles per hour.

Everyone has his or her own style of fingerwave—one finger, two fingers, all five, two hands, twitch, waggle, nod, poke, even vigorous waves of the whole hand. My favorite waver was a pickup driver I once encountered who raised his right index finger from the steering wheel, drew a small circle clockwise with its tip, cocked the finger back, and then jabbed an imaginary hole in the middle of his imaginary target, pointing right at me as I whirled by at an aggregate speed of over one hundred miles an hour. I have never had the presence of mind to get all that in before the other car has gone past, but my admiration for that driver's cool, perfectly timed salute has never faded.

I was once driving through Nebraska's Sandhills and I met a car that struck me as being peculiar. Something about the car was distinctive. I commented to that effect to my companion, and he said that something about the car had struck him as unusual too. We talked about it for a few minutes, and then we figured out what it was that was strange about the vehicle: It was the first one we had seen in two hours of travel.

You just don't shoot at folks when they're the only ones you've seen in two hours. You wave.

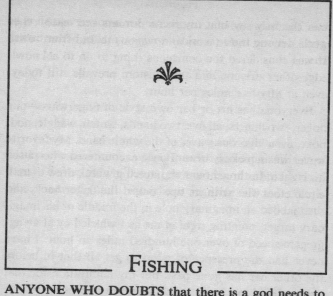

FISHING

ANYONE WHO DOUBTS that there is a god needs to go fishing. Anyone who doubts that god has a sense of humor needs to go fishing with a child. The first story I'm going to tell you is probably the single most clichéd narrative in the *world*. You will know the outcome the moment you start reading it. What makes the tale so blasted annoying is that it is also invariably and absolutely true.

It has been twenty years since I have done much fishing, but I love to catch fish because I love to eat fish. I used to fish for trout in Colorado with Velveeta cheese for bait. As much fun as catching the fish was the look of horror on the faces of the fly fishermen who saw me in action. One guy actually threw up.

In recent years I have run setlines along the beautiful Oak River where it runs along the southern edge of my farm, and I have come to believe that one of the Plains' most underrated natural resources is its superb catfish. I can honestly say that my recipe for smoked catfish is so good, no one in the world—*no one*—makes better catfish than I do.

Anyway, Good Ol' Woodrow and his nephew Paul recently took me out to their secret catfish hole. I was blindfolded as if I were a Beirut kidnap victim, driven in circles for about two hours with the radio to full volume so I couldn't identify cow moos or sheep baas, and we wound up at this incredibly beautiful pond somewhere in central Nebraska. In three hours we hauled in nine catfish of such a size that the stringer was more than one man could carry.

So now I have catfish fever in a big way, and so does Antonia, my four-year-old daughter. She talked her Po-po into giving her a fancy fishing rod and reel and she has been agitating to go fishing. Last Monday was a gorgeous day so I said to Antonia, "Let's go over to Dwaine Dempster's pond and see if we can catch a carp or two."

It was her first fishing trip and she was pretty excited, mostly because she didn't have the foggiest notion what fishing involved. Besides, she liked sorting through my fishing box, lining up shiny hooks, washing the bobbers, that sort of thing.

When we reached Dempster's pond I baited the lines, threw them out, and we sat there in Nebraska's glorious spring sun a few hours, catching only one fish, a nice, *big* carp, which is right now smoking in our smokehouse.

I won't bother you with the details of who caught the fish, but I can say that it was the member of the team who threw sticks in the water, fell into cow pies, dropped a can of pop down the bank and into the pond, got a hook caught in her jeans, fed most of a Braunschweiger sandwich to some minnows, caught a frog for her kindergarten science class and then forgot it in the glove compartment of my car where I found it a couple weeks later, and sat in the car and whined, "Daddy, I'm bored. I want to go home. Is it noon yet? Dad, I have to go number two. Is it time yet? I'm hungry. Dad . . . ?"

The fisherman who knew what he was doing, the *serious* angler, the one who paid attention to his lines, and sat praying quietly and earnestly to Neptune, the god of the fishes, caught nothing, *nada, nichts, rien.* Not so much as a bite.

See? There is a god. And that god has a sense of humor, maybe even a cruel sense of humor when it comes to fishing and kids. No, wait a minute. I don't really believe that, not the part about kids. The gods are cruel to *serious* fishermen, kids or not.

My thoughts go back to two years ago when I was cutting wood—or *making* wood, as they say around here, and I did something hopelessly stupid. I'll admit that the circumstances of this tale are of my own making, but I think I had help. No one is this dumb on his own.

I was pruning and cutting down some scruffy elms up at the top of our place and hauling the wood in a trailer behind the tractor. I'd haul the wood down to a place in the bottom where I could then cut it to fireplace length at my leisure. While I was cutting and hauling, I was indulging in some pleasure—eating my cake and enjoying it too—by running some setlines along the river down under the bridge.

I would cut a load of wood, dump it in the bottomland, make a run out to the river, check and rebait my lines (I almost never have to worry about fish being on my lines—just lucky, I guess), cut some more wood, haul, dump, check lines, rebait, and so on. It was pleasant, working and having a little fun at the same time. Running the setlines was a nice, cool break from cutting wood; cutting wood filled the empty half-hour or so between checking lines.

Somewhere along the course of the morning I noticed some strange tire tracks over my own. Someone had been down to the river since my last trip, and they had driven right along my lines. That gave me some concern, but I didn't see any damage, so I assumed it was just a friend looking for me, maybe.

On my next trip, however, I found the same thing: Again, someone had been down the road to the river since I made the last round of my lines. So I moved my woodcutting operation and started cutting some downed timber closer to the road where I could keep an eye on the road down to the river, so I could perhaps spot who was visiting my fishing lines.

On my next trip, I could see that this same someone— by now I recognized the tracks of the large, badly worn tires—had sneaked past me and again followed the path to my lines.

There was still no sign of tampering or emptying my hooks, but I was beginning to get real huffy about these shenanigans. I looked more closely at the tire tracks. I could see that it was a pickup truck that had been running my lines for me. That the tires were large and worn suggested to me that the truck too might be big and worn.

I sat on my tractor and contemplated the tracks and thought of the vehicles I knew from the area. Well, there are a lot of big, old pickup trucks around here, with worn tires. Worn tires are almost an inherent part of trucks around here—all-terrain tires worn almost to the threads. Sort of like the tires I had on my trailer. The one I was using to haul wood. Behind my tractor. The battered old trailer I bought from Ralph Barker. The trailer made out of an old pickup truck rear end.

At that point I decided to call it a day. Either the day was too long, or maybe I was getting too old, but it was obvious that I had no business running loose on the roads. So I went up to the Town Tavern. When I told Slick about this elegant stupidity, he said that lots of people make mistakes like that.

"But," he added, "most of them are smart enough not to tell anyone about it."

You would think that with experiences like that I would find a sport that didn't make such demands on my intellect or luck—dynamite tossing, maybe. Or grizzly bear wrestling. But I still like to fish. I love fish, but more important than that, I love fishing. There's a big difference there, and an important one. Fishing is not simply an activity. It's not a sport at all; fishing is not competitive. People who think about fishing in terms of outdoing someone else probably make love the same way. You make love best when you do it because it is a joy and a symbol, not when you do it to demonstrate to someone else that you can catch bigger ones.

Fishing has nothing to do with catching big fish, or even little fish for that matter. If there were any sense at all to our tax system, fishing equipment would be deductible on our income tax returns under "Medical expenses, therapeutic."

You think that's crazy? Wait until you hear this one: Our international relations are a shambles, and fishing may be the answer to the problem. For one thing, it's time we took foreign policy out of the hands of amateurs and put some real professionals on the job.

The State Department? The folks over there can't even calm the bureaucratic wars in their own hallways. The Pentagon? Get serious! Diplomats? They're appointed to posts according to the size of their campaign contributions to Washington Winners, which means they aren't even up to managing their own checkbooks, let alone international affairs.

My idea of a *professional* diplomat is Slick, my pal who owns the Town Tavern. He sorts out family disagreements every day. I've seen Slick step between husband and wife in full snarl, and that sort of confrontation makes the Contras and Sandinistas look about as dangerous as a Sunday school picnic. To him it's all in the day's work.

Slick tells guys three times his size that if they don't shape up *right now*, they won't be able to play pool in his bar for a full month. After a scolding from Slick, three-hundred-pound beef luggers behave as if they would be right at home at a Miss Manners' tea party.

Slick tells little kids to sit down and be quiet or get out, and then he tells the kids' mothers to get control of their little hellions or quit having them. Slick is one tough guy. He weighs maybe 110 pounds and smokes six packs of cigarettes a day.

And yet Slick could parachute into Iran or Lebanon, tell the crazies in charge that they'll have to act right or they can forget about playing pool in the Persian Gulf until sometime after the Fourth of July, and they would turn into suitable hosts for a children's television show.

Or how about my pal Luke Bigelow? He once had five girlfriends at the same time and survived. I've seen him successfully entertain two women in the same bar at the same time, and they never so much as suspected they weren't his first and only love. Luke could handle the entire Lebanese debacle between breakfast and coffee break and show no strain whatsoever from the effort. Then, when the dust cleared, the Shiites, Christians, Israelis, and PLO would all think they are the only ones Luke loves.

Woodrow is our plumber and he has taught me a lot about life, but what I admire most about him is that he goes goose hunting without asking his wife for permission. He just grabs his twelve-gauge shotgun, a handful of cartridges, and goes. The man has nerves of steel, and he's the sort of person I would like to see holding America's hand at international poker tables. Can you imagine what a negotiator with cold, steel nerves like that would do to the Russians in our next arms deal?

As you can tell, I spent some time thinking about this problem and its obvious solutions. It all seemed so simple. Perhaps too simple. So I decided to turn to an expert consultant. I decided to ask an expert what he would do with the Persian Gulf mess: I asked my pal Mick—a bricklayer and member of Centralia's leading think tank—what he would do about the disintegrating international situation if he were in charge.

"It's obvious," Mick said without hesitation (obviously, he had thought about the problem too), "that the Iranians have a lot of agitation in their minds. They get a little unhappy and right away they send boats out into the Gulf to lay mines and sink Norwegian tankers, when not one of those Iranian agents of Allah has even met a Norwegian."

Mick explained, "Those boys aren't mad at Norwegians, they're just mad. They outlaw books they want their folks to be mad at, when what they should do is encourage them to read the books so they would *really* get mad."

"Well, I guess that's the situation all right, but what would you do about it?" I asked.

"The solution is simple," Mick said. "The Iranians have boats, right?"

"Right," I said.

"And they control the Persian Gulf, right?"

"Right."

"Panama is only a couple hundred miles wide and fronts on both the Atlantic and the Pacific Oceans."

"Right," I nodded.

"What the Grenadians had the most of was beaches and water, right?"

"Right."

"All those folks need," Mick said, getting deadly serious, "is fishing poles. They don't need guns, and they don't need foreign aid, they don't need missiles, they don't need advisers, they don't need Ollie North, and they don't need our fleet. What they need is fishing rods. Most of the tense situations all over the world could be laid to rest if we would just send over to every hot spot, just as soon as it pops up, a couple of boatloads of fishing poles and maybe a ton and a half of bobbers and bass plugs.

"There's nothing that puts a man's mind more at ease," Mick continued, "than an afternoon watching a bobber or pulling a plug through a good bass hole. Maybe they don't have night crawlers, Rog, but you *know* they got bait. There's not a country in the world so poor that it don't have bait.

"No Iranian is going to waste boat time laying mines if he suspects for a minute that the fish are biting. Ten thousand fishing poles and three weeks and those Iranians will be ready to trade us crude oil for stink bait, Silkworm missiles for night crawlers, death lines for setlines. The Hizbullah will be replaced by The Izaak Walton League.

"No one wants to take over a country when the fish are biting. It's a natural rule just as surely as gravity. There's no need to share the wealth if you got a couple six-pound catfish on your catch line. Even crime, Rog. It isn't 'As the twig is bent, the tree will grow' nearly as much as 'When the bobber bobs, the kid shapes up.'"

Mick turned back to his work, and I sure didn't want to slow him down anymore because I wanted the chimney done before the snow flew, but I guess he'd made his point. And he's right, of course. It's not that George Shultz, Alexander Haig, Ron Reagan, George Bush, Jim Baker, most of the Senate, a couple dozen governors, and damn near everyone in the United Nations are evil or dense.

They just lack the sort of equipment that would equip them to deal with problems of the world. They just don't have the appropriate tools of diplomacy and governance, and that's not their fault.

All they need is some stout line, a couple sharp hooks, a little bait, and more time on the right end of a fishing pole.

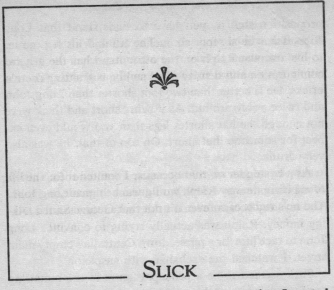

SLICK

SLICK WAS ONE of the first people I met when I started spending weekends at my river cabin outside of Centralia. I have always liked his sense of humor and his ability to see the life of Centralians as worthy of observation. We disagree about politics, but we share a lot of feelings about the world in general.

I think I first saw him in action the time I was up in town at the tavern for a few beers one Saturday night—this was long before Slick bought the place. He and Ralph Barker, a local ne'er-do-well, were drinking hard those days, and they were laying it on good that night. Slick has always described Ralph as "an open five-gallon bucket of gasoline sitting next to a campfire." If there is any potential whatsoever for agitation, you can count on Ralph to go at it with grand enthusiasm.

On this occasion Ralph was doing his best to goad Long John into a foot race. To understand how ridiculous a proposition that is, you have to understand that Long John is maybe six foot six inches tall and his legs go up to his armpits. Ralph on the other hand has the general configuration and density of a bowling ball sitting on two bricks. He is better than two foot shorter than Long John and twice as big around. As if being short and thick were not enough, he has shorter legs than you would even expect for someone that short. On top of that, he was also very drunk.

As a bystander on that occasion I could not for the life of me imagine why Ralph would want to race Long John. The mystery became even murkier when they started talking money. Ralph was actually trying to convince Long John to race him for a purse, down Centralia's empty main street. I watched the exchange with suspicion.

Slick seemed to be a principal figure in the mounting tension, doing what he could to encourage Long John: "Jeez, L. J., are you really afraid to race that short little toad? Why, a horse like you should be able to go three times around the block before he manages to get that belly of his moved off of dead center. This is your chance to make a bundle of easy money. Take Ralph's twenty and add another eighty to it. I can't imagine how you could pick up a hundred dollars any easier. And of all people to let shove you around—Ralph Barker, the town loudmouth."

Slick went on like a sideshow barker for a while, and then Ralph took over the hustling for a while: "Long John, you big cream puff, I think you *are* afraid to race me. You're nothing but a big phony. Would it help if I give you five or six feet head start?" That line got a laugh out of the crowd in the bar; Long John's face reddened, and he could see that it was not going to be easy for him to avoid a foot race with Ralph without the word going out all over Bleaker County by the next morning that Long John Fiala had been intimidated out of a race with Ralph Barker.

While Ralph continued to challenge Long John's ego, Slick started working the crowd. "Anyone else want to get in on this easy action? I'll take even bets on either thoroughbred. Take your choice—Fat Ralph or Long John. How much of the action do you want?" Tens and twenties started to pile upon the bar, and to no one's surprise, every single dollar was put on Long John's nose. It looked to me as if Slick and Ralph were about to lose a lot of money, money they almost certainly didn't have. I felt increasingly uneasy about the situation and was thinking of getting out of the tavern and heading on down to the cabin in case there was trouble when my own fate was sealed by Slick announcing, "Just to show you everything is on the up and up, the Perfesser here will hold the money," and he slid the pile of bills down the bar to where I was sitting.

Great.

"Okay, I'll race the little runt, and here's my fifty dollars for the pot," snarled Long John. Slick laughed at him and noted that for all his talk—to be fair, Ralph and Slick hadn't given him much of a chance to talk on this occasion—fifty dollars certainly didn't show much confidence, and the growing crowd in the tavern roared its approval. Long John emptied his billfold onto the bar—$123. "That's better," said Slick, raking the bills toward the pile in front of me.

"Okay," said Ralph, "the race will be from the front of LaVerne's Beauty Shoppe to the stop sign at the grocery store." Long John nodded in agreement. "And I'll need another shot of whiskey—make it a double." He reached into the pile of wagers and pulled out a five to pay for his drink. He drank down the double shot and turned green. "Whoops," he moaned, "I better get outside. Right now," and he ran out the front door, where we watched him lean his head against his pickup truck, throwing up.

"Maybe we should do something," I suggested, and about ten of the bystanders did: They reached into their pockets and doubled or even tripled their bets on Long John. Slick encouraged the wagering and even bought Ralph another shot of whiskey when he came back into the bar, wiping his mouth on his sleeve. The betting continued, and now some people no one had ever seen bet on anything before were throwing bills onto the pile. Slick was writing down the bets, all the while goading the crowd and Long John into higher antes.

I piled all the money up. The wad was too big to stuff into my overalls pockets. There must have been seven hundred, maybe eight hundred, dollars. Everyone stepped out into the night air. It was cool and still.

"The Perfesser will stand down at the stop sign and give us the official results," yelled Slick. Terrific. Now I was not only holding the wagers, I was going to decide the race. It seemed obvious enough, however, that Long John would win the race with room to spare. There might be a problem over Slick and Ralph paying off their bets, but frankly the race wasn't likely to be very controversial.

The crowd gathered down at the starting line, cheering the contestants. Ralph said loudly, "Any problem with me running barefoot?" I could feel the crunch of gravel and glass under my boots, and I shook my head at the thought of a drunk—even an obnoxious drunk like Ralph—running *barefoot* down the street for more than a couple of steps. "Hey, this is getting silly!" I yelled. "Why don't we just call it good and go back into the bar?"

I was hooted down in short order, Slick leading the booing. On seeing Ralph take off his shoes, Denny Dietz, Woodrow, Dwaine Dempster, and CeCe hot-footed it down to my end of the street to put their last dollars on Long John. As I watched Ralph stand there in the street barefoot and shudder from another wave of dry heaves, I sincerely wished that I had a couple hundred dollars to put on Long John myself.

"On your mark!" Slick yelled, and the runners crouched—at least as far as Ralph could crouch in his condition. "Get set! Go!" The crowd roared their approval.

But the roar stopped almost as soon as it began. Even from my position a hundred feet down the street I could see what happened. Long John's left foot lifted off the pavement as if in slow motion and struck out in front of him like a four-foot rattlesnake. With that one step, his *first* step, he was well in the lead. His left foot hit the pavement like a gunshot and his enormous right foot came off the pavement and lashed out toward me in another three-yard stride.

But that isn't what startled the crowd into silence. It was the next moment of the race that did that. Suddenly Ralph's legs began to churn in a blur that was for all the world like the one in the cartoons when the Roadrunner goes tearing past Coyote. I had never before seen anything like it.

By the time Long John lifted his enormous left brogan for the second time, Ralph had already passed him, yelling "Ouch! Ouch! Ow! Ah! Ouch!" at every step. Perhaps the pain made Ralph move faster, I don't know. I do know that by the time the runners reached the halfway point of the race in front of the tavern, Ralph was so far ahead of Long John—and I am not kidding about this—he turned around and ran the last half of the course backward, waving his hands at Long John and laughing at him.

I was right: I didn't have much of a decision to make about the winner of the race. Ralph limped back past me and grabbed the wad of bills from my hand even before Long John crossed the finish line. "Thanks, Perfesser," Ralph said with a smile.

After the race, everybody walked quietly off into the night. No one had any more money for drinks. No one but Slick, Ralph, and me, and Butch, the guy who owned the tavern then. I watched Slick and Ralph count out their winnings and divide it equally. They tossed out a five to buy a round of beer. "You know," I said, still amazed by what I had seen, "we could take Ralph to Omaha and make ten thousand dollars a night doing this."

"Nah," said Ralph. "The word gets around pretty fast. I can only pull this off every couple of years, and it's not just getting the thing set up. My feet are destroyed for months after one of these routines."

"Try to do something like this too often and you'll get killed, but stick around," Slick smiled. "In a couple years we'll try it again, and if you're smart, you'll have a pocketful of money with you when we do."

Slick eventually bought the Town Tavern. Connie, his wife, said he might just as well own the place since he lived there anyway. Slick quit drinking when he fell asleep at the wheel and plowed his car into Crenshaw's corn bin. I have always been surprised at people like Slick and Goose, who once were such hard drinkers and suddenly decided to stop, and *did*, just like that. Not another drop. Slick says that's the only way he could have ever afforded to own the tavern, when he stopped drinking.

Slick says he misses those drinking days when he used to get so sick, lose three or four days at work, wreck his car or forget where he parked it, and fall down and cut himself up, but he says slowly but surely he is getting used to it.

As far as I am concerned, Slick's finest moment was the time he and I took our wives—he was married then—to Krieger's Restaurant for an anniversary supper. We were dressed up, had a few drinks in Centralia before driving over to Rising City, and were generally feeling pretty good about life.

Once we got a table and settled down, I asked Slick, "Where's the men's room?"

"I'm headed that way myself," he said. "Why don't you come along with me. It'll be easier to show you than to try to tell you. And I'm in a bit of a hurry myself, if you know what I mean."

We stepped back through the reception area and past the cashier's counter, where we had originally come into the restaurant. We went down some narrow steps and around a corner past the pay telephone and into the men's room. I don't recall what we talked about going down to the men's room or what we talked about when we were in there, but on the way back out, Slick said, "Wait a minute. I want to call home and make sure everything is okay with the house. Heather"—Heather is Slick's oldest daughter—"is sitting with the other two kids and she may need some moral support."

I stood by while Slick made his call. While Slick talked to Heather, I heard loud voices above me at the cashier's desk. I leaned around the corner and listened in on the conversation. "What do you mean, I can't have my table by the window?"

"But Dr. Harmon, we already have a reservation for that table."

"It's empty and I'm here first. After all the business I've brought into this dump, Harv, I expect better treatment than this."

"Dr. Harmon, I appreciate your business and if you would help us out in the future by calling ahead, we are always glad to reserve . . ."

"I want *that* table, reservations or not. Let me see your reservations list."

"But Dr. Harmon, I . . ."

"The Carsons? You're holding my table for the Carsons? The Carsons?! You'd rather save the table for a filling station attendant than a medical doctor? Harv, your priorities are really screwed up, if you think that is the way to run a successful business."

"Doctor, if you would like to wait a moment, I could call Fred Carson . . ."

"My time is valuable, Harv, and I'm not about to waste fifteen minutes sitting here waiting for you to call a grimy tractor mechanic to see if you can find a table for a medical doctor who could just as easily be eating at the Country Club. Which I think, by God, is precisely what we'll go ahead and do. Edith! Get your coat. We're going to the club!"

"That miserable cur made me sit in his waiting room and cool my heels for almost two hours last week, and here he is, making a fuss about waiting a couple minutes for a table," Slick said over my shoulder. I turned to him. He had apparently finished his phone call and had joined in my eavesdropping. "And frankly," he continued, "I'd rather have Fred Carson work on my appendix than have that pompous Harmon ass work on my carburetor."

I started up the steps, but Slick tugged at my sleeve. He had returned to the telephone booth and was punching buttons furiously. I went back down the two steps to the telephones.

"Yes, is Dr. Harmon there?" Slick asked quietly into the telephone.

"He is just on the way out," I could hear Harv say just above me. "Oh, Dr. Harmon, it's a call for you." I could hear the sharp clack of the good doctor's wing tips crossing the reception area floor. Wow, I could tell from his *footsteps* that he was still furious about Harv's lack of appreciation for his high station.

"Yes," Harmon snapped into the telephone.

I leaned back down the steps and around the corner to where Slick was speaking calmly and quietly into the phone. "Dr. Harmon, I am wondering why it is that you think you should be treated any differently than anyone else in the restaurant? Fred Carson is a topnotch mechanic and you are at best a mediocre doctor. If you amounted to anything at all, you would be in Omaha, not Rising City, after all. I would say you are making a complete ass of yourself, acting the way you are, but the fact of the matter is, everybody in the restaurant already knows you are an ass. All you're doing is confirming what is general information. Put on your coat and get out of here with your polyester wife so the rest of us can enjoy a civilized meal with people who are decent and friendly. No matter what they do for a living, every single one of them is worth three of you. By the way, you are going to be getting a cool reception at the Country Club too because you didn't fool anyone when you filched the bottle of Glenlivet from the bar during the Christmas party."

Slick quietly hung up the phone and motioned me up the stairs. I almost exploded in laughter as we passed by the cashier's desk where the good Dr. Harmon was still standing stock-still, staring blankly into the telephone receiver.

Back at the table Slick explained, "Carla was bartending at the club for their Christmas party and she saw the cheap rat lift the bottle while she was taking care of the other end of the bar. She wasn't happy about having to pay for it out of her wages, but she knew that if she spilled the beans, she would have to go to Lincoln the next time she needed a doctor for the kids. I had an idea that the information would come in handy sometime."

"What's that all about?" asked Slick's wife.

"Nothing," he said, working on his salad.

I looked at Slick with admiration and said, "Eat up. Tonight the steaks are on me."

The Bleaker County Juice Wars

THE FIRST PERSON through the tavern door every morning is Worm Dower. He's not a drunk, and in fact that's the problem. Worm Dower doesn't drink at all. He plays cards. Every morning, all morning, he plays cards. And he cheats, but that's not the point.

When Slick opens that front door, there's Worm, waiting on the steps. Not far behind him will be Dietz, another old fart who sits at that card table just like Worm, nursing one thirty-five-cent glass of orange juice all morning long. And then Goose. He doesn't drink either. And then Emma Fahrquar and maybe Claire Finch. They don't drink.

Sure, there's only room for four card players at the table, but the others pull up chairs and sit around or stand around watching the game. None of them drinks. None of them, that is, drinks beer or wine or liquor, but as a matter of fact, they don't really *drink* much of anything else either. Every single one of them buys just one thirty-five-cent orange juice and nurses that thing along for three or four hours.

That's not easy to do. Just try to make a little dinky glass of orange juice last four hours some time. You really have to work at it. It gets warm and ugly. You can't take even more than a tiny sip every fifteen minutes without it all at once disappearing. You have to have remarkable self-control to make a thirty-five-cent glass of orange juice last four hours.

But Worm Dower, Dietz, Evan Cool, Goose, and a few other regulars up at the Town Tavern can do it, and do it all the time.

While you're thinking about how hard it is to keep that little glass of juice lasting so long, think too about how this must have worked on Slick, standing back behind that bar, paying the rent, the lights, the price of the cards, the wages of the barmaid, and then cleaning up the mess after those card players left every morning, all the while contemplating the magnificent twenty cents' worth of profit he makes every time he takes ten minutes to cater to the demands of that entire card table of misers.

It bothered Slick—we could see that. On one occasion Evan Cool walked over to the bar and put down a penny. "I found that over by the card table and none of us lost it," he said, obviously proud of his evident honesty.

"Why don't you four just split it," Slick replied. Evan didn't know he'd been insulted, but the rest of us did.

From the very moment he bought the tavern Slick had grumbled about the situation, but it was about four years before he ever put together enough anger to do anything about it. By that time he had accumulated sufficient indignation that he was *determined* to do something.

So one momentous day—although at the time we didn't know it was momentous—Slick raised the price of juice to forty cents. The next morning there was a good crowd of onlookers gathered at the tavern just to see the fun. The usual parade of card players came in, led by Worm Dower, and they ordered up their glasses of orange juice, fully prepared once again to spend the whole day and only thirty-five cents nursing the soon-to-be tepid contents.

They each flicked their thirty-five cents on the table as Slick brought the tray over to the table and Slick made a move as if to pick up the coins, then hesitated, and said, "The price of orange juice has gone up to forty cents."

He might just as well have said, "Jesus has returned to this earth and he just bought this bar."

"What?!" they cried in concert, and Slick repeated, "The price of orange juice has gone up to forty cents." Well, they paid the extra nickel apiece, but there was a lot of muttering throughout the day about obscene profits and just how many glasses of juice Slick was getting out of one carton.

At one point Worm Dower shouted to no one in particular, "I think this is outrageous." "Outrageous" was the biggest word we had ever heard him use.

"When was the last time anyone cared what you think, Worm?" Slick asked quietly.

Worm shouted, again to no one in particular, "I went to Rising City to the Hunky Dory Market yesterday"— which means that once again Worm had driven forty miles to save a dime—"and they have orange juice there for eighty cents for a whole damned quart."

"And just how long do you suppose they'd let you sit in the aisle and play cards at Hunky Dory?" Slick shot back, pretty much shutting off further comment.

The next morning the card players were all in their places again, but this time all four corners of the table ordered coffee. Their strategy was evident: Coffee cost forty cents too, but Slick gave free refills. Which meant that now Slick was having to walk back and forth to the coffee table fifteen times a day, refilling cups. One at a time, of course, because no two cups were ever in need of refilling at any one time.

Slick put up a big sign, right behind the card table: COFFEE REFILLS 10¢ NO COFFEE SERVICE AFTER 12 NOON.

Well, that imposed a pretty mean situation on the card table, as you can imagine. It is one thing to nurse a warm orange juice all day long, quite another to stretch a cold coffee through the morning.

But this was now a matter of principle, and the card tablers rose to the occasion. The general laughter was slowly turning to admiration—of the tactical ingenuity, not the tight-fisted approach toward Slick, which all of us high rollers deplored. We had to admit, the card players might be impossibly cheap, but they sure as hell were determined.

The next day Slick dimmed the lights so you could hardly see across the bar. It was obvious he had been thinking about the situation overnight. It made no difference; the card players simply squinted. Slick turned up the volume on the jukebox and gave every little kid a quarter to plug into the infernal noisemaker. The players recoiled but stood their ground.

It was getting uncomfortable for all of us, what with it being so loud and dark, but the struggle had become the stuff epics are made of. The card players didn't give up. In fact, they struck back.

I wasn't there that day, but the word quickly spread

through town that Worm Dower had outflanked Slick: Now the card players were ordering two cans of soda pop and four glasses, splitting the soda and thereby cutting down the price per player to thirty-seven and a half cents per serving. Before the day was over, Slick was charging a dime for extra glasses and the card players had retreated temporarily back to coffee. And taking seconds, one person at a time. They kept Slick running, and we could see his anger growing.

Slick initiated a new program: He started to charge a dime a game for the use of the cards. The card players stiffed him for more than half of what they owed (although when they were playing, Emma and Claire paid whatever Worm and Dietz shorted Slick because that was just a little too close to dishonesty for them).

Now the card players were paying more and going through hell—drinking warm Dr Pepper and cold, bad coffee—to do it. Whenever possible, they paid their card table fees with Canadian quarters.

Things were tough on Slick too. It probably shouldn't have made any difference to him, but it obviously did. He stopped buying new cards, letting his protagonists play with the old ones until the pasteboards were battered and soft, dog-eared, stained, and dirty, the pips barely visible. As Slick put it, "Those damned cards are getting so worn out, it's like dealing seat cushions. When those bastards at the card table try to shuffle them, they might just as well throw 'em into a bushel basket and stir 'em with a stick."

He raised the price of coffee again, started reusing grounds, and served it cold. Then he only *rinsed* the coffee cups. Maybe it was because it was so dark in the tavern by this point, but the card players proceeded as if they didn't even notice the spots and rings. The next day Slick just dipped the cups in the dishwater but *didn't* rinse them. The coffee was thin enough by that time in the war that the soap must have been obvious even to the less than sensitive card table. It made no difference. The card players gritted their teeth, brought their own cups, and played on.

Nothing made a difference. The Bleaker County Juice Wars had now been going on for a couple weeks and Slick might as well have posted daily updates on his front door, except that he was doing excellent business just on the basis of the people who came in every morning to check on any new developments. No one talked about anything but the Juice Wars, but never to or with the combatants, of course. All information was gathered by witness or report. No testimony was taken.

Of course, by now, it was a matter of principle for Slick too; he would have just as soon watched the tavern go up in smoke before he'd give up or back down. He bid up the price of coffee to forty-five cents. The card players anted back to orange juice. Slick saw them by charging forty-five cents for orange juice and raised them by simultaneously increasing the price of tomato juice just in case the enemy thought of that option.

Slick began serving all his juices in different-size glasses. A beer glass of orange juice cost forty-five cents. A mixed drink glass of tomato juice was forty cents. The mixed drink glass was slightly smaller but of a very different shape so it was hard for the card players to judge exactly how much smaller it actually was.

To compound the confusion, Slick added a small ice-tea glass of apple juice to the menu, a generous serving for thirty-five cents, knowing that no one liked apple juice. He also knew that the card players wouldn't be able to pass up such a good deal and would therefore wind up drinking something they really didn't like, simply because it was cheap. It would never have occurred to this bunch to order the juice and just use it as the price of admission, leaving it untouched when they finally left for home.

Slick licked his lips, anticipating watching them squirm. He *knew* they wouldn't be able to pass up the bargain.

And he was right: They couldn't. But Slick finally took apple juice off his menu altogether when it became clear that his opponents were *beginning* to like it, or at least led him to believe they liked it. One day the card players even ordered a second glass of the stuff before noon. They had never ordered a second glass of anything, and even if they were only pretending they liked it, Slick couldn't handle the possibility and withdrew the offer.

Sure, it was the most net he had ever made off that table, but he simply could not abide the idea that he was somehow doing them a favor.

To add to the annoyance of it all, one day right in front of Slick, while he stood behind the bar and watched them, the card table conspirators ordered a glass of orange juice, a glass of tomato juice, a can of Dr Pepper, and a cup of coffee and laid out two dimes for two extra, empty glasses. While Slick steamed behind the bar, they spent the better part of an hour pouring liquids back and forth and taking careful notes until they had determined the precise schedule of values for all nonalcoholic drinks available at Slick's Town Tavern, down to the closest one-tenth of a cent.

Then all of a sudden, it was as if Slick had surrendered. There was a temporary lull in the Bleaker County Juice Wars. Was it a truce or only the calm before the storm? we wondered.

The lights went back up, the jukebox was turned down,

and decks of new cards appeared at the card table without explanation. Slick began to serve all his juices for forty-five cents in the same-size glasses. He was whistling again, and smiling, and served the card table without complaint, or even comment, which is not at all like him. He even bought a round of drinks for Woodrow, Lunchbox, and me even though he knew we were going to have another and would have paid for it without fuss.

As we learned, Slick had a plan.

One day Lunchbox, Woodrow, and I just admitted our concern and curiosity, and we asked Slick what was going on. He smiled knowingly and nodded toward his back storeroom. We hesitated. He smiled knowingly again, signaling us to go to the sacred territory back behind the bar and take a look for ourselves.

We stepped around the end of the barstools, back to the storeroom, stopped at the doorway, and peered into the gloom. What we saw chilled us, probably much like the first glimpse of the atomic bomb must have chilled Truman. We saw a stack of four cases of prune juice.

"Starting tomorrow, I will be selling a large glass of prune juice for a quarter." Slick smiled knowingly again.

"So what?" Lunchbox shrugged.

"You big dummy," snarled Woodrow, "one stiff jolt of that stuff and those cheapskates at the card table are going to be scooting out the front door trying not to cough."

"What if they just stick to their orange juice?" I asked.

"There's no way in hell those pinchpennies are going to be able to pass up a bargain like a twenty-five-cent juice, even if it's horsefly juice," Slick said.

"But all that means, you know," said Woodrow, "is that the card players will be spending forty-five minutes a day in your toilet."

"Not in *my* toilet." Slick smiled knowingly.

We stood there thinking for only a moment about Slick's toilets, which he cleaned twice a year whether they needed it or not.

And then we *all* smiled knowingly. It *was* the atomic bomb, and within the week the card table would be petitioning for peace, unconditionally.

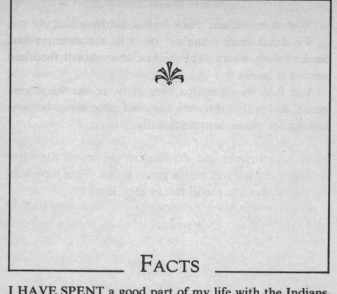

FACTS

I HAVE SPENT a good part of my life with the Indians and my principal conclusion from that experience is that far from stealing the Indians blind, we non-Indians haven't stolen nearly enough. When it comes right down to it, all we've taken from the Indians is some land, some names, and a few products like corn and canoes—the easy stuff, but to our eternal loss we have left the Indians with the best stuff—ideas.

The old Indians knew things worth knowing. They knew about jerking—or drying—meat, for example. But the pioneers didn't want to be mistaken for being low class so they didn't eat Indian food like jerked meat. We can forget for the moment that the pioneers were, generally speaking, from the Pilgrims to the homesteaders, the bottom of the social barrel anyway.

Anyway, these poor pioneers, lost and bewildered, were surviving on green hams, rancid bacon, maggoty beef, and wang-leather venison when they could have had the sort of food that even today we enjoy as delicacies in bars around the country. The Indians knew about food and medicine, about the way of man and nature, of man and woman, of the gods and the powers, the Mysteries, and the truths. And guess what: A lot of Indians still know such things. These wily rascals have managed to cloud our minds so that all we see are the feathers and bells at pow-wows, the drunks and derelicts in the cities, the silver workers and lawyers on the reservations. They have kept to themselves the useful things they know.

Well, maybe they haven't exactly kept this stuff to themselves. Okay, they've said all along we are welcome to it. And okay, the only reason we have not accumulated this treasure chest of wisdom is that, well, we haven't asked.

An old Lakota once laughed at me when I asked him if he was passing along all the things he knew about medicine plants to young Lakota or if perhaps he was writing things down. "No, Roger," he said, "I'm not writing them down and I'm not teaching them to anyone."

"But, Mr. Fool Bull," I pleaded, "if you don't do something to preserve everything you know, it will be lost. Your knowledge is like a treasure and it would be a great loss to all of us, including the Lakota, if it disappears."

He laughed and laughed. It took him several minutes to regain control. "You white people," he chuckled. "You're amazing. Roger, if a treasure is lost, it isn't gone. It's still there, where it has always been. It just so happens that at the moment no one knows where its place is. The knowledge isn't lost. We are. The truth never sleeps."

"If everyone were to forget for a moment that aspirin cures a headache," he asked me more seriously, "does that mean that aspirin no longer cures headache? No, it simply means that for a moment we don't *know* that aspirin cures headache. Aspirin would still cure headache if we knew about it but for a moment we don't know about it—just as it was when we had the willow but didn't know about the willow."

Plains Indians still today chew on willow twigs to ease headache, taking advantage of the salicin in the inner bark, a substance that metabolizes to salicylic acid—aspirin.

"The knowledge is still there to be found again. The truth never sleeps."

Many Indians, especially older ones, have told me that their impressive knowledge was not so much a matter of them knowing things that I did not know, but that I had been educated out of things that any human being should know by virtue simply of being a human being. Since my time among the Indians I have found this to be remarkably true: As a mainstream, Protestant, middle America, middle-class German-American I had been taught to attribute the most remarkable sorts of things to coincidence, or to ignore them altogether. The Indians taught me to see those things as signs. Not to *understand* them—simply to *see* them.

There were other things they taught me, things not so mystic, not so magic. Simple common sense but a common sense that has often been totally lost in mainstream American culture. The most striking example I can give you was the time Clyde Sheridan, an Omaha Indian friend, called me and asked if I would be the head dancer at a Tiapiah Society dance.

Well, Clyde didn't actually *ask* me because asking is not something you're supposed to do in Omaha culture. It's not polite to ask questions. You're supposed to sit quietly and observe the Omaha way of doing things, and then that's the way you do it. What Clyde said on that occasion was, "Roger, we would like to have you be our head dancer at the dance on September sixteenth."

"Sure, Clyde," I answered. "I would love to do that." It was a marvelous honor he had offered me, especially since I was an outsider, a non-Omaha who had been taken in as a friend and relative by these fine people. I was offered a responsible position as head dancer, and I had obligations to fulfill in that post.

Clyde hung up the telephone, and then I realized that while he had told me the date of the dance—a Sunday—he did not tell me the time or location. Well, that's very Indian. Time is not so important within Indian culture. The more time I spent with the Omahas and Lakota the more I realized that they are not too casual about time; we are too *preoccupied* with time. More about that at another time.

Anyway, I listened closely the next few weeks, hoping to hear someone in the Indian community mention the time and location of the Tiapiah Society dance, a ritual dance that embodies song, dance, history, culture, religion, and tribal and ethnic adhesion. But no one said a word that helped me out of my uncertainty.

Finally, the day before the dance was to be held, I went to Clyde's brother Frank and asked. Frank was a traditional Omaha, but he understood more clearly the anxieties that non-Indians feel about such things and he was best equipped to handle the rudeness of the white man's question asking. In short, he was what a good anthropologist should be but rarely is.

"Frank," I said, "I still don't know when and where

the dance is tomorrow. I've been listening but haven't heard a thing. Do you know what's going on?"

"No, Roger, I haven't heard either. But I'm going over to Clyde's place for breakfast tomorrow, so why don't you come over about noon and I'll let you know what I find out."

So the day of the dance I went over to Frank's home, still not knowing where and when the dance was to be held. I sat on Frank's front porch waiting. Finally he drove up midmorning and I strode over to his car, by now very nervous. "Well, Frank, what did you find out? When is the dance? Where is it going to be?"

"Well, Roger, I was over there all morning"—Frank shrugged—"and Clyde never said." And of course as a good Omaha Frank was not about to ask.

I was in despair. I so desperately wanted to play out my role in this Indian ritual I admired and respected—but how could I do it if I didn't even know when and where I was supposed to be? Then I struck on an ingenious solution to my frustrating dilemma. I had followed the same course before in non-Indian situations: I shifted into my Indian gear. Thirty years later I still do that now and then. When I am in an airport, my plane is delayed, there is some considerable doubt about whether I will make my connections in Chicago, the weather is worsening, the lines are getting longer, my pulse is pounding in my temples—I shift, haarruuum, down into my Indian time gear.

There are things we cannot control—the weather, for example. There are things that do not matter—an hour or a day, for example. There are things that matter above all—the Powers and Mysteries, for example, and the storms they give us, the people around us, our lives and our loves.

On those occasions I see things suddenly in focus, my pulse slows, I can smile, I think, I watch people, I wait. And I wonder at the wisdom the Indians have that we have not yet found the wisdom to steal. And that's what I did on the occasion of the Tiapiah dance. I tried to think like my Indian friends. What would an Indian do? I asked myself.

So after a quiet lunch—after all, they couldn't start the dance without the head dancer, so there was no sense in me worrying about the dance starting before I got there!—I got in my car and started driving and enjoying this pleasant fall afternoon. Why not? It was a beautiful day. Why not take this opportunity to soak it up?

There were only five or six places in town that a big dance like this could be held—the armory, the swimming pool bathhouse, the community center, Antelope Pavilion, Pioneers Park, the Indian Center. That shouldn't be so hard to sort out. I picked one at random. I started out the road to Pioneers Park. About halfway down the lilac-bordered lane I met a car full of Indian friends coming toward me. They honked and waved. I honked and waved.

Well, hmmm. I guess the dance isn't at Pioneers Park, I thought, because they're coming back! I turned around and headed back toward town. My Indian friends were already out of sight, but one of my choices was already eliminated—the most distant one at that—so my task was already much simpler.

At the park I turned around and headed back into town. I checked Antelope Pavilion. No one at all there. I went to the bathhouse. Well, there's Clyde's car. And there's Clyde up in the bleachers watching a softball game.

I parked beside Clyde's car and took a seat beside him. He smiled a greeting. My theory was, if I had Clyde in my sight, I couldn't miss the dance. We watched the two remaining innings of the game and stood up. We turned, and I saw in the parking lot behind us ten or twelve cars of Indians, the men standing around, leaning on the hoods of their cars and talking, the women sitting in the cars, the children running around, playing in the dust.

"Well," Clyde said, "it looks like everyone came here. We might as well have the dance here."

My God! I suddenly realized that Clyde had decided *at that very moment* that the dance would be at the bathhouse. That meant that for the past three weeks I had been seeking information that did not, in fact, exist. Neither Clyde nor Frank nor anyone else could have told me where the dance was going to take place because there was no such information. No one knew where the dance was going to be. They couldn't have told me even if they had wanted to. I had spent my white man's energy futilely searching for a fact that did not, in fact, exist.

You see, we now think of a "fact" as a thing, a noun, when it is linguistically, historically, and probably philosophically, a *verb*, not a thing at all but an action. A fact is not a thing that exists but a process that occurs. The Indians still know that.

That *fact* of where my participation in the Tiapiah Society gourd dance was to occur only came into being—a process—later, as all the Indians knew it would. That the fact—"When will this dance take place?"—did not exist three weeks earlier was really of no consequence other than to the degree that I manufactured the consequences within my own anxiety. The information I sought was not only unknown, it was unknowable.

We Westerners, especially we Americans, tend to think that there is an answer to every question, *one* answer to

every question. The Indians know that is not at all true.
There are questions to which there are no answers at this
moment; there are questions to which there are many answers; there are questions to which there will never be answers.

I don't know about you, but that makes life easier for
me. And a lot more reasonable.

Skunked

LILY AND I moved out to our place—we call it Primrose Farm—a few years ago from the city. We bought a 100-year-old house and rebuilt it almost from scratch, so while it looks like an old home from the outside, the inside smelled all too much like new lumber. Therefore, we have rejoiced whenever the place has filled with the lush smells of baked apples and smoked turkeys.

One night we discovered a new country delight—a skunked dog. Slump the Wonder Dog made a new friend about 2:00 A.M. and shared his good fortune with all of us. We woke up in the middle of the night smelling this terrible odor that we could not quite identify. Lily went downstairs and tried to isolate whether the furnace was about to explode, the stove was loading up with ignitables, or sewer gas was backing up. She came back suspecting that "something electronic is burning up."

I went downstairs. It was Slump. No doubt about it.

I had a mountain of work to do the next morning, but instead I spent an hour trying to wash Slump down with tomato juice and fighting to keep him from drinking it or shaking it on our newly painted walls.

Antonia surveyed the canine chaos and said she sure would like to see a skunk sometime, which reminded me of my own first encounter with this inevitable joy of rural living. I was just a kid, visiting my Uncle Fred and Aunt Mary at their farm near Yoder, Wyoming. Someone mentioned skunks at some point one evening, and I said to Uncle Fred that I sure would like a skunk tail to hang from my bicycle handlebars back in Nebraska.

Uncle Fred told me that he just the day before shot a skunk down by the hired man's shack. If I took a sharp shovel down there, he said, I could just chop off the tail and take it back to Lincoln with me.

Full of excitement, I grabbed a shovel from the tool pile in the barn and headed down to the hired man's house about thirty yards west of the house. Sure enough, lying with his forequarters under the shack, tail out behind, was a beautiful, silky skunk. I stepped right up and gave that tail a good chop.

I was surprised by the results, but not nearly as surprised, I suspect, as the skunk. The *dead* skunk, I later found out, was on the other side of the shack. The one I applied the shovel to was just looking under the house for something he had left behind the night before.

Well, I returned to the house howling like a bad transmission. My reputation preceded me, as they say, and I found the house closed up and locked tight. Aunt Mary yelled to me from a window that I should go over to the downwind side of the yard, shed all my clothes, and go to the horse tank. My cousin Dick, she hollered, would bring me some soap.

Cousin Dick was three or four years older than I was anyway and had the additional advantage of being a farm kid while I was a dummy from the city. So he regularly taunted me with snakes, needled me into riding a calf in the cowyard where there was not a single square foot without a fresh cow pie, or "giving me a ride on his wagon," a trip that put me in the middle of the pond.

On the occasion of my skunking he took obvious pleasure in strolling out to the horse tank from the house, mocking my tears, holding the soap away from me so I had to come out of the water tank to get it, and then laughing at my white and stinking carcass.

There was only one comfort in the whole affair: Cousin Dick was awarded the task of burying my clothes, and by the time he was done he smelled as bad as I did. So Aunt Mary made him take a bath in the horse tank.

I got to take the soap out to him. I dropped it twice in the cowyard.

BEERING THE FARMERS

YOU SEE, GOOSE used to drink real hard. He has been solidly positioned on the wagon—not a drop—for almost five years now, but there was a time when you wouldn't see Goose without a bottle of blackberry brandy under the seat of his pickup truck.

I see him almost every day now and that's the way it was then, but there used to be a ritual I could count on as regularly as the spring and autumn equinoxes. Goose would come by my cabin down by the river sometime in April and again in September and announce, "It's time." He didn't have to say it. I knew already "it was time" because water was dripping out from under the bed of his truck. In that truck bed he would have about five hundred pounds of ice and maybe ten cases of beer, and so the one or two coon dogs he always had with him had to ride up in the cab, which they preferred and he really didn't mind. Sometimes if it was real hot, Goose would sprinkle ice cream salt over the top of the ice so that the beer was nearly frozen by the time he got to my place and he'd pull a canvas cover over it to keep it that way.

I'd jump into Goose's truck, grabbing a cold beer on the way and pushing one of the ever-present coon dogs aside, and we'd go out and just drive the back roads all day looking for farmers—farmers planting in the spring and harvesting in the fall. The way Goose explained it to me, it used to be that farming was a community operation: No one harvested by himself. Fifteen or twenty fellows would get together and work one fellow's crop and then move on to the next's.

In part it was because the big old steam traction engines and threshers needed a lot of hands to operate them, but it was also a matter of them knowing in those days that things just go better when you have some company. At noon they would go to the farmhouse and have a huge meal together, one the women had joined together to prepare, which meant the women had a chance to have a couple social days together too. In the evening, after the work was done, they'd pull the gallon of moonshine up out of the well and the home brew from the creek, and the evening was a chance for everyone—men and women—to talk, relax, even sing a little. It was hard work, and it was good times.

Anyway, Goose told me that he felt sorry for today's farmers, sitting in that tractor cab for twelve, sixteen, twenty hours a day, just running back and forth down those rows in the hot Nebraska sun, hearing nothing but the whining voices of country-western singers on their tractor radios, doing what they could to make life seem even more miserable than it already was.

So Goose and I would drive all day long hunting for

lonely farmers around Bleaker County. Then we'd stand at the end of a corn row and wave them down. Mostly they would stop even without us waving, wondering what these two big guys were doing standing there at the end of the row—grinning, stropping their overalls straps, two beers in their hands. Grizzled, dusty, red-eyed, exhausted, they'd crawl down from the cab.

"We brought you a cold beer," Goose would say.

"Jeez, you guys, I appreciate the effort and I'd love to drink a beer but I just don't have time!" they'd growl. Then they would turn around thinking that they were going to crawl back into the roaring monster they had been wrestling for days. But Goose's enormous hand, bigger than a grain scoop, would reach out, envelop a shoulder, and pull the farmer back to the ground. "You'll drink a beer or you won't be *able* to climb into that piece of junk you call a combine," he'd snarl. When Goose snarled, it was a little like meeting a grizzly bear at close range.

The first time I saw this performance I felt like a real jerk, taking this poor hardworking farmer away from his work for something as trivial as sitting in the shade and drinking a beer, not to mention seeing him bullied like that.

I soon learned that a curious thing happened on those occasions when Goose waylaid a farmer: The farmer would smile, his shoulders would loosen—even sag. Then the farmer would sigh, he would wipe the grime and sweat from his face, he'd lean against the truck chilled from its icy load, or maybe his combine, which we sometimes preferred because it threw more shade. Then that farmer would let that cold beer run down his throat, maybe some down the front of his shirt, inside his overalls bib.

Okay, Goose and I took him away from his work and

made his day, maybe his week, a lot longer, but he'd smile a smile that had nothing to do with resentment. We'd stay only long enough for one beer. If he would take one, we'd give him a cold one to take up into the cab with him. He'd get back to work, and we'd move on to our next "victim." Those trips got to be the favorite ritual of the year for me. The thing is, Goose might have been a drunk those days, but he wasn't all bad.

Now, on the occasion in question, I was sitting in the Town Tavern slopping down a few beers with some buddies and in came Goose, five days into a beard, smelling of the beer he'd lived on for the last five hundred miles and fairly well loosened up from the women he'd entertained over the last five nights. Goose has straightened up pretty much these days but at the time he had something of a reputation.

Problem is, all those distractions had somehow blurred Goose's vision and he didn't notice that CeCe was in the tavern too, sitting right where she had been sitting during his protracted and unexplained absence, slugging down wine coolers for the same five days, calculating and categorizing all the vengeful things she planned to do to remind Goose that he had a happy home.

For just a minute Goose must have thought that he had accidentally walked into a chain-saw store with about eighteen samples stuck on wide-open. CeCe's fury was explicit, well documented, and generously public. Woodrow, Lunchbox, Lily, and I sat there at the bar, genuinely happy we were who we were, listening to CeCe remind Goose of everything he'd ever done wrong during the seven years they'd been married, from the way he smelled when he came back from running his trap lines to her curiosity why he thought it was such a great idea for her to cook with cast-iron pans, from the fart that he'd unleashed at their wedding dance while dancing with her sister Wanda to her observation that he seemed more concerned that his coon dogs had fresh calves' liver once a week than that his children had hamburger to eat the rest of the week. "And if they're *your* dogs, why is it *I* am the one who has to feed, water, and clean up after those mobile tick farms you call 'dogs'?" That hurt. She hit him where he lived: his dogs.

Then, at about ten thousand decibels, CeCe reviewed Goose's employment record over the past seven years, or maybe his unemployment record, she blamed him for everything from the Korean War to the loose gravel on Main Street, and she inventoried every unfulfilled promise he had made, suggested, or mumbled in his sleep since that night he proposed when they saw Brigitte Bardot in *And God Created Woman* at the Rising City drive-in movie.

She guessed that he never snored with his lady friends like he did with her, that he probably never asked them to skin a muskrat, and that those fancy girls in Omaha probably had poodles that never so much as growled, while *she* had to put up with those damned coon hounds howling every time any two cats in Centralia exchanged feline phrases *d'amour.*

CeCe did not ignore a single one of Goose's many failings during her marathon recitation, which is sure evidence of some kind of memory. The rest of us sat there silent, cringing whenever Goose's indiscretions happened to correspond with our own, hunched down and hoping that CeCe wouldn't notice us and start announcing those failures to the community at large. Jeez, if she knew all that about Goose, God only knows what she had on us, the thinking seemed to go.

The tavern echoed with CeCe's fire-breathing and the walls shook with the thunder of her indictment for nearly an eternity, so help me. And yet there wasn't another sound to be heard. The floor was CeCe's.

Finally she paused and took a deep breath. It was clear that she had arrived at some sort of conclusion, and it promised to be spectacular. She stood over Goose, her face now not an inch and a half from his. His was bigger and uglier, but hers was madder and more determined. "And what," she asked Goose, "and what are you going to think, you miserable plowboy playboy, if sometime you come home from one of your weeklong, shit-faced drunks and you just find that there's no one to come home to?"

There was nothing but silence. Goose studied his hunting boots as if checking to see if they needed new laces. The rest of us tried to look busy too, in case CeCe looked in our direction.

"You know, one of these days you're going to come back to Centralia from the fancy girls in Omaha, after a five-day drunk, and you're going to wonder why your car is gone and why the door is locked." She tapped him on the back of his bowed head with the long nail of her forefinger as if to make sure he was awake.

Goose looked up at CeCe, beginning to figure out what was coming.

"And then just what are you going to think when you finally get into that house and I'm gone?"

Silence.

"And the kids are gone?"

Silence.

"And the furniture's gone? And the clothes are gone? And the food's gone?" There was a long, dramatic pause, and then she shouted at him, her nose touching his, "*What are you going to think when you come home from some orgy with the fancy girls and* everything *you thought was yours is gone?"*

The silence in the tavern was now total. The pool players stood frozen just exactly where they stood when the tirade started. Not even the ice machine was running, and, believe me, there are times when you can't even hear the jukebox over that dinosaur.

Now there was a sound—the sound of Goose's mind working. He looked at CeCe intensely and leaned forward to speak. He spoke quietly as if he hoped that his words might have been private, or maybe it was just because he had loaded so much meaning into his words that there wasn't any room left for volume. It didn't matter. By that time we were so intent on what he was about to say, we could hear his heart pounding in his ears.

"CeCe," he gasped, his voice choked with passion. "Don't you take them dogs!"

ADDRESSES

ABOUT ONCE A week I get a call from someone back east about one thing or another. A standard part of the conversation goes, "We need to send you this stuff, but the shipping company won't send it to a postal box. What's your address?"

"I don't have an address," I reply, knowing what's coming next.

"Everyone has an address. There's no such thing as having no address."

"*I* don't have an address."

"Then we can't send this package to you. To get a package, you have to have an address."

"Okay, how about 'Roger, Centralia, Nebraska?' That'll get it here."

"No, that's not an address."

"But that's enough to get the package to me."

"Maybe it will, but it's not an address. The shipping company won't accept a package without an address."

"Okay, how about 'Roger Welsch, 147th and Y streets, Loading Dock M, Bin 14A, Centralia, Nebraska 68831-0160?' Is that an address?"

"That'll do it. Give it to me again. R-O-G . . ."

You get the idea.

The thing is, Frank, our UPS man, will look at that address, laugh, drive up to our house, pat the dogs, say "Hi, Slump! Get down, Blackjack," open the door, stick in the package, say "Hi, Lily! Hi, Rog! Package from CBS. Looks like a script. *Great* address! Where did you get the stuff about 'Loading Dock M'? I *love* it!" Frank doesn't need to know an address for us because he knows *us*.

I was once in Germany and sent a post card to my grizzled friend Bojack. I addressed it "Bojack, Centralia, Nebraska, USA" and Bojack got that post card a week later. I was really impressed. Four words and out of all the people in the world, Bojack got the card.

I recited that wonder one day after I got back to America to a bunch of my buddies in the Town Tavern. Al Simmons dismissed my amazement with a wave of his hand. "That's nothing," he said. "Just last week a fellow came into town and asked Slick, 'Where's that big, dumb, ugly son of a bitch live?' and Slick said, 'Al Simmons? South of town about a mile on the gravel, across the bridge, and then east two miles."

Besides, there are a lot of folks who maintain that it doesn't matter what you put on your envelopes anyway because Dwaine the Mailman can't read. Well, that's not at all a reasonable assumption in my opinion: Dwaine likes it when I come in to pick up my mail or if I am out at the box when he drives up to throw our mail into the box out by the road because then he can provide instant synopses of what I am getting in the bundle: "Hey, Rog! You got a card from your son, Chris, and he's doing fine, but it's been real cold up in Minneapolis or wherever. Sometimes it's hard to read his writing. Where did he go to school anyway? You got two checks from the *Nebraska Farmer*—what's going on there? And it looks like you finally got that issue of *Penthouse* with the naked woman who's a game warden—page one forty-eight if you want to take a quick look. And Lily's mother finally sent her that rhubarb pie recipe she asked for on a postcard a couple weeks back, but I guess late is better than never."

See? Dwaine can read just fine.

And what about the time Orville, Jr., filed the complaint about Dwaine reading his *Playboy*? Orville, Jr., was mad because he got his copy one month later than everyone else. Dwaine finally compromised by announcing that he would no longer read Orville, Jr.'s *Playboy* every month. He decided to spread out the burden a little, reading Slick's copy in January, April, July, and October, Denny's in February, May, August, and November, and Lunchbox's in March, June, September, and December.

A lot of people, when writing postcards to anyone in Centralia, add a little P.S. on the bottom of the card saying, "Hi, Dwaine!" Don't tell me Dwaine has trouble reading. Lily and I once got a card from a friend in New York whom we had told about this little quirk of country living. Just for fun she added to the bottom of the postcard, "Hi, Dwaine!" When we got the card a couple days later, Dwaine had added in pencil below her greeting, "Who is this? I don't know this woman."

*   *   *

I suspect the accusation came from people who misinterpret another of Dwaine's problems with mail delivery. See, Dwaine bundles up everyone's mail early in the morning up in the back room at the post office. He puts all my mail, for example, in one pile, rolls it up, and bundles it all together with four or five big rubber bands.

Then he puts my bundle with all the other people's bundles in order on the front seat of his car and he drives along his route, stopping at each farm's mailbox, opening it, tossing in the next bundle, closing the box, and driving on down the road. It's a long route and he doesn't have time to spare.

The problem is, if anyone along the route doesn't happen to get any mail that day, then the mail for everyone down the line is one box off. If two people don't get mail, then everyone is *two* boxes off. If it's a really slow day and three people get no mail, then you may have to drive a mile or two and visit three or four neighbors to find your mail, and of course several neighbors downstream will be dropping in at your place to see if maybe you got their mail.

My favorite delivery was the time we got Dwaine's mail. I took it over to Daisy, Dwaine's wife, and she explained that Dwaine does that every once in a while: "It takes a day or so longer for the bills to get to us that way."

Royal Cupp says cynically that Dwaine is the best thing that ever happened to Bleaker County's social life because his delivery system means that we all get to meet our neighbors and chat with them on a fairly regular basis, whether we want to or not. Royal usually doesn't.

I don't know when this address nonsense is going to be sorted out. We live on Ormsby Road, but all the signs say HIGHWAY 2, and not a single sign anywhere says ORMSBY

ROAD. Everyone knows it's Ormsby Road except strangers and the people who make the signs, I guess.

About three years ago Centralia celebrated its centennial and one of the projects was to put up street signs. Someone dug out an old map of the town, and the village board ordered the signs from some street sign company in Ohio. The Booster Club put the signs up when they arrived. The only problem is, the founders of the village named a street "Main Street" that they thought would be the main street. But things didn't work out that way. All the businesses in town are on Mill Street; Main Street has nothing but homes, a shop for saw-blade sharpening, and a dozen vacant lots. There's no depot on Depot Street— not even a railroad, and they're thinking of closing the park entrance on Park Street. So a lot of the street names don't make any sense at all.

There are probably parts of the world where addresses are a good idea, but out here, where everyone knows where everything is, we just rely on Dwaine to know where the mail goes and Frank to know where UPS packages go, and we cannot for the life of us understand why, if we trust Dwaine and Frank, the rest of the world doesn't.

If you agree with me, drop me a line. That's "Roger 68831-0160." Dwaine will get it to me.

GROVER BASS

THAT'S THE PRETTIEST name I have ever heard: Grover Bass. It's like poetry. It's possible I suppose that the reason I like it is because of the man who wore it. My Uncle Grover. Grover Bass.

Uncle Grover was already forty by the time I came along and that means he was fifty by the time I had any appreciation for him, but he was still tougher than any other man in Nebraska, regardless of age. He was famous for his trick of spotting someone with a new pair of pliers in his overalls pockets in Centralia, and Grover would ask if he could take a look at those pliers. If the fellow was a greenhorn, he might hand the pliers over; anyone who had lived in Bleaker County very long knew better. What Grover would do is admire the pliers for a moment, comment how light they felt, maybe even flimsy, and then he would take them in his huge right hand and squeeze. There was no sign of struggle or strain, but all at once the

67

handles of the pliers met, bent together in that powerful grasp. Most men kept their ruined pliers just so they could show them off and tell others what had happened. A story like that needed proof. I wasn't in Bleaker County at the time so I have only heard the stories, but I have heard them over and over, and I never tire of them.

And yet Uncle Grover could be the gentlest person you ever met. I was just a little boy still living in Lincoln when he first came to visit us—my folks and me, that is. His second day there he asked me if I had time to go downtown to do some shopping with him because he had a couple special errands to run. I didn't get many chances to go downtown so even though I felt a little uneasy about spending a couple hours with this huge man I really didn't know much about, I said sure, I'd go. If he would check with my mother. He said he already had, and she had said it would be okay.

It was a warm spring day and we drove downtown with the windows open. The wind noise was enough of an excuse for us not to exchange more than a few words before we parked the car. Then we went into Walgreen's and he bought me a candy bar and a cold bottle of pop.

While we sat in the cool booth, he asked me how I was doing at baseball. I was surprised he even knew I was playing in the Small Fry League. I told him I was doing pretty good—I was working at playing catcher. He asked about my batting style, said he had played a little ball in his own time, and maybe he could give me some tips later when we got back to the house. I said I'd really like that, and I meant it. He said he'd like to see my uniform sometime, and I told him we didn't wear uniforms yet. He asked about my glove and I told him with some embarrassment that I was using my dad's first-base glove until I could get together enough money to buy a catcher's mitt, which didn't seem like much of a possibility this year. They are a good twelve dollars even in the Sears catalogue.

We stopped at the Surplus Store where he bought some fishing gear he needed. He bought a tackle box and everything that went with it—bobbers, hooks, pliers, a skinning knife, swivels, everything—and asked if I would mind keeping it for him at my place so if he ever wanted to come down to Lincoln, everything he needed would be right there. He said in return for my taking care of it in my room, I could use anything in that tackle box any time I wanted.

He asked me to take him up to the top of the Capitol Building, because I knew how to take the elevator and he wasn't sure, so we did that, and then we had an ice cream cone. Then he asked me, since I seemed to know quite a bit about catcher's mitts, if I could take him over to Lawlor's sporting goods store and help him pick out a good one for a young friend of his who was just about my age.

Well, I did it, but I sure didn't like it. It had been a great day—getting use of all that fishing gear, going up the elevators to the top of the Capitol, the candy, the ice cream, the pop—but this next task wasn't going to be that easy.

It was bad enough that I ached for a mitt of my own, but here I was helping Uncle Grover buy one for some other kid. For a good half-hour I tested pockets in catcher's mitts, slamming my fist into soft, moist, redolent leather until my arm was sore. I thought about selecting a third-rate glove for this kid I'd never met, but I knew I couldn't do that to Uncle Grover. Finally I settled on a fine mitt that brought tears to my eyes when I put it on.

"Best glove in the store," the salesman said, "and the only one of that quality we have left. Can't buy a better glove than that for nineteen ninety-five." It would have hurt me knowing that this was the only glove like this left in the store, meaning I wouldn't have one, but it didn't make any difference anyway. If twelve dollars was impossible, then nineteen ninety-five . . . ?

"Are you sure that's the best catcher's mitt you've seen?" Uncle Grover asked.

"Yeah, it is, Uncle Grover," I said with a catch in my throat. God, it hurt. "Then we'll take it," he told the clerk and handed over twenty dollars. The clerk put the glove in a nice solid box and then into a large paper sack and thrust it toward me. It would have been nice to carry the sack saying "Lawlor's" down Lincoln's main street to the car. Maybe someone would see me and know I had been shopping in the best sporting goods store in town and think that I had a quality item of some kind instead of whatever it was we could afford, but I didn't have the heart for it. I handed the sack to Uncle Grover.

"If you're going to be a catcher, you'll have to learn to carry your own glove, boy," he said sternly. It's a good thing he didn't say any more because I would have dissolved in a puddle on the floor, right there at the cashier's counter in Lawlor's.

When we moved from Lincoln out to Centralia, where Uncle Grover lived all his life, he was nearly eighty. He still lived alone as he had all his life and was still running the farm by himself even though we all worried about him. His place was up in the hilly northwestern part of Bleaker County. His lane was almost a half mile long, so whenever we had a blizzard, Uncle Grover was stranded, sometimes for as long as a month. We once took groceries in to him on a tractor when the winter was long and hard; he hadn't been able to get out of his place for almost six weeks. We thought we should at least check to see if he was still alive.

He said he was glad to see us, accepted the groceries, and waved us back out the lane, saying he'd be just fine. "Except for the trouble of playing host for all you uninvited guests," he said as we left.

One morning five years ago Uncle Grover stepped out onto his back porch and slipped on a bit of ice. He hit the concrete apron off the stairs and broke his hip. He managed to get to his car and get it started, and then he drove the thirty-two miles to the Rising City Hospital where he sat outside the emergency entrance honking the horn of his car until someone finally came out to see what was going on and got him into the hospital for care.

When I drove him back out to his farm a few weeks later, I asked him why he didn't stop at a neighbor's and ask him to call me or the hospital or the Centralia Fire Department. "Whenever I went by someone's place I knew I watched for a light, but no one was up yet that morning and I didn't want to bother 'em. And I'm not the sort who bothers someone I don't know just because I was dumb enough to fall down and bust up a hip," he said.

"Look, you tough old goat," I scolded, "I'm not at all happy about leaving you out here as it is. I want you to get a telephone."

"I am not going to have one of those things in my place."

"But Uncle Grover . . ."

"Now, don't say any more because I won't hear it. I'll tell you straight out what I'll do and straight out what I won't do, and I'm telling you straight out, I won't have a telephone in my house. All that clattering and ringing and prying people bothering me. If I want to talk with anyone, I'll go see 'em."

"Okay, Uncle Grover, no telephone, but I won't even drive into your lane unless you promise me right now that you'll go to the neighbors or somehow let them know if anything like this happens again."

He grunted.

"That's not enough," I said. "I want a promise."

"I promise."

"You'll promise to let a neighbor know if something happens."

"Yeah, I promise, Roger," and I could tell by the way he said it that he was promising, and I knew from the way he was that his promise was good.

I didn't know how tough an old goat he really was until we reached his farm that day. "When I came here the day after your accident to feed the dogs someone had already closed your new gate for you," I said. He had put up a nice new pipe gate only a week before he had his accident.

"I closed it," he said.

"You closed it?"

"You don't think I was going to drive through a brand-new one-hundred-and-fifty-dollar gate, do you?"

"What did you do? Crawl out of the car and open the gate?!"

"Yes, then I drove the car through the gate, crawled out again, closed the gate, crawled back to the car, and drove to the hospital. Nearly ruined a good set of overalls."

It was just like the time we drove downtown in Lincoln when I was a boy. I didn't know what to say in the presence of this giant. I once broke my ankle, slipping on a piece of ice just like Uncle Grover; when I tried to stand up, I fainted and bounced my head off a kitchen cabinet. I remember that pain. What Uncle Grover had gone through to save that new gate was what most people would do to save their lives. It wasn't a matter of being cheap; for Uncle Grover, it was simply a matter of being practical.

I got him settled in his house—Lily had already cleaned the place up, put new food in the refrigerator and cupboards, remade the bed I moved downstairs for him, and washed out the sinks. He was obviously glad to be home and smiled—"Place looks good"—by way of acknowledging what we had done by way of sprucing the place up.

He did pretty well for a couple years. We dropped in every few weeks and then every month or so to make sure he was in good health and didn't need anything. He was soon driving his car again, even his tractor. He rented most of his land to neighbors and he got rid of the livestock all except some poultry, but he still planted a little garden and grew some grain for his ducks, chickens, and geese. He never ate any of them or gathered the eggs, but he said it wouldn't be a farm if there weren't the sounds of some critters around.

The neighbors found Grover dead one Sunday. They were driving back from the Farwell Church, they told me, and saw a sheet hanging from the windmill tower in Uncle Grover's yard. They went to the house to check on him and found him in his kitchen, lying dead on the floor. He had been dead only a day. He had written a note telling us what had happened:

"Roger made me promise to let you know, so here it is. I fell off the tractor Wednesday. Same hip. I got to the house, fed Benjy"—Benjy was his dog—"and got a sheet just before the rain started. Tough goin but good for the corn. Rain let up that night and put sheet on the windmill just before train came thru. Got back to the house just in time to see Rode Runner. Haha. I'm not doing so good now, so make sure Slick gets Benjy."

It wasn't until Uncle Grover's funeral on Tuesday that my cousin Mark and I figured out what that note really meant. The only rain we had had that week was on Thursday. Grover fell off his tractor Wednesday. That means it took Uncle Grover a full day and night to crawl to the house from out in the field. The train goes by Grover's place on Friday, about sundown, so it had taken him another full day to struggle back out of the house, across the yard, and up the twenty steps of the windmill ladder, where we found the sheet. He got down off the windmill and back to the house twelve hours later and spent the next few hours dying and watching cartoons on his television. I don't believe a twenty-year-old athlete could have survived that marathon of pain.

Now, I don't want you to think for a moment that I consider this to be a sad story. Dying in a hospital bed is a sad story.

God knows, Uncle Grover didn't spend his last days feeling sorry for himself. He just did what needed to be done. When I think of him, I think about the time the parish priest dropped by on Friday and found him sitting at his table eating sausage. The priest was shocked and told Grover that by way of a penance for having eaten meat on Friday he would have to deliver a load of wood to the church the next week.

"But sausage isn't meat," Grover argued.

"Indeed it is, my son," said the priest sternly.

The next week Grover traveled the extra miles to the mill in Centralia and back so he could deliver a load of sawdust to the church, telling the stunned priest, "If sausage is meat, then sawdust is firewood."

Uncle Grover was full of stories like that. For example, he said that when he and his father came out here, the first year they planted potatoes. "Planted twelve bushel of seed potatoes by hand," Grover used to say. And that fall, he told me, he and his father harvested exactly twelve bushel of potatoes. When I expressed sympathy, he said, "Was our own fault. We could have planted more."

He said that in the thirties it was so dry his well water only tested out at 60 percent moisture content. And that the wind blew so strong one of his hens once laid the same egg seven times. One day he told me it was too windy to load rocks, and when pressed for why he had never married, he said he was looking for a rich old widow with a bad cough.

He used to say that he got his bad eye because he was once polite to a lady on a trolley in Lincoln. He said he got up to give her his seat and when she thanked him for his courtesy, he explained to her, "I'm that sort of fellow. A lot of the men these days, you know, only give their seats to good-looking women," and that, he said, was when he lost his eye.

It wasn't often that we could get Uncle Grover to tell us stories like that, but I'll never forget the times he did. Uncle Grover never laughed, even though all the rest of us did.

What always amazed me about him is that he could tell stories like that when I knew what a series of tragedies his life had been. He had lost two sisters in the influenza plagues of 1918 when I lost two of my grandparents. He had seen the floods in the Oak River valley that destroyed so many farms and even took lives. There were the dust storms and grasshopper storms of the thirties. There was the time his barn burned down, the accident when he lost three fingers to a grain auger, the loss of his life savings when the Centralia Bank went broke, the money he had spent taking care of his aunt at the Rising City rest home.

And yet Uncle Grover never mentioned such things. If he did say anything, it was something either kind or funny, but it was always gentle. And all that from this giant who could crush pliers with his bare hands. I once asked him, "Uncle Grover, how can you tell such funny stories when you have obviously had more than your share of tough times?"

I've never forgotten his answer. He said, "Roger, I'm not an educated man, you know, and I can't give you the philosophy or the psychology of the matter but I can tell you another story. Once old Benjy and I were down in the Cherry Creek bottoms hunting and Benjy ran right smack into a bobcat three times his size. Benjy took off running, that bobcat right behind him. Now, you can look at Benjy over there and see that he was at a principal disadvantage in this matter: He could see that that bobcat was gonna get him, so he ran up to one of those big cottonwood trees that grows down there along the creek and he run thirty feet right straight up the trunk."

Uncle Grover paused to let that soak in, he looked me straight in the eyes, and said, "Now that dog didn't climb the tree because he could, Roger; he climbed it because he had to." What Uncle Grover was telling me was as simple as it was articulate: He didn't laugh because he could, he laughed because he had to.

After his funeral I sat down with my cousin Mark at the Town Tavern and we talked about what we remembered about Uncle Grover. "I was always uncomfortable when I had to spend time with him because he was so old and big and rough," laughed Mark, "but all my life I'll remember the time he came to Denver to visit the folks and me and he asked me to be his guide in downtown Denver. I hardly knew what I was doing, but I managed to steer him over to the Botanical Gardens, which was always my favorite place, and then he took me to Elitch Gardens and had me show him how to ride the roller coaster and play all the games. And then he asked me to take him to May D and F because he had a friend who had a boy who needed a football helmet. And I'll tell you, Rog, it damn near killed me because I was in Peewee Football at the time . . ."

Grover Bass. The name is like a poem.

FANCY DRINKS

IT'S NOT VERY far from the village of Centralia, Nebraska, to Rising City. Maybe twenty-five miles. But it's a long ways from a lounge in Rising City to Centralia's Town Tavern.

You probably wouldn't take a little kid into a *lounge*, but in a town like Centralia the tavern is the equivalent of the town hall. It's not just a place to drink. In fact, a lot of people who are regulars here don't drink alcoholic beverages at all. Goose doesn't drink, but he's in the Town Tavern every day. I think maybe Oscar doesn't have anything against drinking, but I don't think I have seen him drink in here. In fact, my pal Slick who owns the tavern doesn't drink. Not a drop.

This is a place to meet, to talk, to laugh, and almost incidentally to have a drink now and then. Actually, for a newcomer to small-town life, one of the toughest things

78

to get used to is how to order a drink in a place like Slick's Town Tavern.

The first time I walked into the Town Tavern I asked for a beer and whoever was tending bar at the time asked me, "Plain?"

I was nonplused. "Plain?" What's the alternative? Well, out here on the Plains the alternative is *red* beer. It's a mug of whatever beer is on tap plus a healthy proportion of tomato juice, or better yet—if you want to get fancy— tomato juice, a dash of Worcestershire sauce, some Tabasco, celery salt, and pepper. Yum.

Red beer—sometimes simply "a red one"—is the standard morning-after drink out here on the Plains and is very popular with the ladies at all hours, but it is not considered a breach of tavern etiquette to drink a red beer any time of the night or day.

The argument often goes that a red beer is a lot like a good, solid breakfast—cereal in the barley and vitamins in the tomato juice. And breakfast is the most important meal of the day.

Red beer is sometimes thought of as a morning drink, sometimes as a woman's drink, but it is not at all unusual to walk into any small-town tavern on the central Plains and find someone drinking a *red* beer.

Now and then I fancy an after-dinner liqueur or wine, and one of the things I learned early on is that if you want anything without ice, you'd better make that point early and firmly because otherwise, *everything* comes with ice.

Another thing: Don't order anything fancy. Let me explain fancy. My friend Oscar once went into a Sandhills bar and ordered a screwdriver—vodka and orange juice. The grizzled bartender looked him in the eye and said,

"Mister, if you want a fancy drink, you can just go to a fancy place!"

A couple days ago another Bleaker County friend was laughing about a stop he and some friends made in another small-town tavern even farther west than Centralia. He said that the four couples were returning from a wedding in Alliance and stopped for a cool drink on a very hot afternoon.

The bartender in the small, simple tavern greeted them and asked what they would like. He listened patiently as the orders came: "One light beer, two Millers, two raspberry wine coolers, a vodka tonic, a sloe gin fizz, and a whiskey sour." He looked at the nicely dressed visitors a moment, obviously trying to think of how he was going to deal with this problem diplomatically. Then he said with a sigh, "Okay, let's make this easy. How many whiskeys? How many beers?"

I once went into a tavern in a town of no more than one hundred citizens, and I suggested to my first wife, Betty, a woman who wouldn't take a suggestion on how to swim if she was drowning, that we might order a drink. I knew enough about village taverns that I issued a warning before the bartender approached us: "Don't order anything fancy, Betty."

"I'll have a Jack Daniel's on ice," I said. "No water," thinking I might head off problems.

My erstwhile wife said, "I'll have a gin and tonic."

Oh no. The bartender left our table and I said, "Good grief, woman, I told you not to order anything fancy. A place like this may not have any gin, probably doesn't have tonic water, and certainly doesn't have a lime."

But the bartender came back a few minutes later with my whiskey and ice and something that looked pretty much like a gin and tonic. "Excuse me, folks," he said. "I checked the book on how to make a gin and tonic but I don't have any limes, or tonic water, or even gin, so I hope vodka and soda water will be all right."

When he came back to ask if we were ready for a second try, I again warned my wife not to order anything fancy. I asked for a refill on my whiskey and ice. What do you think *she* asked for? A brandy. She ordered a *brandy.*

Again the bartender drifted off and again he returned, this time with my whiskey and ice and with her brandy—a tumbler of blackberry brandy on ice. In Centralia blackberry brandy is not so much a drink as it is a medicine—good for colds, flu, and the drizzles.

A fancy television guy from New York came through Centralia last summer while working on a program about drought and failure, which certainly made Centralia a matter of type casting. He came into the Town Tavern and ordered—get this—a martini. He at least took the caution of asking if Carla, the barmaid, knew how to make a martini. When she didn't seem sure of herself, the guy with the necktie said, "That's gin and a little vermouth."

"Easy enough. Gin and vermouth," Carla must have thought. "Let's see, for a whiskey sour you mix a shot of whiskey and a cup or so of mix, so that should work for a martini: a shot glass of gin, a cup of Wahini Wine Cooler, since we don't keep vermouth, and *lots* of ice. There you go, Mr. Tourist. Your martini."

If you want a fancy drink, believe me, go to a fancy place. In a small town you drink beer and vodka, maybe whiskey. The fattest guys in a little town drink light beer, don't ask me why. Women drink wine coolers, and don't ask me about that either. In towns like Centralia wine comes in bottles with screw caps and *never—never!—*

bears a label saying what year it was made. It may, however, have a little tag that says, BEST IF DRUNK BEFORE MARCH 1989.

In Bleaker County you should never pay more than three dollars for a bottle of champagne and you should be careful when and where you order it: Any bystanders will know what you're up to because nothing puts a woman into bed with the passions quicker than a little champagne.

And you better make damned sure no one is within hearing distance when you order yourself a Tom Collins or Old Fashioned.

"If you want a fancy drink . . ."

THE WEDDING

LILY AND I have been married for almost ten years, but folks around here are still talking about the wedding. There were a couple of times during our courtship, it didn't seem to anyone, least of all us, that the marriage was ever going to happen. Our romance was electric, but early on in our time together we decided there were too many differences between us and that we could probably save everyone a lot of trouble by calling the whole thing off. We weren't mad at each other or anything like that; everything just seemed to be so much trouble.

We were here at the farm when we were breaking up, saying good-by for the last time. Lily was crying. I wasn't feeling very good myself. Lily said it would be heartbreaking, never seeing the place again, and I understood that because I love the farm almost as much as I love her. Little did we suspect that a year later her name would be on the deed. I tried to comfort her by saying that I would always

83

try to be her friend—and of course I do, but not in the way I thought I would—and that given the opportunity, by golly, I would dance at her wedding. Which, as it turns out, I did. But, as you'll see, not with her.

Eventually Lily and I got past all those problems and decided to get married on April 25. The boys in town accused me of picking April 25 because that year it was the night we changed to daylight savings time and they figured that since Lily is nearly twenty years younger than me, I was trying to make things easy on myself by taking advantage of the one night of the year that is an hour shorter than all the rest.

We finally found a minister who would marry us. We wanted to be married outside on the farm, down by the river, but one preacher told us that that wouldn't do because God is in His house, not down by the river, which pretty much confirmed my estimates of the relationship between religion and God. But the Lutheran minister here in Centralia had spent some time watching birds on our place so I thought he might cooperate with an outdoor wedding, and he did.

He said that before he could marry us, however, we would have to "take instruction" with him. Lily felt that we should do whatever we could to sanctify a marriage that would almost certainly need all the help it could get. Take a look at this inventory:

Lily is a Czech; I am German.

She is Catholic; I am something else.

She is female; I am male. (I know that seems self-evident, but you'd be surprised how many couples don't take that very important difference seriously).

She is quiet and gentle; I am loud and obnoxious.

At the time she was twenty-seven years old; I was forty-five.

Neither of us were members of the church we were asking to marry us.

So I told Lily that I had no problem with "taking instruction." Even as he told us his requirements, the minister seemed a little uneasy. I am older than he is, I already had a reputation for being a little peculiar, and as I told him, I really didn't think I would need much instruction, having been married once before for nearly twenty years and having endured damn near everything any man should have to put up with in a marriage.

The first night Lily and I walked up to town and met the minister in his study at the church. After a couple of preliminary niceties, the minister opened his Bible and announced that we would be discussing in this first of four sessions the duty that a woman owes to her husband. He told us that just as only one person can drive an automobile, and that of course is the man, only one person can steer a marriage, and that too is the man. The "instruction" continued along those lines for about an hour, and I enjoyed every minute of it.

As we walked home I could tell from the silence that Lily was not happy about the idea of "submitting and cleaving," as the minister put it. But I didn't say much and neither did she.

The next time we met with the minister, I was a little uneasy, since we had gotten off to what I sensed was a shaky start. Again we exchanged pleasantries with the minister, and oh boy, he started on submitting and cleaving again. I wondered if he had any idea how thin the ice was that he was stomping on with both feet.

To make a long story short, the third session dealt with

pretty much the same topic as the first one. On the walk home Lily said that if it was all the same with me, she'd probably had all the "instruction" she needed and she was going to ask the minister if maybe we could forgo the fourth meeting. I have no idea what she said to him when she called, but he agreed to skip the last seminar and marry us anyway. Maybe Lily convinced him that we had a good grasp on submitting and cleaving. I've never had the nerve to ask her.

The wedding itself was beautiful, peaceful, and private. The day was glorious, and we were surrounded by a small gathering of good friends and family. We stood in a circle of towering cottonwood trees and sheltering cedars. The songs of the birds seemed to echo our own joy. Not twenty feet away the river water rippled soothingly. It was warm for April, not a cloud in the sky. Everything went smoothly. It was precisely the wedding I had imagined and hoped for. We invited everyone we knew for the reception, and it was not so serene.

You have to imagine hundreds of Lily's Czech Catholic relatives coming to grips with all my German Lutheran relatives. We were married in Centralia, which is Danish Lutheran, but the dance was in Stanford, which is Polish Catholic. It's the only wedding I've ever seen where there should have been a couple of field judges and a referee.

Not until the next day did we discover that the pals I had asked to help us with the food had gotten their noses wet, as the phrase goes around here. When they skidded to a stop in front of the dance hall to deliver the food, the turkey loaf slid off the back of the pickup truck into the gravel of the street. They told us a week or so after the wedding that they had done their best to wash the gravel off the turkey loaf in the sink in the dance hall's kitchen and CeCe arranged it nicely on the banquet tables. They suspected, however, that their gaffe had not gone undetected when they noticed that the guests devoured all the liverwurst and baloney, all the pickle loaf and deviled eggs—but no one ever took more than one slice of the turkey-loaf-and-gravel canapés.

Lily and I also noticed, but only peripherally, that none of the buckets of sour cream and French onion chip dip we had bought showed up on the food tables, but we were too swept up in the festivities to give the deficiency more than a passing thought. Stan Kopelski told us that he found them mid-July when he tossed a bunch of fence posts into the back of his pickup truck and broke open the paper sacks there, sacks he had occasionally wondered about. It was the dip that had been sitting for three months in the Nebraska sun. He says that after all these years, if he drives real fast he can hardly even smell the stuff anymore.

Lily and I had been to Stan and Beth's wedding two months before and had tried to learn things from their experience that we could apply to our own upcoming wedding. We noticed, for one thing, that at the Kopelski's wedding dance, Stan and Beth had almost no chance to be together. Even worse, no one had a chance to talk quietly because of the loud music and laughter, so Lily and I decided not to have a dance.

Now think for a moment about the cosmic craziness of trying to have a German and Czech wedding without a dance. In retrospect we realized that it was a dumb idea, but at the time it seemed like a good one. So the day before the wedding we moved dozens of tables and hundreds of chairs out into the hall and set everything up for drinking, eating, and comfortable, cozy conversation. It wasn't three minutes into the reception before revelers were moving furniture and someone came in with a sound system they had dug up someplace around town and a stack of polka recordings. Whether we wanted a dance or not, we had one.

The one person I didn't get to dance with that night was Lily, so our peculiar prescience about my dancing at her wedding was true—I did dance at her wedding—but contrary to what any of us thought, it was not with her. She danced with her brothers, her father, her uncles and cousins, my buddies and relatives. I danced with her aunts and her mother, CeCe, LaVerne, and some women I had never seen before in my life. But in the confusion and joy, the whirling dancers and joyful drinkers, we never found each other.

Slick, Goose, and Ralph tended bar for me at the reception. Everyone told me, even before the wedding, that that was another dumb idea, hiring the three biggest drunks in Bleaker County to tend bar, but my theory was that if I could keep those three busy, the bar bill would be a lot less than if they had had only themselves to take care of.

As it turned out, it didn't make any difference. Such heroic quantities were consumed that minor variables like Goose, Slick, and Ralph wouldn't have made a dent in the eventual refreshment totals. At one point Goose came over to me and said, "Rog, those bohunks"—that's what Czechs are called around here, even Lily's relatives—"those bohunks want to mix their own drinks, and believe me, they mix 'em strong."

"That's okay, Goose," I told him. "Let them mix their own drinks."

It wasn't long before he was back again. "Now they want to take the bottles to their tables."

"That's okay. Let them take the bottles."

Another pause and here he came again. "Now they're taking the bottles home with them."

"Well, jeez, Goose, do you think we can stop them?"

He looked at me and considered my question. "No way in hell," he said and returned to his post at the bar.

I later heard that I missed the best part of the party. At some point in the evening Woodrow told me that my pal Luke was fooling around with a local farmer's young—very young—daughter, so I stormed out looking for him. (I later found that he was already having his share of problems with his wife and wouldn't have had time for any more complications in his life.) While I was outside roaming around among the parked cars, CeCe, Woodrow, and Lunchbox conspired with Lily's two sisters, Claire and Faye, and together they kidnapped Lily.

If you are not familiar with Midwestern ethnic weddings, this is not as sinister as it might seem. The custom is to take the bride off to another town to a tavern and try to get her as drunk as possible, hopefully too drunk to consummate the marriage. Even if the kidnapping is not that successful, the kidnappers will at least try to keep the bride away from the celebration long enough to extort some tribute from the groom.

Well, Woodrow, Lunchbox, CeCe, Claire, and Faye took off to Barnston with Lily about the time I went outside. When they got to Barnston, they ordered a pitcher of red beer and Woodrow called back to the reception-turned-dance with a ransom demand: "Either Welsch comes up with a case of whiskey for us or he won't have a bride tonight."

I don't know who Woodrow talked with on that occasion but whoever it was looked around a while and finally came back to the phone to tell him, "Sorry, but Roger isn't here. He left about a half-hour ago."

Assuming there must be a misunderstanding of some sort, Woodrow returned to the abductors and victim, figuring that they would have a few more red beers and then try calling again. Now, Woodrow couldn't have known Lily very well at that point because if he had, he would have known that you can put red beers into her with a fire hose and there isn't a pumper in the county that could keep up the pressure.

To make things worse, by that time Claire had gotten into a pool game with three cowboys from the Sandhills. She was pouring it on good, winking, leaning over the table to take long shots, and laughing coyly. Sweat was pouring out from under the cowboys' big hats, and it was beginning to look as if Woodrow, Lunchbox, and Slick were going to have a lot of explaining to do to the amorous cowboys when they decided to take Claire back to the wedding or to Claire's folks if they didn't take her back.

To make matters worse, Lily's other sister, Faye, had walked too close to a table of card players on her way back from the ladies' room and she was in the process of telling four burly guys that if they were brave enough to pat her on the fanny maybe they would like to step over to the bar and talk with Woodrow, Lunchbox, and Slick. These guys were big, railroad construction workers in town for a little rest and recreation. They took one look at the Centralia trio in their wedding clothes and started making remarks about the sissy shirts the Centralia boys seemed to be sporting those days. All in all, things were not looking good.

Woodrow drifted back over to the pay telephone and made another call to the dance. "Is Welsch there? Tell him that if he wants a bride tonight, he better have a good bottle of whiskey ready."

As it turned out, Marv Casperson had been working out in the fields all day but made a special trip into town just to have a drink with me on my wedding day. It was a nice gesture, so we stepped out to his grain truck to drink a couple quick ones. And Marv had some advice he needed to give me about women. At least I guess it was advice. He said, "Rog, me and some of your friends have been talking, and we're worried about you. You're getting on in years, you know, and . . ."

"Jeez, Marv, I'm only forty-five years old. It's not as if I'm decrepit," I complained.

"Now just listen to me here, Rog. This girl's a lot younger than you and, well, let me tell you a story. Once there was an old dog like you and he married his young hired girl. And he told her, 'Honey, when I'm out working in the fields and you feel like you need a little loving, you just step outside and fire the shotgun and I'll come running.' "

Marv paused for dramatic effect, put his big, farmer's hand on my shoulder, looked right into my eyes, and concluded, "You know, Rog, that old guy died two weeks into pheasant season," and he exploded into laughter.

Then it seemed as if everyone had an old-man-marries-a-young-woman joke to tell me, and by the time I got back into the dance, whoever it was who answered Woodrow's telephone call this time had told Woodrow that I wasn't anywhere around and that most folks at the dance had the impression that I had gone somewhere with Casperson, maybe over to Farwell. Or even into Rising City. No one knew.

As Lily later told the story to me, Woodrow returned to the kidnapping party in the Barnston tavern with a look of concern on his face. Lily was finishing off the second pitcher of red beer and was ready for more, she announced cheerfully. At the pool table, one of the cowboy's girlfriends was making noises about ripping out Claire's eyes and at the card table Faye was making it clear that if the four construction workers had any manhood at all, they would take their roving hands over to the bar where any one of the men in her group would be perfectly happy to rearrange the ugly faces of any one . . . any *two* . . . heck, all *four* of them, free of charge.

This time Woodrow waited only ten or fifteen minutes before trying another call to the dance. "Yeah, we have the bride and if Welsch will buy us a beer, we'll bring her right back," he tried.

Once again Woodrow's timing couldn't have been worse. One of my best friends, a man who had told me there would be no way he would be able to come to the wedding, had managed to make his way all the way from Oregon to Nebraska, and all at once there he was. We shook hands, hugged, and decided to walk down to the river and sit on the bridge talking a while and enjoying the cool of the evening.

So the woman who answered the third call to the dance could only tell Woodrow, "I asked around and someone says he's down at the bridge fishing. No one here has any idea when he'll be back."

Lily later told me that Woodrow came back from the pay phone, pulling on his jacket. He announced, "Time to go," grabbed her, and led her out to the car, telling

CeCe and Lunchbox to do what they could to rescue Faye from the railroad workers and the cowboys from Claire. There was a lot of shouting and screaming, some really nasty threats, during the kidnap party's exit but no damage was done when everyone was back in Woodrow's car.

"We're going to make one short stop at the Rising City airport and then we're going back to the dance," Woodrow said, making it clear that the question was not up for discussion.

"Could we stop in Rising City so I could use the powder room?" Lily asked. "And maybe another red beer? It's my wedding night after all."

"Yeah, one more stop," Woodrow sighed.

I was back at the dance and had just asked Goose what happened to Lily when they all walked through the door. Lily and her sisters were instantly swept onto the dance floor by eager polka-ers and I got a brief report from CeCe. Later in the evening Woodrow cornered me over behind the bar. "Rog, I just spent nearly two hours with your bride and her two sisters."

"That's what I heard from CeCe," I answered. "Sorry it didn't work out. I wasn't around to get your ransom demands. I'll buy you a drink for your trouble anyway."

"After what I've seen tonight, buddy, it's obvious to me that this ransom stuff needs to be the other way around," and he handed me an unopened bottle of Jack Daniel's. "There you are, buddy, and if I were you, I'd drink some of that before you dive out of here and head for the Sea Breeze Motel."

"Well, thanks, Woodrow, but . . ."

"That's not all," he said, shaking his head seriously as he handed me an envelope. I opened it and found a

$100,000 trip insurance policy Woodrow had bought from the machine in the lobby of the Rising City airport. "I don't know, Rog, but I think you're going to need this," Woodrow said.

PIGEONS

"NOW, THERE'S SOME kind of coincidence for you," said Lily with unaccustomed irony. "Here I am setting the table for supper, and Lunchbox and Woodrow drive into the yard. When was the last time that happened?"

"Yesterday, I think," I answered, trying to eat as much of the meat loaf on my plate as possible, knowing that once those two were in the house and at the table, there would be no mercy.

Lunchbox and Woodrow are a lot like my dog Blackjack. His heart is full of good will and happiness, but wherever he goes he leaves destruction behind him. His tail flails from one side to the other, clear-cutting a path four foot wide of furniture, children, beer cans, whatever happens to be there. Then Blackjack turns around, surveys the damage, and wonders how all that came to be.

Woodrow and Lunchbox never call ahead and ask if they can drop by or come early enough that they can transact whatever business they have—seeing if I can go fishing, for example, or borrowing my shotgun—and get a proper invitation or be sent along their way. They come unerringly at the moment Lily sets the table because they don't want to be any trouble. That way, they explain, they don't have to hang around. We're eating after all. So they can just say what they need to say and then go.

But they never do. Lily always invites them to sit down. Her Czech blood denies her the possibility of not inviting hungry men to sit down at the table. And they always do, their male heritage denying them the possibility of saying no.

Antonia and Lily watched with a horrified fascination as the supper disappeared along with the meat loaf still on the stove that Lily had planned to use for the next day's sandwiches. The bread disappeared, the salad, the potatoes and gravy, and the peas. I wondered if Lily was going to have the discretion not to say anything about the chocolate pie in the refrigerator.

One of Lily's culinary peculiarities is that when she serves radishes, she puts them on the table in a little, wide-mouthed jar of water. She says it keeps them crisp and fresh, and besides, that's the way her mother served radishes. Even Woodrow stopped eating and watched Lunchbox with admiration as he ate the last six radishes in one mouthful. *And then drank the water from the radish jar.*

To my horror Lily also brought out the chocolate pie. (Only later did I learn that she knew our situation well and had stashed two pieces toward the back of the lower shelves of the refrigerator, well out of sight, probably out of danger.) She suggested then that maybe "the men folk would like to repair to the back porch to wash down supper with some cold beer." Woodrow and Lunchbox took kindly to the suggestion, I grabbed a six-pack from the cellar, and we stepped onto the screened porch into the cool of the evening.

We sat there quietly for a good hour, picking our teeth, making adjustments for the generous supper, and looking out over the river and the bridge down below my place. In the summer it stays light until nearly ten in the evening, so we just sat there enjoying the cooling of the day, listening to the evening sounds, and enjoying the cold beer I retrieved regularly from the cellar. I've noticed that city people get nervous if no one says anything on occasions like this, but I had learned when I spent time with the Indians that sometimes it's nice simply to be in good company. You don't really have to say anything to express good feelings like that. Country folks are like that sometimes too. But finally, when we had polished off maybe five or six beers apiece, Woodrow broke the silence, "Boy, that's a mess of pigeons circling the bridge."

"Yeah," I said, "there are maybe thirty of them and they live down there somewhere. What I don't understand is that they just keep flying in circles like that. Round and round they go. They come under the bridge—see, there they go right now—come up the other side"—I hesitated long enough for the birds to come out from under the span—"then come upstream by that willow"—another pause—"and turn back . . . go back over the bridge . . . drop down again . . . and back under. Sometimes they do that all day long."

We watched them a few minutes and Woodrow said, "What do you suppose those birds think about all day long circling around like that? All they do is fly over the bridge and then under the bridge, over the bridge, under the bridge. They must look around and see the world under 'em. What do you suppose they think about?"

We sat there a long time in silence, watching the pigeons circle, pondering that philosophical question, and then Lunchbox said, "You know what I think those pigeons are thinking, boys? I think they're thinking, 'Look at those guys sitting down there. All they do is drink beer and then go take a leak, drink beer and go take a leak. Sometimes they do that all day long—drink beer, take a leak, drink beer, take a leak. What do you suppose those guys down there think about?' That's what I think they're thinking."

It was a long time before anyone said anything else.

INDIAN TIME

IN OMAHA INDIAN culture, you don't ask questions. It's just not done. It's part of their way of life. Imagine what it was like the time I spent seven days camping on the reservation during the Omahas' centennial powwow— for one hundred years they had been holding their annual powwow dances on the same site—and I couldn't ask questions.

By the time I went up to the centennial powwow I had spent enough time with the Omahas that I was comfortable with their ways. A lot of whites wonder why the Indians haven't adjusted all that well to white culture when, "Heck, my grandparents came over here from Holland— didn't speak a word of English and didn't have a dime— but they managed to do all right, and they never went on welfare either." That's the way Royal Cupp put it, and you've heard the same thing from other people in other places. Well, there's a much bigger jump from Indian to white than from Holland to America.

Once I knew a little about Indian ways I took great pleasure in being with the Omahas. If I ever got into real trouble—went broke, got real sick, just went to pieces, had a world of problems—I'd go to my Indian friends and relatives before I'd go to my blood relatives, and that's for sure. Part of my pleasure in being with the Indians is that I genuinely love to learn things and there weren't many stretches when I was with the Indians when I wasn't learning more than I could easily absorb within the allotted time. And the things I learned were big things, things that changed my life.

It doesn't seem like much, I know, but one night during that centennial powwow I woke up in my tent and there was all kinds of noise going on outside. It wasn't fighting or anything like that. In fact, it sounded for all the world as if I were camped in the middle of a baseball game.

I checked my watch, and it was about two-thirty in the morning. I crawled out of my sleeping bag and raised a window flap of the tent. There was a full moon, some lights over the camping ground, and a lot of car headlights, so I could see pretty well what was going on. And sure as hell, I was in the middle of a baseball game, not far from second base.

Having never been in that situation before—camping at second base—I just went back to bed and did my best to get a little sleep. I wanted to be ready to go for the next day's events after all. The next morning I went over to Frank and Clyde Sheridan's tents and sat down at their campfire with them. They poured me a cup of Indian coffee—boiled with the sugar already in it—and we sat there just appreciating the cool morning and warm coffee for a while. You see, I knew I couldn't *ask* what had been going on the night before. It would have been rude.

"I guess there was a ball game here last night," I suggested.

"Yeah, the Little Warriors just stomped the living daylights out of the Legion Boys," Frank laughed. "In fact, we were kind of wondering where you were."

Well, I didn't want to be rude, but Holy Cow, "daylights" is an interesting word to use in this situation, Frank. I was sleeping! It was the middle of the night and I was in my tent and I was sleeping—oh, I'd say about ten or twenty feet toward left center field from second base, I wanted to snap. All I said, however, was, "I was sleeping."

Frank and Clyde laughed, and I could hear Clyde's beautiful wife, Lillian, and his sons, Matt and Dewey, laughing from inside the tents. "See, I told you," Clyde yelled at his family in his tent. Then he turned to me. "I told them. I said, 'That crazy damned white man is in that tent down there, I know it.' "

I grinned and looked to Frank for an explanation, Frank looked at Clyde, and they all laughed again. A gentle laugh. They weren't making fun of me; they were just kidding. Omahas don't make fun of anyone.

Clyde said, "I told them: 'That crazy white man is down there sleeping during the cool of the night and I'll bet he'll be sitting around in the sun all afternoon tomorrow. Just you watch. All our relatives here for one short week, and he could be meeting them all here in the cool of the night, and what do you suppose he's doing? He's down there sleeping away the best time of the day. Put him in charge of next year's powwow and I'll bet he'd have everyone playing baseball at two in the afternoon.' "

I suspect I would have too.

I can't give you the appropriate footnotes, but my favorite musical group used to be an outfit—just three kids actually—called "The Incredible String Band," and they *were* incredible. Their music was wild and haunting, and it had a lot to say. One of their songs was about time, and Time—with a capital T—was talking to man. Time was bragging about how he had taken over. He sang to mankind, "Once I was your slave . . . but now you are mine."

I was sleeping at night because night is the *time* to sleep. It didn't make sense to be asleep when it was so cool and so much was going on, but it *was* time to sleep.

As I spent more time with the Indians, I also realized that I ate not because I was hungry but because it was time to eat. I too had become Time's slave. But the Indians set me free. Indians today still speak of "white man's time" and "Indian time." "White man's time" is when everyone gets all sweaty and nervous about ten minutes after something is supposed to have started; "Indian time" means that you start things when things are ready to start and no one gets excited.

Let me give you a good example of the problem. The Omahas once decided to throw a big dance for the white community in Rising City. They wanted to share the beauty of their culture with everyone else, so they issued a general invitation in the newspaper and over the radio. They even planned to feed everyone who showed up for the occasion—corn soup, brown fry bread, sweet coffee.

The day of the dance came, and it turned out to be a beautiful September day. It was cool and sunny, the leaves were gorgeous, there was no wind—all in all, it was about as fine a day as you can imagine. Only about a hundred white folks showed up—because, it turned out, the Boy

Scouts were having a big Indian dance at the town auditorium and everyone was over there watching them pretend to be Indians—but the Omahas were still pleased with how things had turned out.

It had been advertised that the dancing would start at one P.M., but it was already after two when the Indians started to get things together. It was just too nice a day to rush things.

By two-thirty things were starting to fall apart. I went over and talked with some of the whites who were starting to get pretty hot about the delay. I tried to cool them down, but they were ready to forget the whole thing and drive back to Rising City. I hurried back toward where the Indians were slowly getting ready to tell them that they better put things into gear.

As I stepped up to some of my Indian friends at their camp area, I heard one say, "Take a look at those poor white folks sitting over there. They're about ready to go crazy. Here they are in about as pretty a place as they'll ever see, in this fine weather. They haven't got anyplace to go or they wouldn't be here. But they are working so hard at getting riled, I can hear their stomachs growl all the way over here. They're mad as hell, because it's *time* to be mad as hell."

I decided not to say anything. Instead I took off my watch and haven't worn one since.

Most Indian tribes around here have clown dancers at their powwows. The clown dancer does everything wrong. He dances the wrong way around the drum. Instead of stopping precisely on the last beat of the drum, as any good dancer *must* do, he pounds on ten or fifteen extra steps. Everyone howls in laughter as they watch him foul everything up. He helps himself to the food before it is served in equal proportions to everyone. He has a big grin painted on his face. He puts his arms around dancers—male and female—something no one should ever do.

His costume as often as not is a double-breasted suit and a fedora, his face is a white flour sack painted with red cheeks and lips and blue eyes. The clown dancer is a white man. No wonder he does everything wrong.

The most striking thing to me on these occasions is that the clown dancer/white man doesn't carry a staff or eagle-feather fan like the other dancers; he carries an alarm clock. He constantly consults it, stares at it, shakes it, holds it to his ear, and if the alarm goes off, he runs around the dance ring wildly. You see, he *is* a white man.

We are just that goofy when it comes to time. Do you know what white people do to white people in airports? The next time you're in a big airport where they have those little food areas with stand-up tables and no chairs, look around for a clock. They don't very often put up clocks in places like that in airports. They want to get rid of you. They want you to go away. They need your place at the table so the next gulper can choke down his food and move on. They get rid of you by making you a nervous wreck. They take away your clock. And man, you're on your way.

All of which is to explain why I had trouble finding a job for Clyde's son Dewey when he came to town. He had known my Indian friend in Centralia, Calvin White Shell, for some time, so he stayed with Cal and Jacinda for a couple days until he could get established, insofar as Indians ever get established. Dewey knows me and he knows I know some people around town. Most of all he knows I'm a white man and so other white men will talk with me even when they aren't all that anxious to talk with people like him.

I went over to Rosewater's Lumberyard in Rising City and asked to see Martin Rosewater. When I was trying to get some money for Cal when he wanted to go back to school—another story—Martin had been real generous even though he didn't know where the money was going. (I don't like the kind of charity where the recipients have to be properly beholden.) I explained to Martin that I had an Indian friend who needed a job.

"Is he willing to do work like loading the trucks in the morning and cleaning up under saws in the afternoon?" he asked. "Will he straighten up stacks of lumber? I can't find anyone around here who wants that kind of work. It's dirty. Lots of splinters, you know."

"Martin, I have known Dewey a long time and I know he wants to work. I think he'll do anything you need done, and I believe he'll do it right. He comes from a good family and has a nice family of his own."

"Tell him to be here at eight o'clock Monday morning." Martin smiled. We shook hands and I hurried back to Cal's to tell Dewey. He was pleased too, and I felt like the world was going pretty well, considering.

I was crushed when Dewey came down to the house only a week later looking pretty glum. Seems he had been fired after only five days on the job. "Damn, Dewey, what happened?"

"I just don't know, Rog. I liked the job, and I did my best. But I came in today and Mr. Rosewater said he just couldn't keep me on if I didn't want to work. I told him I *did* want to work and he said it sure didn't look like it to him."

"Let's go, Dewey," I said, and we jumped into my

pickup truck and headed for Rising City. At the lumberyard we had to wait a little while to get into Martin's office, and when he saw us, he was obviously uncomfortable. "I didn't want to fire Dewey, Roger, but he really didn't leave me much choice."

"What happened? Dewey tells me he liked the job and did his best to keep the saws clean, the trucks loaded, and the stock straight."

"Well, he did that, all right, but we just can't have people drifting in and out of here whenever they want. We open up at eight and that's policy."

"You mean he did the job but didn't keep the schedule?"

"He wasn't here on time one day out of the five this week. Not one. And he asked to take Wednesday off after only two days on the job."

I turned to Dewey. "What's the deal, Dewey? What was going on Wednesday?"

"Grandma Saunsoci was having her birthday."

"That's what he told me," said Martin, shaking his head. "His grandmother was having a birthday party. You don't take time off work for a birthday party."

The problem was that Grandma Saunsoci was ninety-seven years old. She was the grand matriarch of the Omaha tribe. She was the last member of the tribe who spoke only Omaha. She was believed by the tribe to be the last full-blood Omaha, although she probably was not.

More important, she was part of Dewey's family. I had *told* Martin that Dewey was a family man, and I meant it. Indians are family people. The only thing more important to an Omaha than family is tribe. The real question in my mind was what was Dewey thinking? He must have been amazed to see before him a grown man who had so little regard for his grandmother.

"What about not showing up on time, Dewey?" I asked.

"During the day I worked hard keeping the saws clean and the stock stacked." I turned to Martin, and he shrugged an acknowledgment.

"By the time five o'clock came around, I had the saws all set, the trucks all loaded, and the lumber all dressed up about as neat as it was going to get dressed." Again Martin admitted with a wave of his hand that what Dewey was telling us was indeed the truth.

"So when I left, everything was ready to go for the morning. Now, if I came in here at eight and the saws were dirty, the lumber scattered, and the trucks empty, something sure as hell would have been wrong. Everything was as ready as I could make it, and if I came in at eight I would just stand around waiting for something to do, so I just came at nine when there was work to do."

I turned to Martin. He said, "Roger, it's a matter of principle. We open at eight and that's when I want the help to be here. *All* the help."

I looked at my racial brother Martin and wondered where my people had gone wrong. Time is not a principle. It's a tool, like a hammer or a car. It doesn't tell us what to do; we tell it. We can't ignore everything that makes sense and do what the clock tells us, but that's what Martin was indeed doing. When did we decide to flail around meaninglessly like this? Were we doomed to do it forever?

My shoulders slumped. I couldn't imagine how I was going to undo the generations of cultural misdirection that were going into Martin's position. Dewey's logic was irrefutable . . . but futile.

Martin leaned forward over his desk. He was in agony.

He had so wanted to do the right thing, but he could only go so far in abandoning all of the principles that make the world work smoothly. "Let me put it this way," he tried. He leaned back in his chair, tapped his fingertips together, and blew air out his pursed lips. "Dewey, around here time is money."

I saw Dewey smile and nod. He understood that all too well. "Time is money," he said, and Martin smiled that they had reached some sort of cultural détente.

Good grief, that's it, I said to myself, and I got up to leave. From dead in the water we had gone to reverse, full all engines. Dewey thought he knew what Martin was saying, but he didn't at all. Martin meant, "Time is money. They are the two most important things in the world—the only thing in the world—and we will worship them, as we damn well should."

Dewey, I knew, was thinking like an Omaha, "Time is money. Neither of them are worth a moment of our consideration; they are no consequence in this world—they are not of this world—and we will disregard them, as we damn well should."

I explained it all to Dewey later over a cup of coffee on my back porch. I think he understood. I just told Martin it was okay. I don't think he understood at all.

CeCe

I SUPPOSE CECE is the way she is as a matter of heredity. Her father, Orville, was one of the founders of Centralia. There's no statue of him on main street, but there is no end of tales about how he saved the town at one time or another. For example, when things were really tough, he was the primary industry here.

It seems that the old Ord–Rising City road passed on the eastern edge of town, right through Orville's place and when not a dime was coming through the town from any other source, Orville was bringing in dollars for himself and, when he could, seeing to it that others had their chance too.

There was a big hole in the road right where it crossed his place, and even in the driest years Orville could make a pretty fair living pulling travelers out of that mudhole at four dollars a tow. Four dollars was a lot of money in those days. And when Orville couldn't handle the volume of business, he'd have neighbors and friends come over with their teams (and later, tractors) to pull out the grateful tourists.

For Orville and Centralia, it was a matter of doing well by doing good. The only drawback of the whole operation was that Orville died when he was only fifty-four years old. Worked himself to death, the doctor said, what with hauling wagons and automobiles out of that mudhole all day and hauling water all night.

Bumps, an old-timer here in town, used to say that Orville really came to the town's rescue in the thirties when times were so tough that folks couldn't even afford chicken feed. Orville saved everyone the trouble of worrying about chicken feed by stealing their chickens.

Now, don't get me wrong. CeCe is not by any stretch of the imagination dishonest. She just has a different sense of how things are done. Woodrow says one of the most interesting things about eating over at the Chew 'n' Chat where CeCe is the waitress is to get your check. You never know what it is going to be because CeCe never charges you the same thing two days in a row for the very same thing. We think she takes into account how she feels, what the weather's like, how polite you were when she waited the table, where you sat, what Goose is up to these days, and other factors we haven't figured out yet.

Occasionally Slick has her work as a barmaid over at the Town Tavern. He knows when she's working she eats at the rate of about seven dollars an hour, but he also knows that when she tabulates meal tickets she makes mistakes in favor of the house about three out of four times so he still comes out ahead.

When *I* think of CeCe I think of how she handled things when we got eleven inches of rain in one afternoon and

Cherry Creek ran right through the middle of town as if it had forgotten entirely where its channel had been for fifty years. I'm not going to bother you with a lot of detail, but CeCe is not held in regard by the high-class, and even what passes for middle-class in Bleaker County. She's loud, abrasive, and irreverent. One thing for sure: She doesn't take any sort of trouble from anyone. Perhaps as a result of that, she is not generally thought of as one of the town's solid citizens. Solid citizens do what they're supposed to do. That's not CeCe's style, doing what you're supposed to.

The June flood hit town with no warning. It began raining at one in the afternoon, and by three water was waist deep on main street. The mayor of Centralia at the time was a nice old gentleman—thoroughly pleasant, thoroughly ineffective. When the flood came through, we might just as well have had Pooh Bear in charge of things. Everything by way of civil defense and emergency operations had to go through the mayor's office, of course, which means nothing went through. No one wanted to hurt the mayor's feelings, so no one was willing to do anything.

No one but CeCe, and she did it in spades. She called the civil defense office down in Rising City and said we needed sandbags, tools, relief supplies, manpower, and whatever else they happened to have on hand. Are you the mayor? they asked. Hell yes, I'm the mayor, CeCe snarled, and you better get those supplies here right now because even before I'm the mayor I'm one pissed-off woman.

The supplies were in town within the hour and then CeCe mustered the men of the community, much the same as a mule skinner puts together a team, and put them to work, and she made the guys from Rising City who delivered the sandbags and supplies stay and work too.

As far as I am concerned, whatever the election commissioner says, CeCe is Centralia's mayor for the rest of her life. Next time there's a disaster, I'm going to ask CeCe what to do. Anyway, CeCe is a remarkable figure, no matter how you see her—town bawd or town savior, loudmouth or philosopher, deadbeat or paragon.

CeCe has had her share of problems with her husband, Goose. For that matter, Goose has had his share of problems with CeCe. It's hard to imagine how life could ever be easy with either of them let alone both of them. The passion of their relationship has been either love or hate, rarely anything in between.

Everyone in town knows when there's been trouble over at Goose and CeCe's house because whenever there are problems in paradise, as Lily says, Goose moves out of their house and into his trailer behind their garage. It's not much more than a box where Goose can keep a bed, his guns, and some decoys. It is tucked away back in the trees, but folks keep their eyes on it, sort of like a barometer. Whenever you see lights on in that trailer, you know things are not going well for CeCe and Goose.

Things were not going well for Goose and CeCe when the Mexican came into town to kill his girlfriend. No stranger comes into a town of 380 without being noticed in any event, but when it's three Mexicans driving a battered '67 Plymouth station wagon with Kansas license plates and one flat tire that has been flat for maybe sixty or eighty miles, anonymity is out of the question.

The three Mexicans went into Slick's Town Tavern and seemed innocuous enough, even though they were, as the phrase around here goes, snot-slinging drunk. Slick kept his eye on them but didn't notice that one had gone out the front door until he heard the shots over by the trailer court.

Russ Brown's mother lives over there next to the trailer the Mexican was shooting into, and she told Russ that the guy emptied his .357 into the trailer door, which was probably true. One bullet went through the door, out the other side, through Bert Finch's front door, disabled his recliner chair, continued out the back of his trailer, hit Old Lady Perly's kitchen window, blew her begonias all over the cupboards, and lodged in her copy of *Life's History of the Second World War.*

A .357 makes a lot of racket in a trailer park when it goes off. What with all the yelling and shooting, as I understand it from Russ's mother's account of the events, about fifteen people called the sheriff over in Rising City, all at the same time. Centralia is too small to have any sort of law enforcement officer of its own. Well, that's fine, but Rising City is a good half-hour from Centralia, and so the citizens of Centralia all had to settle back and watch things develop for a half-hour, hopefully without getting shot.

When the sheriff did show up, he spent fifteen minutes drawing down on and handcuffing Dietz Miller, who was leaning up against the back wall of the grocery store across the street from the Town Tavern, looking suspicious, throwing up. By the time the sheriff was done sneaking up on Dietz, throwing handcuffs on him, and then getting them back off without getting anything on his uniform, the Mexican had disappeared into the dark.

For that matter, all the shooting had happened before the sheriff got there, and that's where CeCe comes in. When the Mexican emptied his gun into the trailer where he thought his girlfriend was living and kicked in the door, he found the place empty. And then he was really mad. He broke up what furniture was left, used a mop handle to knock all the windows out of the trailer, kicked in a few doors, reloaded his big revolver, and then went back outside, yelling for his Maria. And it wasn't anything at all like a Leonard Bernstein libretto.

As we reconstructed his route later, he apparently went through Co-op George's backyard and shot his barbecue when it got in his way. Then he fell over Emma Barberry's rhubarb patch and fired a couple rounds into it. He killed the Coke machine at Mel's Sinclair with two shots to the coin slot and then disappeared somewhere down the creek bank.

Even in this little town there's no one could keep track of his erratic path, and so even when the sheriff came into town, no one could tell him where the wild gunman could be found. As it turns out, the Mexican saw the light in the kitchen of the Chew 'n' Chat Cafe where CeCe was working on the Wednesday specials and he came up out of the creek bed and walked in.

For once, CeCe was not fast or loud with her mouth. The Mexican's .357 took a little wind out of her sails. And the Mexican was slowed down a little too. CeCe is not someone to be taken lightly. The Mexican could see that. So he sat down at the table in the café kitchen and demanded a cup of coffee. CeCe, being what she is, said she wanted to see the color of his money before she started pouring coffee, and he put three dollars on the table. Nothing softens CeCe's heart more than a hungry, heartbroken man, so she got him a cup, made some coffee, and cut the frantic fugitive a generous slice of raisin-cream pie.

Well, that calmed him down quite a bit and he started

to talk. He told CeCe that his girlfriend—one of the Golddust Twins, it turned out—had cheated on him and was pregnant and he wasn't the father, and on and on—just the sort of thing CeCe understands. He explained that he didn't want to hurt any innocent parties, that all he intended to do was blow that miserable woman into country-western heaven. CeCe let him know that she understood his complaint and had nothing but sympathy for him, and there is no doubt she was telling him the truth.

The Mexican thought it was great that someone finally understood him and his agony, not to mention the appreciation he had for CeCe's great coffee and pie, but the best was yet to be revealed to him. As he finished off the pie, CeCe told him that she knew precisely where his girlfriend was, apparently forgetting for the moment that both the Golddust Twins had left town for Del Rio almost a month before. To the best of her knowledge, CeCe told him, the wretched, ungrateful slut was at this very minute wiggling—that's what CeCe calls it: wiggling—with her white boyfriend in their secret love nest.

Whatever calm the food and conversation had given the Mexican disappeared in a moment when CeCe told him that. He was a university boy from the city, she continued, and he was already married. With two children. He was just using this girl the Mexican loved for a quick and easy good time.

By now the Mexican was livid. He pushed the empty cartridges out of the cylinder of his revolver, dug into his pockets for more shells, and reloaded his cannon. "Just one thing I want to know," he seethed. "Where is she? Tell me where she is."

"Down the road here two blocks, go west past the schoolyard to the white house on the left," said CeCe, leaning out the café door and pointing so he would not mistake her directions. "See, right over there? There's a little trailer house down in the trees behind that big white house with all the damned ducks in the front yard and the two dead water heaters. That's where they are. In that trailer where the light is on. They're in there, doing God-knows-what." The Mexican plunged into the night and CeCe closed the door, wiping her hands on her apron.

The sheriff and his deputy spotted the Mexican marching down the road at the school just fifty feet short of CeCe's house and the trailer where Goose was sleeping. It wasn't easy getting him stopped. He told the sheriff where he was headed and the sheriff told him that there was no one in the trailer but Goose, but the Mexican didn't believe him for a minute.

He believed CeCe, and you can't blame him. She seemed so honest, so certain about her directions, so understanding about his pain, so sympathetic with his intentions. It wasn't the sort of thing about which she could have made a mistake, after all.

LUNCHBOX

LUNCHBOX IS HALF my age and twice my size, which would impress you a lot more if you had any idea how big I am. Once Lunchbox, Woodrow, and I were standing at the pool table up at the Town Tavern and Marv Casperson walked in. He walked over to Slick, pointed his thumb in our direction, and said, "What's going on back there? A convention of sumo wrestlers?"

Lunchbox runs an auto body shop. I don't have much occasion to use his work (1) because I'm a careful driver, (2) because I really don't care all that much what my cars look like, and (3) because there's not much you can do with bent or dented rust anyway.

I once bought a pickup truck as a Christmas present for Lily from Lunchbox. It took him two months to get the truck over here. I quickly found that the lights didn't work, the horn didn't honk, you had to jiggle the key to get it to start, and he didn't have a title for it so I couldn't get the damned thing licensed. None of the gauges worked, even though there was two of everything—two gas gauges, two oil pressure gauges, two temperature gauges, and two ammeters. It wasn't a week before both tires on the left side went flat, and when I shoveled the trash out of the bed it turned out the bed had holes in it that were so big Lily couldn't have hauled four-by-eight sheets of plywood in it without worrying about a few of them falling through.

As Lunchbox was quick to point out, the eyes of the bulldog on the dashboard both still lit up when you hit the brakes.

As I and later Lily complained on a weekly, sometimes daily, basis about the failings of this piece of junk he unloaded on me, a *friend* after all, Lunchbox just shrugged and reminded me of some feature or another of Old Blue, as it came to be called—"Now, it's not going to take five minutes on some nice warm day to fix those tires, but you know as well as I do that you'll be driving this old truck for a good twenty years. So a month or two up on blocks won't seem like much of anything in the long run, now, will it?"

To give you some idea how things go in negotiations with Lunchbox, I called his attention to one of the most glaring problems with this truck shortly after we had complained for the fifty-third time and he had finally delivered it to our yard: It became immediately apparent to us that it really didn't matter where you put the gearshift lever. The transmission went in reverse when you put it on N for neutral instead of R for reverse. Nothing happened when you put the lever on R, which should be reverse. The truck went forward only when you put the shift indicator on 2, rather than D, which I had always presumed means "Drive." When set on D, the truck just sat there and roared. When you put the shift indicator on P for "Park" the truck lurched forward.

"What the hell is this all about?" I huffed when I finally ran down Lunchbox at the Town Tavern taking advantage of Taco Tuesday, which fell on Wednesday that week.

Lunchbox looked at me as if I were an idiot, walked straight out the tavern door to where the truck was parked, and crawled into the driver's seat. As if instructing a first-time driver, he said, moving the lever from gear to gear, "Now look here. That P means '*P*ut 'er into gear.' The R means 'Sits *R*ight here.' N means '*N*ot forward,' and that D means '*D*on't go nowhere.' And that number two," he emphasized, jabbing at the indicator with his forefinger and looking me in the eye, "that two means '*two* fast to slow down.'"

Lunchbox's philosophical pronouncements are about that interesting but a lot less frustrating. His business motto, for example, is "A city boy's price at a country boy's pace." You would think that that would discourage potential customers, but the words sound so poetic that most people don't spend much time thinking about them.

I once asked Lunchbox why the sign outside his shop says, "OPEN 8 A.M. TO 5 P.M. WEEKDAYS," when everyone around here knows he is never there anything close to those hours. "Well"—he smiled—"around here the schedule is pretty much the same for everyone: work one hour, drink coffee for two, and then go to town for parts." Whatever else you think about that, the fact of the matter is, Lunchbox cut through all the theory and confusion and spoke what is ultimately the truth.

I do not mean to give you the impression that he is not a good businessman. Well, that's not, strictly speaking, true at all. For one thing, he is a topnotch body repairman, and that's worth something; what's more, he is honest, and that's worth a lot.

More impressive, now and then he demonstrates a cleverness that suggests he should be running General Motors or the Defense Department. For example, whenever we have a major snowstorm, local television stations announce cancellations of basketball games, anniversary parties, Alcoholics Anonymous meetings, PTA sessions, and pork producers banquets—and, of course, businesses that have closed down because of the weather.

Lunchbox's shop is rarely open even in good weather, you have to remember, and, while he now and then has a part-time helper for particularly heavy jobs, he is by and large a one-man business. Anyway, Lunchbox makes a point, whenever there is bad weather, of calling up the television and radio stations and having them announce, "The second shift at Lunchbox's Body Shop in Barnston will not—we repeat, will *not*—report for work today."

As Lunchbox correctly explains, "It would cost a fortune to buy that kind of advertising on television and radio during nice weather, and me? I just get it for a discount when the snow blows."

One of the reasons I love Ol' Lunchbox is that his best stories are ones he tells on himself. For example, he likes to tell about the time he was out at Marv's place to help him butcher a steer. Butchering is heavy, dirty work. It's a matter of wrestling around a ton or more of dead weight and then cutting and sawing and pulling and pushing and packaging for the better part of a day. It's always easier when a bunch of folks work together, but it's never really easy.

Anyway, Lunchbox and a bunch of Marv's friends, including me, had gathered at Marv's place early that morning to butcher one of his steers for his freezer. After some coffee and cinnamon rolls we ambled out to the corral where Marv kept his livestock. We stood there looking over these beeves, as they are called here, and Marv finally decided which one we would dress out. There was a certain amount of grumbling about Marv having only a .22 rifle to kill this steer because all of his animals tend to run a little on the big side anyway. A .22 long rifle or .22 magnum can drop a big steer if you are at very short range and have a good shot right between the animal's eyes, but there is still a good deal of uncertainty about a good, clean kill with an animal that big and a gun that small.

Marv, even though he is a big, loud lug, has always been a little tenderhearted when it comes to his livestock, so he handed the rifle over to Lunchbox and indicated that he should go ahead and drop the steer. Lunchbox waited until the animal in question was a little in the open, a few feet away from the rest of the herd, and he shot.

Well, the steer seemed mildly annoyed by the noise, but he didn't seem the least bit inclined to drop dead. "Hit him again! Hit him again!" everyone yelled. So Lunchbox fired another round. The steer again jumped a little bit at the noise of the shot but didn't seem to be the least bit injured by the bullet.

"Well, damn," someone grumbled, and Marv said to his boy, Craig, "Son, why don't you run on up to the house and get that .30-30 deer rifle, and make sure there are a couple of shells in it."

Well, that deer rifle should drop a steer at two hundred yards, so we all were breathing a little easier about the prospects of getting this butchering operation finally under way. We strolled over to the pickup truck, refilled our coffee cups from the thermos, and waited ten minutes or so for the boy to return from the house with the rifle.

After a few minutes he came running back with the rifle and handed it to Lunchbox. We walked back over to the corral. Lunchbox took careful aim and fired. The steer dropped as if hit by a cannon. We stepped through the bars of the corral and tied a chain onto the back legs of the steer to pull it out of the corral and up into the pickup so we could drive over to the building where we were going to skin it and cut up the meat.

We were all huffing and puffing at this dirty, heavy work, when we heard Marv stutter, "W-w-w-well, I'll b-b-b-e d-d-d-damned!" The outburst was a surprise, since Marv doesn't usually stutter, but when we followed his gaze across the farmyard and saw what he saw, we were all cussing and stuttering.

Over at the other side of the corral the *first* steer Lunchbox had shot also dropped dead. You see, the steer Lunchbox had hit with the .30-30 wasn't the same one he had shot with the .22. Now we had *two* huge steers to take care of in one long day of butchering. Not a butchering season comes around that Lunchbox isn't reminded of that morning when he shot two steers, and, as you can imagine, no one ever hands him the rifle when the killing time comes.

Another time Lunchbox was trying to get a little something going with his sister-in-law Punkin', who was visiting from Missouri. She had been staying at her sister and Lunchbox's house for a couple weeks during the summer. Punkin's a cute little thing, inclined to tight denim shorts, peasant blouses, and bare feet, and she made it pretty clear to Lunchbox that anything good enough for her sister was good enough for her.

Well, Lunchbox did his best to resist this temptation,

but finally the pressure got to be too much for him. One evening the three of them were sitting around watching *Wheel of Fortune* and Punkin' gave Lunchbox a back rub. While his wife—Punkin's sister, remember—was out in the kitchen making popcorn, Punkin' quietly mentioned something about how she considered her *real* specialty to be her patented *front* rub.

As you can imagine, that riled up Lunchbox's curiosity, so that night he went to bed with lots on his mind. He woke up about two in the morning and listened to make sure that his wife was sleeping soundly. Nothing. He sat up and listened for any irregularity in his wife's breathing. Nothing. He stood up. He waited. He walked to the bedroom door and opened it. He waited.

All clear.

He stepped down the hall of the large farmhouse toward Punkin's room, and the closer he got, the more confident he got, and the more confident he got, the more curious he got, and the more curious he got, the more he hurried to get to that delicious promise in the guest room.

What Lunchbox forgot in his enthusiasm about the extended family was that earlier that same day he had brought in his big metal toolbox from the truck and set it in the hallway, just a few feet from Punkin's room. That night he rediscovered the toolbox with his left foot, while in full stride.

You would think that with all those wrenches, hammers, screwdrivers, and pliers in there, kicking that box would have made a lot of noise, but the fact of the matter is, that toolbox was so heavy, it didn't move so much as a sixtieth of an inch. It just sat there.

On the other hand, all three of Lunchbox's toes broke upon meeting that hundred-pound toolbox in the hallway.

Three weeks later tears still came to Lunchbox's eyes as he told us about the events that evening. "What could I do?" he asked us rhetorically. "I not only couldn't go on into Punkin's room, I couldn't even scream. I just had to stand there while the worst pain I had ever felt in my life ran up and down my leg, into my spine, through my brain, and back down through every muscle of my body, time and time again for about fifteen minutes. All I could do was stand there and scream inside real quiet-like. Between the waves of pain, I couldn't help but think about how that girl smiled when she said 'Front rub.' "

Well, after a half-hour of the most incredible self-control imaginable, Lunchbox told us, he made his way slowly back to his wife's side. "Have you ever for a minute thought about the pain of sliding a foot with three broken toes down between two sheets?" he asked us. None of us had.

"And have you ever thought about laying there in bed for five hours with three broken toes throbbing like three wine-cooler hangovers?" We hadn't.

"All three of those toenails turned purple and fell off the next day." We shuddered.

"And do you want to know what the worst part was?" Lunchbox asked. We didn't, but we knew there was no stopping Lunchbox now.

"Imagine laying there with all that pain until your wife wakes up and then trying to explain to her how you broke three of your toes just laying there in bed sleeping."

He looked at us one by one, as if expecting us to answer but knowing that there was no answer. "I told her that I dreamed I was playing for the Oilers and we were in the Super Bowl. The score was tied fourteen to fourteen, we were on our own forty-yard line, and there were three seconds left in the game. The coach turned to me and said, 'Lunchbox, go in there and kick like you've never kicked before.' So, I told her, I ran out onto the field, the center snapped the ball, and I kicked as hard as I could.

"I told The Little Lady that all I know is that at that point I felt pain like I've never felt before in my life. And I woke up with three toes broke. She believed me, by God, and that's why I'm married to her."

He took a drink of his beer while the rest of us contemplated his quick thinking, and then he added, "And that damned Punkin' laughed at me the next morning and said—right there in front of her own sister—that the next time the coach tells me to kick a field goal I should maybe carry a flashlight."

I suppose that what I love about Lunchbox is that there is never any question about his philosophy of life. It's right there in front of you, and if you don't see it, go ahead and ask; Lunchbox is perfectly willing to tell you about it.

Lunchbox and I were once sitting in the Town Tavern talking with Slick, who was having a particularly hard day. He was moaning and groaning, complaining and whining. Nothing was going right. There were no apparent solutions to his agonies. "Damn, Lunchbox," he complained, "what *is* the meaning of life?"

Without hesitation, as if he had given that question some considerable thought before, Lunchbox replied quietly, "I'll tell you, Slick, I intend to wait until someone else gets the answer and then I'm going to copy his paper. It worked when I was in high school and I figure it should work now."

And I'll bet it will.

ICE FISHING

AS USUAL, WOODROW, Lunchbox, and Long John didn't bother to tell their wives they were going fishing. As Woodrow put it, "She knew I was going fishing when we got married. I shouldn't have to tell her again."

"You should at least notify the Volunteer Rescue Squad," someone at the Town Tavern suggested. "You three elephants get out on that ice and it won't matter how cold it's been; you're going to go into the drink, and probably everyone else on the lake at the same time."

"Why in the name of God would anyone go sit on the ice for twelve hours, freezing their rears for maybe three fish the size of your hand? Why, there won't be enough fish in that lake this time of year to feed your cats for a week," I asked no one in particular.

Don't get me wrong: I love to sit on a warm bank in the spring sun, listening to the river and the birds, enjoy-

126

ing a warmth I have almost forgotten during the winter, but this ice fishing does not interest me at all.

"We're talking *fishing* here," explained Woodrow, holding up his load of two cases of Winterfest beer and a fifth of blackberry brandy, "not *fish!*"

There was some more hooha-ing, yelling, laughing, and brandishing of bottles and the jolly fishermen were out of the tavern. Lunchbox's battered pickup lurched to the right as the three of them crowded into the cab, and they were gone in a cloud of exhaust smoke.

Normally it would have been an inconvenience, but I had to go to Rising City to pick up some hardware the next morning anyway, so it was no trouble at all to drop by the hospital to visit Woodrow. He was resting comfortably, but then Woodrow rests comfortably most of the time anyway, even when he's supposed to be working on somebody's plumbing. All I could think of as I looked at his enormous body under the hospital covers was, "God help the nurse who has to give him a sponge bath!"

Out in the waiting room I ran into Long John and Lunchbox coming in with a package that looked suspiciously like a blackberry brandy bottle and a short stack of well-thumbed *Playboy* magazines. I have often wondered if the Hefner organization realizes that the men who read their publications are not at all the tuxedoed dandies with the Boodles martinis and the skinny ladies in white, low-cut gowns they show in their ads but fat guys in coveralls like Woodrow, drinking blackberry brandy out of the bottle and, having learned their lessons and more, doing whatever they can to avoid any and all contact with the women of Bleaker County.

"Lunchbox, how did Woodrow get all his hair burned off like that?" I asked. "How come you guys got out of the fire and Woodrow didn't? How did a fire get started out there on the ice anyway? Are you guys all right? How bad is Woodrow? Just what was it that happened over at the reservoir yesterday anyway?"

"What question do you want me to answer first?" Lunchbox grinned. "We probably should have brought another bottle of blackberry."

"Just tell me what happened."

"We got out to the reservoir," Lunchbox started, "and parked over at the boat dock just fine. We got the ice house out of the truck, got it set up on runners to slide out onto the ice, and took off. It was pretty easy pulling except when we hit the really rough spots. The ice was booming like thunder, but it was solid as a rock. We found a good spot, pulled all the stuff off the skids, and started to set up. We put up the sides of the shelter, pulled the canvas up over the top, and got inside out of the wind. We drilled a couple holes in the ice, set up our lines, and got Long John's kerosene heater to cranking out the heat."

Lunchbox pulled on the bottle of blackberry brandy he'd brought to the hospital for Woodrow. "We were having some luck—some good solid bites, and we were having a good old time. Pulled in a couple of nice perch, had a couple hard hits that might have been walleye or bass, maybe even a Northern.

"The blackberry and Winterfest was going down smooth. Woodrow got to talking about the time he took the Golddust Twins for a job interview at the Rising City stripper joint. He said the twins and him drank a few wine coolers on the way down there to get their courage up, as if the Golddust Twins ever needed a drink to get their courage up, and then they had a few more when they got there to warm up, and then when they got the job, they had a few to celebrate. Anyway, Woodrow got to describing in some detail how he could testify in court if he had to that they sure aren't identical twins, and all at once there was smoke and fire everywhere."

Lunchbox took another drink of blackberry and passed the bottle to Long John, who was once again so interested in the story about the Golddust Twins that he poured about a half cup of the stuff into the billfold pocket of his bib overalls. "Turns out Long John here had gotten so excited listening to the story he leaned up against the kerosene heater and his coat had caught on fire. He ripped that coat off and threw it aside, but it landed right on the box we had the groceries in—potato chips, cold cuts, and a couple boxes of stick matches—and the whole box of groceries went up like a bucket of gas. There was nothing but flames and smoke, and hollering and yelling."

Long John nodded to affirm the truth of the story as Lunchbox was telling it. "We had all had enough to drink by that time," said Lunchbox, "that we could hardly get the latch on the shack's door open to get out of that inferno, so Long John finally just tore the thing off with his bare hands, and that's how he got that cut on his thumb. Long John dived out of that ice house, and then me, and by that time, my coat and Long John's overalls were on fire, so we got right down on that ice and rolled around. We were hissing and steaming like a couple of Yellowstone Park geezers."

Lunchbox laughed and shook his head. "I'm telling you, we stood there laughing at each other because we looked so funny sitting there on the ice with our clothes smoking, all black and melted, smelling like burnt rats.

"We turned to the ol' fishing shack. By that time the canvas was burned off of it and the plywood was smoking, all the clothes and fishing gear was smoldering and the plastic had melted and gotten all mooshy, smoke and steam was rolling out the open top and the hole where the door had been. And there was Woodrow, still sitting there in the smoldering ruins. His hair was mostly burned off by then, and he looked like hell because he had dumped the bait bucket over his head to put out the fire. He had minnows in his hair and mustache. Parts of his clothes were still smoking. He looked terrible. Worse than usual even.

"And he was still holding his line in his hand. 'Shhh,' he said. 'I think I have a bite.' "

TOBY TODD

ONCE A MONTH Lunchbox's wife, Cookie, goes into Rising City "to get her hair twisted," as he puts it, and he is then required to spend the day in the unlikely position of "being a father," as she puts it. What this means is that for the day Lunchbox is put in charge of his three-year-old son, Toby Todd.

I've always wondered what Lunchbox tells Cookie when she returns from Rising City on these days. At some point she must ask him what he did with the boy all day, and he must tell her something, but it doesn't seem at all plausible that he would have told her anything remotely like the truth.

Not long after Cookie leaves town, Lunchbox settles in with Toby Todd at the Town Tavern. He gets a mess of change from Slick and puts the pile of coins at the end of the bar where Toby Todd can reach it.

For the next three or four hours, Toby Todd eats potato

chips and candy, plays the jukebox and the pinball machine, and clubs balls around the pool table, generally driving Slick and his customers crazy. While all this is going on, Lunchbox sits in a booth drinking mugs of beer fast enough so that it is obvious to anyone with any sense that he is far too busy to deal with Toby Todd.

Then Cookie comes to the tavern "to meet" Lunchbox and Toby Todd. I say "to meet" that way because it was so obvious to all of us that Cookie had the impression that Lunchbox and his boy were busy all day doing dad-and-son sorts of things and just used the tavern as a convenient place to meet her. She would have faded away and died if she had suspected for a moment that Lunchbox and Toby Todd spent the entire time of their monthly exercises sitting in the tavern. Cookie is a Baptist minister's daughter, after all.

Well, one Wednesday Lunchbox came into the Town Tavern with Toby Todd and we all braced ourselves for another long afternoon. Rather than face Toby Todd, the card players simply folded up their cards and left. I thought about doing the same, but I sat down with Lunchbox for a couple of beers and then I went back to the bar to talk with Slick.

Toby Todd pretty much had the run of the tavern that day and was making the most of it, but Lunchbox was slowing down. In fact, his head was nodding. "Looks like Lunchbox had a tough night last night," I said to Slick.

"Yep, he was in here until closing time last night. I'm surprised he made it in here at all today. And it doesn't look, as a matter of fact, like he *is* making it very far."

I followed Slick's eyes to Lunchbox's booth, and there he was, sprawled out in the booth, his head thrown back, his mouth wide open, snoring up a storm.

For the next hour Toby Todd took care of himself much the same as usual, treating all of us much the same as he treated the jukebox and pinball machine, like large toys he could ricochet off of now and then.

An hour passed, Lunchbox snored on, and Toby Todd finally settled down in the booth opposite his father with an ice cream bar he bought out of his treasure trove of coins. Curiously, he seemed better behaved when Lunchbox was sleeping than he was when Lunchbox was awake.

Toby Todd sat quietly looking around the tavern and eating his ice cream bar while Slick and I watched him, surprised by the calm in his conventional storm. Then a little piece of chocolate fell off of the boy's ice cream bar and melted in a little puddle on the booth's table.

Toby Todd put down his ice cream bar and slowly, tentatively dabbed his finger in the melted chocolate. He poked at it, smeared it around in a circle about the size of a dime, and then stuck his finger in his mouth.

It was like a cartoon. You could see the light bulb turn on over his head. He had discovered another dimension of a chocolate bar: You could play with it *and* eat it. He turned to the ice cream bar and found, when he picked it up, that now there was a large spot of melted chocolate and a little ice cream where he had left it on the table. He put down the ice cream bar again, at the other end of the table, and dabbed at this new, larger puddle of melted chocolate and ice cream and drew circles about the size of a supper plate. Now his whole finger was covered with melted confection and he plunged it deep into his mouth.

The circles grew larger. The ice cream was melting faster. The lad's drawings became ever more generous, then exuberant. As the minutes passed, the entire ice cream bar sagged into a puddle. The boy used his whole hand, then both hands to draw his developing abstract work, and he was licking his arms from his elbows to his fingertips.

As you can imagine, Slick and I just stood there, our jaws agape, watching this spectacle develop. Within fifteen minutes the booth table had been transformed from a gray, cold, shiny piece of furniture into a white, brown, and gray palette, an impressionist scene worthy of most galleries.

And the boy? He hadn't come into Slick's tavern in his Sunday best, but his mother always turned him out pretty well, even if he was only going to go to the park or maybe the Chew 'n' Chat Cafe, which is probably where she thought he was bound when she sent him out the door with Lunchbox earlier that day. Now only his shins and ankles were untouched by ice cream and chocolate.

At the height of his artistic frenzy he had smeared the entire top of the table with all of his arms, from the shoulder down, often leaning his whole upper body onto his canvas. Then when he put his fingers in his mouth, his upper arm transferred a certain amount of its viscous load onto his shirt.

When he raised his arm to lick his elbows, his hands rested on his hair. When he leaned over to lick the table— it had come to that—his arms rested in his lap, leaving some of the sticky mess there. Chocolate and ice cream dripped from the edge of the table onto his shoes. Only the vertical hang of his lower legs had saved *them* from the spread of this terrible brown-and-white monster that threatened to take over the tavern.

Through all of this, Lunchbox slept on, totally unaware of the devastation his son was wreaking. When the ice cream bar was exhausted, the boy sat back and admired his work. We all admired his work. There is no way that anyone could have predicted that one ice cream bar could possibly have done that much damage, no matter how thin it was spread.

I finally broke the silence: "My God, Slick, can you imagine what Cookie is going to say when she sees that kid. I mean, you have a mess to clean up in that booth, but look at that kid. When Cookie walks in here, she is going to readjust Lunchbox's constitution in a big way.

"What do you think we should do?" I asked. "Should we make a stab at cleaning the kid up?" Slick didn't say anything but turned and walked toward the kitchen. "You getting something to mop up the mess?" I asked.

"Nope," Slick grunted.

"What are you doing?"

"Getting the kid another ice cream bar," Slick said.

Slick made two more trips to his freezer before Cookie showed up. He walked over to Lunchbox's booth, took the wrapper off the ice cream bar, and handed it to the boy. The boy smiled and went back to his work with renewed vigor.

You can imagine the condition of the boy and the booth by the time Cookie walked into the tavern. Things had gotten to the point where people would walk in the front door, take one look at what was going on, look at Slick and me, shake their heads, turn around, and go back out without a word. None of us could predict what the terrible consequences of all this were going to be, but anyone with any sensitivity at all certainly wouldn't have wanted to be around to see it. Slick and I wouldn't have missed it for the world.

Cookie walked in on schedule, and the look of horror on her face when she saw Toby Todd and Lunchbox was about what we expected. She screamed, "Toby Todd!" which is also about what we expected, and Lunchbox woke up so fast we could hear his mouth snap shut. He tried to stand up while still in the booth and spilled the full mug of warm beer that had been sitting in front of him with a fly spinning lazy circles in the foam. The effect on the ice cream fresco was amazing.

Cookie pulled a few napkins out of the holder on the table so she could grab the boy's arm—no one would have touched him with bare fingers. No one. She said nothing to Lunchbox. Not a word. She clamped her jaw so tight her ears stood out from her new coif and squinted her eyes. She looked at Lunchbox so hard that for a moment he looked puny. Slick snorted—a real mistake—and she turned and glared at us. We turned our gaze from the booth for the first time in four hours and intently watched the stock market report on the television set behind the bar.

Cookie stomped toward the door and Lunchbox stumbled out of the booth and toward the door a few feet behind her—still no words had passed between him and The Little Woman.

We were sure he would turn and give us some sort of sign of anger, or fear, or amazement, or something, but he had to do some fancy hustling to keep up with his wife and child. Just as she went out the door, Cookie said her first words to Lunchbox: "I'm telling you right now, Delbert"—Lunchbox's real name is Delbert, but no one ever called him that unless they wanted to humiliate him, and I guess that's pretty much what Cookie had in mind on this particular occasion—"this is the *last* time I intend to leave Toby Todd alone with you. Do you hear me? The *last* time."

Lunchbox turned to us and winked.

PANKRAS' DANCE

"YEAH, ROG, THIS is Shelton Pankra. Hey, if you don't have anything going on Friday night, why don't you grab your banjo and come on up to the ranch? The folks from educational television are coming out from Lincoln to film some of our music and the way we figure, 'The more, the merrier.'"

"Sounds good to me, Shelton."

"Dinner's about six, but if you want to watch the filming, they're supposed to set up some time around noon."

"I'll be there a little after noon, then, Shelton. Can I bring anything?"

"Only your banjo, an appetite, and a big thirst," he laughed.

The Pankra ranch is a medium-size operation, maybe four or five sections of Sandhills pasture and hay meadows about twenty miles north of Centralia. Shelton is a pleasant fellow maybe fifty years old, but the most notable thing

about him is that he and his family have been an institu-
tion in Nebraska since the days of homesteading. Shelton,
his wife, Nora, his father and mother before them, his
brothers and sisters, even some cousins, all of his children,
and now his grandchildren are all musicians, and good
ones. They play old-fashioned music—the kind of thing
you used to hear before rock and roll and country-western.

Shelton plays fiddle and mandolin, Nora and the oldest
girl play guitars, one son is a good banjo picker, and the
youngest girl plays drums and bass guitar. No one would
think of having a wedding or anniversary dance in north-
central Nebraska without asking the Pankra Family to
play for the dance. I wasn't surprised that the television
people from Lincoln were coming to film them.

I pulled into the yard a little after noon, walked up to
the house, pushing away the various dogs that were jumping on me by way of greeting, and knocked at the back
door. "They're setting up down at the haying grove,
Roger," Nora called from the kitchen. "Go on down.
Close the gates behind you."

"Right," I yelled. "See you later, Nora."

As if the Pankras didn't wear themselves out playing
music for dances and such, evenings during haying season,
when there were more than the usual number of workers
and wives around, the Pankras and whoever else happened to be around would gather evenings down in a beautiful grove of cottonwoods at the edge of Clear Creek. It
was a beautiful site—cool, quiet, out of the wind. The
Pankras had a horse tank there where they could ice down
all the beer it took for a good party, and they had poured
a little concrete slab for dancing. There were picnic tables
for the food the Pankras always provided in abundance
and even an outhouse for the ladies.

As I drove slowly through the dusty stubble, opening and closing the two cattle gates between the house and the haying grove, I could see the activity in the broad, shallow valley where the grove lay. There was a big white truck with television equipment on the sides and top, two dark blue university cars, and ten or twelve pickup trucks—probably the Pankras', their kids', and other musicians' vehicles. There was already music coming from the grove, so I waited in my car well away from the scene of the work until the music stopped and it was clear that I wouldn't be interrupting the filming.

Shelton came over and greeted me, and I exchanged greetings with the musicians I already knew, introduced myself to those I didn't, shook hands with the television people, and settled back to watch the afternoon's work. "Beer's in the horse tank," yelled Shelton. I sat at a picnic table in the shade of a big, old cottonwood and the crew and musicians went back to work. It was a big crew—a couple of cameras, two sound men, a lighting director, a couple of technicians in the truck, and a director. There were six, later eight, musicians and two other fellows who had just dropped by to watch the fun.

It was an interesting process to watch. The director was a nervous little fellow who didn't seem at all at home with the ranchers or even ranch country for that matter. He was constantly brushing away bugs that most of us around here would hardly have paid any attention to. He tied a hanky across his mouth and nose because he thought the dust was kicking up his asthma. He kept asking Shelton when the last time was that he had seen a rattlesnake. Shelton said just last week, mostly, I suspect, to make the guy even more nervous. The director fussed and fussed, but none of his crew seemed to pay much attention to him so he really wasn't in the way all that much.

The cameraman who was carrying the mobile camera was a big burly guy with a thick black beard, and he seemed to be just the opposite of the director. Nothing seemed to bother him. He stood out in the sun as long as it took to get his shot, never so much as wiping the sweat away. The director's complaints bounced off of him as if he didn't even hear them.

The other cameraman, the one operating the dolly-mounted camera, was thin and pale. He was wearing white canvas pants, white boat shoes, and an almost transparent white cotton shirt, the kind that come from India. He had a flower earring in one ear and thin bracelets on his left arm. His blond hair was pulled back in a thin braid. He was a nice enough fellow, but he talked in a way that made us nervous—too friendly, I think, and too high-pitched.

One sound man handled a long pole with a foam-padded microphone on the end. He was a big, heavy-set fellow and had earphones on almost all the time, so we never really had much chance to get to know him until we sat down to eat.

The other sound man was actually a sound woman. She saw to it that all the mikes on the musicians and their instruments were in order, and she operated a switchboard that turned them off and on, so far as I could tell.

She was gorgeous. Not just pretty. Gorgeous. She was slim, hardly much of a figure at all, but there was enough there that no one would mistake her for a boy. She was wearing jeans and a man's cotton workshirt. Her long hair hung loose almost to her waist, and her eyes were light blue. She looked straight at you when she talked, actually straight *through* you. About the time I got to the haying grove, she kicked off her shoes, pulled her shirt out of her jeans, and tied the two front panels together at her waist.

"My God, look at that pretty little thing," one of the other bystanders whistled to his companion. "Makes you wish you were single, don't she?"

"And young," said the other.

The filming went well, as far as I could tell. The music certainly sounded good and the weather was beautiful—cool, clear, and just a hint of a breeze. Every so often through the afternoon another vehicle would come slowly down into the grove, some folks the Pankras had invited and others who had spotted the festivities from the highway about a quarter mile from the grove and decided to come down and see what was going on down at Pankras' haying grove.

At five-thirty a couple more pickups came in from the house—the women with the food. They spread plastic cloths on the picnic tables and laid out chicken, ham, barbecue beef, rolls and biscuits, potato chips, baked beans, ten or twelve pies, two gallons of cole slaw, another two of potato salad. As we ate, another eight or nine loads of visitors arrived and someone commented that the haying grove must by now have been about the second or third largest city in Carson County.

After we had all gone through the food line a couple of times, everyone started hauling out his instruments and began some preliminary picking and tuning. Roxie—that was the sound lady's name, we all knew by now—asked one of the cowboy musicians in attendance if she could give a little try at his Martin. He was thoroughly flattered by even this little bit of attention from the prettiest girl he had probably ever seen in his life, and he handed the guitar over without hesitation even though he had never let anyone else ever touch the thing in the six years he had owned it.

Roxie pulled the flat pick from the strings and ran through a couple of country-western riffs that set everyone back on his heels. "Whoa! It's a female Chet Atkins!" yelled Shelton from over at the beer tank. And if Roxie hadn't been enough of an attraction just as she stood there, barefoot and long-haired, once she started picking on that guitar, every young man in the grove crowded around her as if she were giving away hundred-dollar bills.

I was sitting at the picnic table with the rest of the television crew, and the other sound technician chuckled and said, "Same thing happens every time. Roxie knocks 'em out every remote we do." The crew was thoroughly enjoying the music now that they could relax. They were helping themselves to the food and beer and letting down from the tough afternoon they had put in. All except the strange cameraman in the white outfit. He sat quietly, almost sadly at the end of the picnic table, as if he felt left out, abandoned.

"This past two years we've been filming local and regional musicians all over the state, so we've hit a good twenty dances just like this one—except Greek, Czech, Polish, Irish, Mexican, all kinds, you know—and it's always the same. Roxie draws men like honey draws flies."

"She's a beautiful woman, all right," I agreed.

"They act as if she's the only person on *earth*," the cameraman in white said. "She's *pretty* and all, but it makes me so *angry* when she gets all the *attention* like that."

"Well, jeez, Bob, I would think that you of all people should be grateful to her. God knows, she certainly takes care of you," said the sound man.

"I'm grateful all right, but it's a *shame* that it *always* has to be this way," he huffed.

The musicians finally got organized, and while the Pankras were good on their own, the rich mixture of instruments, styles, and traditions, the beauty of the scene and the cool evening, gave us all the feeling that this was something special.

That's one of the nice things about living in a small town: There's no such thing as a band with a fancy name and suits and all. We all belong to one big band, and whoever happens to be around when the music starts is part of that performance. Moreover, while everyone here understands what makes a good singer or musician—we have radios and see the best performers from Barbara Mandrell to Itzhak Perlman at the county fairs and on television, after all—what's important on occasions like this one in Pankras' haying grove is who has their instrument with them and who's willing to step up to do what they can to make the occasion a happy one.

Now, you can imagine what went on once the dancing started. A few fellows got out on the concrete slab with their wives or one of the older women—I danced a couple polkas with Mrs. Pankra, a couple of the older women danced together, but the crush around Roxie almost reached riot stage the moment the music got started.

"Happens every time, just like that," said the sound man, nudging my elbow.

"They're like a bunch of rutting *bulls*," piped Bob, the thin fellow in white.

Roxie danced with a couple of the cowboys, but other young men tried cutting in every half minute or so, and some of the fellows wouldn't let others cut in. There was some grumbling, and after just a couple dances a few rough words were exchanged.

"Same thing, every time," chuckled the sound man. "It's coming up. The big announcement. Watch this."

Finally two cowboys grabbed Roxie by either arm, and each tried to take her out on the dance slab. When she shook herself free from them, they pushed at each other a couple times, snarled a few insults, and then squared off. The music stopped and there was a tense moment while the two angry young bucks stared at each other and muttered threatening noises, a little like mountain goats banging heads.

"Here it comes," said the big sound man. Bob stood up at the end of the table and moved toward the dance floor.

"Now, look, you big dopes," Roxie said, stepping between them. "This is getting entirely out of hand. I don't mind dancing with you guys, but I don't want any more trouble. There are plenty of people to dance with, so there's no need to argue. Here's what we'll do: From now on there'll be no more cutting in. When I dance, I'll dance the whole song through with the same guy." There were mumbles of approval from the herd of cowboys. "That will cut out some of the nonsense. And to calm down some of the confusion about who's dancing next, what I will do from now on is dance with whoever dances first . . ." she paused . . ." with Bob," and she pointed.

The silence was absolute. No one moved, and frankly I don't think anyone breathed. A couple of the cowboys turned, mouths open, and followed Roxie's point to Bob, who by now had moved to the edge of the dance floor, now lit by headlights from three or four pickup trucks. It seemed like hours before anyone moved. Then it was only Shelton, who coughed.

"Well, whoever is going to dance with whoever better get to dancing," Shelton said, and started sawing a lively tune on his fiddle. The musicians played the entire song through, but this time only a few couples ventured out onto the floor. The twenty-five or thirty young cowboys who were in the grove stood stock-still—not so much as moving, let alone dancing.

During early settlement of the Plains, when women were scarce, it was a common practice for a couple of men at a square dance to tie kerchiefs around their left arm, thereby designating that for the purposes of the dance, they were . . . well, women. The old-timers knew that, but they also knew that this was not, strictly speaking, the same situation. Even the young men whose egos were being challenged understood that Roxie was not so much being cruel to them as kind to Bob, but . . . this city idea was going to take some time getting used to.

When the cowboys did begin to move again, slowly and stiffly like bugs after a frost, they could only look from Roxie standing at the musicians' corner of the floor, plucking furiously at a borrowed Martin guitar, to Bob leaning between the headlights of one of the parked pickup trucks, smiling, back to Roxie and again to Bob.

The musicians played two or three more songs with no movement as yet from the circle of cowboys. Roxie sang a couple verses of "Your Cheatin' Heart," then put down the Martin and did a couple pretty little dance steps by herself in the area in front of the musicians. Shelton whooped and tore into an even more furious rendition of the fiddle tune he was playing and Roxie danced faster.

"Well, that does it," snarled a big, rawboned cowboy who had been in the altercation that set off Roxie's New Order. Red-faced, the muscles in his jaw rippling, he strode across the concrete dance slab toward Bob and the pickup trucks, and I don't believe there was anyone at the scene who would have bet one way or the other whether the big cowboy was going to kill Bob or ask him to dance.

To our surprise, he did neither. He strode right past Bob without so much as looking at him, jerked open the door of the pickup truck Bob was leaning against, and jammed in the light button on the truck's dashboard so hard the truck shuddered. He wheeled and leaned far in the window on the passenger side of the next truck and hit its light button too. He marched around to the third and final pickup, opened the door, and shut its headlights off too, leaving us with nothing but the dim light of a thin crescent moon, the stars, and a few glowing cigarettes.

From the dark the cowboy announced, "I'll dance with that son of a bitch if it's the only way I'll get to dance with that pretty little filly, and I'll keep on dancing with him just as long as she'll dance with me. I'll dance with him, but no one said I'd have to dance with him so's everyone can see it."

"On the floor everybody," Shelton hollered. "Let's dance. You don't have to see your feet to make 'em move."

RACING HORSES AT THE
CENTRALIA FOURTH OF JULY

I DON'T GAMBLE. Gambling is something I've never enjoyed. I once put a quarter in a slot machine in a little casino on an island off the Gulf coast of Mississippi and hit the jackpot on the first pull—I think it was ten or twelve dollars. It seemed to me that if I quit then, I would be ahead the rest of my life, so I did.

I did sort of bet on a horse race once, but it wasn't the same thing at all. Three of my buddies and I took off for Storm Lake, Iowa, in a red convertible for a wild weekend thirty years ago. A town cop stopped us for speeding in a little town in western Iowa before we had been on the road three hours and the village justice of the peace cleaned out our billfolds, leaving us each two dollars to get home on. The next day we ate some green apples we had with us and we looked longingly at the roller coaster in the amusement park, but that was about all we could afford. That night we slept in an abandoned dance hall.

We started for home the next day, buying four dollars' worth of gas, which left our pooled reserves at four dollars. We got to Sioux City and noticed that there were a lot of cars parked in the lot outside the Atokad race track. We decided to send in the most knowledgeable race enthusiast from the group, using one dollar to get into the track and two dollars to bet on the best chance he could find in the remaining races of the day.

You can imagine how that went. An hour later we were down to one single dollar bill. We were again getting low on gas, so we stopped in a small Nebraska town and looked up a fraternity brother, who wouldn't so much as loan us ten dollars. We coasted into the next town late that night and slept in a cornfield just down the lane from the home of another fraternity brother, knowing that he would help us out. After all, he once lived at my home in Lincoln for half a year at no cost. In the morning we approached the house and good old fraternity brother Ron let us fill up our tank with farm gas—and made us leave all but one of our drivers' licenses for collateral until we repaid him the eight-dollar cost of the fuel.

On that occasion I learned a few things about the nature of fraternity brotherhood and confirmed my understanding of the processes of gambling, I guess. All of which is to explain why I went to my first Centralia Fourth of July celebration twelve years ago with no intention whatsoever of betting on the horse races.

I had heard a lot about the celebrations down at the river, but I had never been in town for the occasion, so I was looking forward to it. I was not disappointed. I took my three children—they were twelve to fourteen years old then, and they were in hog heaven. There were carnival rides, basketball throws, a target-shooting booth, pony rides, fireworks, and free pop and ice cream. There were kiddie parades with homemade costumes, which I always enjoy, and when the afternoon got too hot to move around, I spent a good hour watching the old-timers pitching horseshoes. Well, *listening* to the old-timers pitching horseshoes because what they said was what was interesting. "Guess you must be saving your arm for your next game, huh?" "You'd think that if you just closed your eyes and threw overhand you'd hit the peg more often than you've been doing this afternoon." "I'll bet you don't even have the paint wore off those horseshoes you bought new two years ago, throwing like that." Turns out that horseshoes is more a psychological than a physical game.

And that Fourth of July was the first time I saw Marv Tyler pitch. He used to say that he had had a chance to try out for the New York Yankees when he was a young-ster and when they *were* the New York Yankees, but I had always shrugged it off as so much small-town baloney until I saw him throw. No doubt about it, Marv probably once did have a major league arm. Even those many years later and with a lot of Budweiser in him, he was still an impressive pitcher (for a small-town Fourth of July game).

I talked with Marv a little after the game about his pitching. We sat in the shade of a big cottonwood tree drinking cold beer and talking in between the times Marv was "on the air." He had rigged up a speaker under the seat in the ladies' privy and run a wire over to the tree where we were sitting, so whenever he would see someone go in there—especially someone he knew—he would wait just a second or two and then say something like, "Excuse me, Clara, would you mind waiting until we get our work finished down here," and almost instantaneously the poor lady would come exploding out the privy door to the delight of those of us who were in on the routine. Marv did the same thing every year, so we had plenty of time to talk; most Bleaker County women were onto Marv's Fourth of July trick.

The highlight of the day, not just for me but for everyone in the park, was the horse races. Since my college friends and I had had only enough money to get one person into the Atokad track on that desperate occasion thirty years before, I had never even been to a race track or seen a race, but I don't think having been to a track would have prepared me for the Centralia races anyway. I think you could go to horse races all your life and not be prepared for the Centralia races.

For one thing, the betting was done with a system called a Spanish quintilla. Before a race each rider and horse were brought to the pickup truck that served as the announcer's booth. The announcer—Martin Cogsworth on this occasion—would give a brief description of the team: "This is Craig Tyler and his mount, Dragon Fly. They won the river race last year, and I'm going to start the bidding at fifty dollars." Martin would then auction off the horse and rider to bidders in the audience. If Craig and Dragon Fly were "purchased" by Dick Whitefoot for one hundred dollars, then twenty dollars would go to the volunteer fire department for their new tank truck and Dick and Craig would split the remaining eighty dollars half and half if Craig should win.

The truly fierce bidding, I quickly learned, concentrated on the most unlikely riders. A little blond, brown-skinned farm girl would come forward on her saddle horse—clearly not the stuff race winners are made of—and the bidding would quickly soar to $200, $225, $350. No grandfather, I learned, was about to let his granddaughter be anything but the race's favorite. If the bidding boiled down to two rival grandfathers, it knew no limits.

I got involved with the betting through no fault of my own. I was standing around the stand watching the proceedings—it was like a new world to me—when a lithe young black girl rode her nice-looking bay mare up to the announcer's stand. I knew who she was—the adopted daughter of a friend of mine and one of the two or three black people in the entire county. I dreaded what was coming and almost turned away and left.

Racism is a reality in Bleaker County, and I feared that this child would sit there on her horse, met by crushing silence when Martin Cogsworth called for bids on her for the upcoming race. I looked around for the girl's father. He wasn't there; I remembered that he had driven the ambulance to Rising City with the most recent racing casualty. She wouldn't even be able to count on his pride to raise her bids. I stayed and watched with morbid fascination.

"Here we have Dusty Stevens, on her fine bay mare, Challenger, and I want to start the bids at fifty dollars." God, why did Martin start so high? I thought. It would have been politic, I would have thought, to start low in hopes of getting something by way of a charity bid. Fifty dollars seemed high for charity.

"Do I hear fifty dollars?" There was a moment's hesitation, but only a moment's, not enough time for anyone to anticipate Martin's next words: "I have fifty dollars, right over here, from Roger Welsch. Do I hear sixty?"

"Roger Welsch?!" I didn't bid. I didn't raise my hand or shift my weight or blink or anything that Martin could possibly have interpreted as a bid. Maybe he saw someone else bid and thought it was me.

"Okay, I have sixty over here from Lunchbox!" It just so happened I had had my eye on Lunchbox at that very moment and he wasn't even facing the announcer's stand. When he heard that he had bid, he turned to Martin, smiled, and shrugged.

"Yessir, and Roger Welsch says he'll bid sixty-five dollars," Cogsworth shouted into his microphone.

And so it went. It was one of the gentlest gestures I have ever seen. The girl sat quietly on her horse, never noticing the auctioneer's diplomatic kindness and therefore never realizing the cruelty it masked. Okay, I thought, there is racism in Bleaker County, but there is also a sense of brotherhood I have rarely seen elsewhere.

As it turned out, Dusty and Challenger won the race, and so the very first time I bet on a horse race I won a little over eighty dollars. Not bad money, I thought, for no more than I did to get it.

Not more than a half-hour later I was at the other end of the race track when I heard my name called over the public announcement system: I was to report to the horse-racing announcer's stand. I walked the quarter mile back and asked what the problem was. "You didn't pay for your horse," the cashier said, shuffling papers. "Sure I did, and then I collected from you because Dusty and Challenger won."

"Not that race, the other one, the relay that the Casper-son boy won."

"I didn't bet on that race. I wasn't even here," I protested.

The cashier caught Martin Cogsworth's attention just as he was starting the bidding on another race. "Hey, Welsch says he didn't bid on that last race, Martin. What do you think?"

Martin smiled and waved to me, turned to the crowd, and said, "Terrific, we just got a *sixty*-dollar bid from Roger Welsch to start things off on this race! Do I hear seventy?" This was obviously not an auction where you wanted to call attention to yourself, especially by arguing! By the time the day was over I had lost perhaps twenty dollars more than I had won on Dusty and Challenger, but it was all done with such open, goodhearted fraudulence that the loss was more than covered by the entertainment.

The races themselves are powerful and passionately run contests. I imagine that when you go to the Kentucky Derby or even the Nebraska fairgrounds races, you sit up in a stand, well removed from the mud, violence, and smell of the race, but not at Centralia. At the Centralia Fourth of July races, the viewers stand along the track— nothing more than a two-hundred-yard stretch of grass on a piece of river bottoms—and the horses pound by within feet of your face. The ground shakes. You can see the rolling eyes of the horses, hear the pained grunts of horses and riders, smell the sweat of man and animal.

The horses come from farms in Bleaker County and the surrounding counties and the riders are men and women, boys and girls we all knew—not a professional or even trained rider in the lot.

The races are not simple horse-and-rider races like you see on television. They are relay races, where riders take off from one end of the pasture to the other, jump off, another rider then leaping into the saddle and then riding back full-tilt to the start line. And a "boot race" in which a boot is taken from each rider and put in a pile at the other end of the pasture. The riders ride to the pile, jump off, find their boot, put it on (all the while trying to hold on to the frantically pitching and lurching horses), throw themselves back into the saddle, and ride back to the start-finish line.

It is exciting, but it isn't pretty. There are big horses and little horses, big riders and little riders, good teams and poor teams. That means that one rider might reach the end of the pasture, change riders or pick up a boot or whatever and be riding back toward the finish at the same time other riders are still heading toward the far end. Two-way traffic is not a good idea on a race track. Horses and riders are injured; a couple riders are occasionally hauled off in the ambulance, and now and then an animal has to be destroyed.

The size of the animal or rider is of no consequence or consideration, and no quarter is given for sex or age. The longest race starts near the announcer's position in the truck bed, plunges down the riverbank into the water, follows red flags on the sand bars perhaps two hundred yards to the bridge, passes under the bridge and then back out, across the channels two or three more times, and then back up the steep bank to the finish line.

Last year twenty riders entered the race, hard cowboys and schoolgirls, athletic young men and leathery-necked women. Three horses went down, and one rider's arm was broken at the very start as the horses plunged down the bank into the river. Another horse went down at the edge of the sandbank and limped off leaving the rider lying prone in the sand. Two more riders pulled up short at the channels. The winner was a big burly cowboy who rode his horse as if it were an extension of his own body. But second prize went to a slip of a girl on a Shetland pony.

Horse racing in Bleaker County may be sport, but it is deadly serious. That's why I was not at all amused when my daughter Jenny, a skinny little Indian girl twelve years old, came up to me that afternoon leading a shambling forty-year-old cowboy behind her: "Dad, this is Mr. Hunkins from Gibbon. He is gonna ride in the pickup relay race, and he needs someone to pick up. Can I ride with him in the race, Dad?"

"She's little and wiry, just what I need for a pickup." The grizzled cowboy smiled.

In my mind all I could see was colliding horses, riders with broken bones, lacerations and cracked heads, wrenched limbs. "Are you out of your mind, Jenny? Hell no, you can't ride in a race. Look out there. I wouldn't even ride in that mayhem. Your mom would *kill* me if I let you do something that dumb. The only horse you've ever been on in your life is Woodrow's swayback nag, Peanuts. This is not like riding Peanuts."

"Well, we didn't think it'd hurt to ask," the cowboy said. "Thanks, girl," he said to Jen, patting her back with his leathery paw. She didn't complain, didn't say a word, but I saw the tears well up in her black eyes as she turned and started away.

My other two kids are homemade and Jen was adopted, so she's always felt a little on the outside of things. She has a different way about her too—quiet, apart, a little peculiar—so not much had happened in her life that stood out as something special. My mind crackled with thoughts about what the thrill of this race could mean to her. If she dies, I thought, she'll be dying at the moment of her greatest triumph.

Somehow the fears of my own pain should she be hurt seemed insignificant in comparison with that. "Hey, Jen,"

I called to her. "Run grab that cowboy and ask him if he's still looking for a pickup rider on that race. If you want to ride, you can ride." She ran like the wind, her black hair flying, dust kicking up from her feet. I saw her intercept the cowboy before he reached the edge of the track. She talked a moment with him and shook his hand. She came back and kissed me, telling me that Hunkins was going to get his mount and he would be right back.

The bidding for the pickup relay was not all that high and I thought I might get by cheaply, but as soon as Martin Cogsworth saw that Jenny was going to be the Gibbon cowboy's pickup, he found a raise to counter my every bid. And I never saw a hand rise or a head nod during the entire process.

I "bought" Jen and Hunkins for something less than one hundred dollars and found a good place on the sidelines to watch the action. In a pickup relay, the pickup stands at the far end of the track, waiting. At the gun the riders take off at a full gallop down the track, circle at the end, grabbing the pickup and swinging him or her onto the saddle behind the rider, then riding full-tilt back to the starting line. I didn't even think what that meant until the moment I saw my eighty-pound daughter, Jenny, standing there, looking for all the world like an abandoned orphan while ten half-ton horses pounded down the track straight at her. I comforted myself again: "She'll die happy."

I saw Hunkins reach her well up in the pack of riders. Still at a full gallop he reached out his huge hand like a hay rake and grabbed her outstretched arm, swinging her like a limp rag doll onto the saddle behind him. He didn't "lift" her and "place" her, he hurled her and slammed her onto the saddle. Dust quickly obscured the scene at the end of the pasture as the other horses and pickups milled around and leaped into the return dash. As the riders pounded past my position all I could see was my precious little wisp of a daughter—black hair streaming behind her—clinging frantically to the cowboy's shirt as he lashed the horse and occasionally Jenny with his reins.

I ran to the finish line along the sidelines of the track. I found Jenny and the cowboy, covered with sweat and dust, standing beside the cowboy's big roan. "Well, she did just fine until the end and then her air guv out," he apologized. At first I thought he meant Jenny, but then he patted his horse. He turned then to Jenny. "And this little girl of yours rode like a professional. Just as I come up to her she looked like she was about to take off into the plum brush over against the end of the track and I thought I'd have to run her down like a rabbit, but she stood right still. Think I pulled her arm out of her socket. We're out of the money, but you can have the second-place ribbon, little lady. And next year I hope to work with you again."

Well, Jen's arm *was* nearly wrenched from its socket, we found later. She was sore for a month. She was bruised from end to end and had welts on her sides and back from the pounding she had gotten from the flailing reins.

The worst part, she grinned, was that Hunkins's elbows kept hitting her in the head and she had cut her hands with her own fingernails from hanging onto his shirt so tightly. All the next week she wore her wounds like badges of honor.

She had never shown much enthusiasm for anything, especially life in Bleaker County, so I was pleased when she asked me if we could go back the next Fourth of July, and I said we could. And it brought tears to my eyes when she handed me her second-place ribbon and asked me to keep it for her. But the best part of that Centralia Fourth of July was the smile on her face that night as she went to sleep.

CAL

I AM PROBABLY the only guy in town who knows him by his first name because everyone else calls him "Geronimo." His name is Calvin. Calvin White Shell. In town they usually say, "Here come the Cherokees" when he comes into the Town Tavern with his daughter, Jacinda, even though Geronimo was an Apache and Cal and Jacinda are Lakota. Brule Lakota, to be specific.

It's nothing anyone gets excited about. Almost everyone here has a nickname. They call me "Hippie" or "The Perfesser," for example. You can see that it grates on Cal, though, when they call him "Tonto."

I guess I also got to know Cal better than most folks in town because unlike most of the others I'm not at all uncomfortable about being seen with a man with a braid hanging down the nape of his neck, which Cal has. I was a hippie twenty years ago, you see, and I remember well

159

the days I used to wear a ponytail down my back and a turkey feather hanging down behind my left ear.

You can imagine how a getup like that used to go over here in Nebraska. There were days back then when I would have been relieved to have someone call me Geronimo or Tonto. That's the reason I get along with Cal. I've never called him Geronimo. Or Tonto.

It wasn't easy to get to know Cal even at that. He keeps pretty much to himself, or at least to himself and his daughter. He has never mentioned Jacinda's mother and I have never asked. He comes down under the river bridge at my place to throw out a few lines for catfish now and then, and whenever I see Cal's brown pickup parked down in the chokecherry brush, I make a point of throwing together some Braunschweiger sandwiches and a cooler of Coke or root beer—Cal's favorite—and going down to interrupt his peace and quiet.

I've always figured that the sandwiches and root beer are a small price to pay for what I get in return. That's the way it's always gone for me when I have fallen in with Indians—give a dime, get a dollar. Every once in a while, at the most unlikely moment, I learn something from Cal, and it's always worth a lot more than some sandwiches and root beer.

For example, just last week I spotted the dust of someone driving down under the bridge. I try to keep track of such things because I worry about people going down to the river on my place and leaving trash there or tearing up the sand bars and destroying the calm of the river critters. The worst ones are the folks from Rising City who come in with their all-terrain vehicles and grind around on the sand all weekend long. The noise and mess would be bad enough, but it's the stupidity of it that really gets to me.

I usually also go down there to see what's going on in case it's Woodrow or Lunchbox rigging up for some philosophical conversation, Slick with his saucy new barmaid, Rose (I love to see him squirm when I settle in as if I'm ready to spend the evening with them under the bridge!), or Cal.

On this occasion it was Cal. He had already hauled out his bait bucket, rods, and reels by the time I got there with my cooler. He had, as usual, helped Jacinda get her lines set up first. That way she would have a chance to get a bite or even a catch before he even baited up. She got a kick out of that and so did Cal. You could see it.

"Ho!" he grunted without looking at me. "Ho! back at you," I grunted. "About a week back I caught a nice six-pounder just downstream from that log, about where Jacinda has her line." I handed Cal a root beer.

"Here we go again," Cal said quietly. "That little poop is going to catch the first fish, and then the biggest fish, and then the most fish, just like always, and I'm going to be skunked."

Jacinda turned and smiled shyly at me. She has hair as black and coarse as a horse's tail. Her eyes don't have a white and then a ring of color and then a black center like the rest of us in town. There is a little white and then a deep pool of pure black. Her skin is olive, and at thirteen she is about as pretty a thing as you can imagine.

Of course they call her "Pocahontas" at school and don't like to stand next to her at school programs. The kids treat her well enough in class and the teachers bend over backward to be nice to her, but when parents are watching, well, it just seems to be easier for the kids to avoid trouble at home by not being too friendly with her. The fellow who dated my own adopted Indian daughter, Jenny, is known in the area as "Squawman" to this very day.

Jacinda knows her fishing. Cal never baited her hooks for her from her first trip to the river, or took fish off of her line, or even cleaned her catches. "Woman's work," he laughed.

"And if you ever manage to catch any fish, it might just be man's work too," she would snap back.

I was always a little uneasy about that traditional exchange between them because Cal had told me during a couple of previous conversations that Jacinda was having her share of problems—not just with being Indian but also with being female. And thirteen years old, and for that matter, everything else she is. That's not unusual for a kid, you know.

Cal and I went through all the rituals of our sessions under the bridge. He refused the root beer and sandwiches and then helped himself. He asked about Lily, Antonia, and the dogs. And then he got serious about his fishing. He pulled in one nice three-pounder; Jacinda landed two small keepers and a handsome carp that would come out of Cal's smoker tasting like premium northwest coast salmon. I worked at putting a pretty good dent in the soda pop supply.

Before long it was obvious to all of us that it would soon be too hot for the fish to bite until later in the afternoon when things started to cool down again. It was also too hot to do anything besides fish, especially leave the cool shade under the bridge, where even the sound of the river was refreshing.

I handed Jacinda a cold bottle of pop and stepped over

to the chokecherry bushes to pee. That, I guess, is what started things off for the afternoon. "Man, that's just not fair," Jacinda complained. "You guys just get to step over there and write your name in the sand while I have to go lean up against some rough old cottonwood tree and try to stay an inch or so above the poison ivy. It just isn't fair." Her complaint wasn't entirely in jest, even though it struck Cal and me as funny at the time.

"Yeah, and in the winter *we* have to go out in the cold and snow while you sit comfortably on the chamber pot, and that isn't any fun either," Cal said. She still wasn't happy, but she laughed.

I picked up the pace. "That's God's way of punishing you women for what you did to us men in the Garden of Eden. You can read about it right there in the Bible, Jake." She liked it when I called her Jake, Cal had once told me, so I always made a point of doing it at least once when we ran into each other. "That," I explained, "is why God cut off your wienies."

Even Cal laughed at that one, and Jacinda blushed, at least insofar as her olive skin let her. Then she was serious again. "I mean it, Mr. Welsch. Now they won't even let me play baseball with the school team because I'm a girl."

"But . . ."

"Yeah, I know: They let me play with the girls' team. But the girls all play like girls. You know it's true. And I'm the best shortstop in Bleaker County." And I did know that. "They tell me you can't win them all, Mr. Welsch, but you sure would think I could win one now and then."

Now she was very serious. "I'm a girl, and I'm an Indian. Don't get me wrong, Dad"—she turned to Cal—

"I'm as proud as I can be about being Lakota and a White Shell, but you know it isn't easy." We all three knew that.

"And I'm skinny. Every single girl in the seventh grade has boobs except me." She stood up to show us just how skinny she is. "Jeez, Dad, I could go out skinny-dipping by the bridge right now and not a single car would so much as slow down and honk. There's nothing here"—she put her hands on her chest—"to honk at."

She didn't give us time to talk with her about the beauty of her hair and her eyes, her poise and grace, the subtle texture of her skin, but for that matter she probably wouldn't have listened to us even if we had tried to tell her. She wasn't in much of a mood to listen.

"You know what I wish. I wish I was white, Dad." I saw Cal's knuckles whiten on his fishing rod handle. I sincerely hoped he wouldn't say what he was thinking.

"I wish I was a boy, Dad. I wish I had a mom, and I wish we didn't live in a trailer house. I wish we had a toilet, I wish we lived in the city, I wish . . . damnit, Dad, I just wish I wasn't me."

Tears welled up in her eyes, but she just stared out toward her lines at the river's edge. I wished uneasily that I weren't in on this particular conversation. I couldn't look at either her or Cal. Like a white man, I reached out, patted Jacinda's shoulder, and said, "Hey, Jake, it's okay. Don't let it get you down." What a dumb thing to say, I thought, even then.

Like an Indian, on the other hand, Cal sat in silence for a quarter hour to gather his thoughts. I almost jumped when he cleared his throat and said, "Coyote lived in a lodge . . ."

". . . at the edge of the village . . ." Jacinda continued without looking at either of us.

". . . with his grandmother . . ." Cal went on.

". . . who was blind," Jacinda said.

It was clear to me—*very* clear—that they had been down this narrative road before.

" 'I think I'll go outside, Grandma,' Coyote said, and his grandmother said, 'Now, don't you go over that hill where the Big Bull Buffalo is tearing up the sod all the time. With those horns and hoofs of his, he'd grind you up like a rabbit pellet.'

"And what do you think Coyote did?" Cal asked Jacinda, and they both laughed in chorus, "Went over the hill to where the Big Bull Buffalo was tearing up the sod all the time!"

"That's right. And Coyote lay there on that hill in the sun, his tongue hanging out, and he spent most of the day watching the buffalo. Pretty soon though that Big Bull Buffalo sort of drifted over close to Coyote and said, 'What do you want, you scruffy little pipsqueak? You better watch yourself or I'll turn you into food for the magpies.'

" 'Oh no, Mr. Bull Buffalo, I have just been sitting here all day watching you, and I have been thinking how handsome you are and what a fine life you lead.'

"The Bull Buffalo looked at him and kind of rolled his eyes like buffalo do when they aren't sure what is going on.

" 'I mean, look at you,' Coyote said. 'You don't have to chase mice and rabbits for your supper; you get to eat this nice, tender grass, and there's no shortage of that here. Everywhere you look, you see food.

" 'When there are storms I have to find some dark, wet hole to crawl in, or a hollow tree, but you . . . you are so big and your fur is so thick that you stand there like a mountain and let the storm blow around you.

" 'And you have such a big family'—Coyote pointed out to the herd—'and all I have is my grandmother.

" 'Me, I'm afraid of bear, and elk, and even you. Any time I hear something a little scary, I run off and try to find something to hide under. But you. You are so big and strong and powerful. You don't have to be afraid of anything.

" 'So what I am wondering, Mr. Bull Buffalo, sir, is this: Is there any way I can be a buffalo like you?'

"Well, now, as you can imagine, that proposition took Big Bull Buffalo by surprise. He'd never heard anything like that before, but he remembered from the old days the way those things are done.

"So he said to Coyote, 'You just stand right there and don't move. I am going to come running and hit you with my horns and that will change you into one of us. But if you really want to be a buffalo, you have to stand still.'

" 'Yessir, I sure will, sir,' said Coyote, and he braced himself. But when he saw that Big Bull Buffalo coming at him, he just couldn't stand still, and at the very last moment he jumped aside and let the Big Bull Buffalo run past.

" 'I thought I told you to stand still,' roared the Big Bull Buffalo, and Coyote just stood there shivering, so scared all four of his knees were banging together." Jacinda laughed out loud at the thought.

" 'I am going to give you another chance, you scruff ball,' Bull Buffalo said, and he went off about a half mile to get another run.

"But the closer he got to Coyote, the more scared Coyote got again, and once more, he jumped back just as Big Bull Buffalo passed him.

"Now the Bull Buffalo was really getting mad. 'I told you to stand still, and I mean it.' He pawed the dust and his tail was standing straight up, which means he was really mad. 'Don't you budge from *right there*, you scrawny piece of poop,' and all Coyote could do was nod.

"Well, just as you might guess, coyote jumped back on the third pass too, and this time Big Bull Buffalo was so mad he hooked his horn hard at Coyote, and Coyote could see that with those iron-hard, black horns, Big Bull Buffalo could tear him apart if he ever decided to do the job on Coyote good, so the fourth time Big Bull Buffalo came running at him, Coyote shut his eyes and hummed his death song as loud as he could so he couldn't see or hear Big Bull Buffalo bearing down on him.

"And *pawow!* Big Bull Buffalo hit him, and when Coyote came to and looked around, sure enough, just like Big Bull Buffalo had said—he had been turned into a buffalo. Not as big as Big Bull Buffalo, but a lot bigger than he had been when he was only Coyote. 'Hey, this is great,' he said to Big Bull Buffalo and trotted off to join the herd.

"Well, Buffalo-that-had-been-Coyote set to eating that grass, but jeez, it turned out it was peppergrass, and it tasted terrible. And then he got hold of some ripgut and it cut up his mouth. And he got a cactus stuck on his nose. 'Well, this isn't quite as great as I thought it was going to be,' he thought.

"Then he strolled over to some other bulls in the herd about his size—to make friends, you know—but they pawed the ground and threw dust up over their shoulders. Then they proceeded to pound on him with their horns and hoofs until he was covered with bruises and blood.

He retreated over to the back of the herd where he had to breathe dust all day long. He sure wasn't going to mix it up with those guys again.

"Then a storm came up. Instead of finding some nice warm shelter like he used to when he was Coyote, now he had to walk straight into the storm like the buffalo do. Lightning was everywhere, but he couldn't get away from it. There was cold rain and wind, and he thought, 'This is getting to be less fun all the time. I wonder if this was such a great idea, me turning into a buffalo.'

"Then some Indians came running up over the hill. Well, when he was Coyote he hadn't paid much attention to the Indians except to slip into their camp for scraps of meat and bone now and then, so he wasn't too worried. He had never bothered the Indians, and they had never bothered him.

"But then he realized, 'These guys are shooting arrows at me. Hey, know what?! They're trying to *kill* me!' And he took off running, but even then he had a couple arrows stuck into his rump and they hurt like crazy, and he stumbled in a gopher hole and fell down and broke one horn.

"Well, that did it. He limped back over to Big Bull Buffalo—hungry, battered, cold and wet, and bleeding from where the arrows were still sticking out of his hide and from his broken horn. 'Mr. Big Bull Buffalo, sir, I think a mistake has been made,' he said.

" 'What are you talking about?' grunted Big Bull Buffalo, and he continued eating grass.

" 'I think I want to be Coyote again.'

" 'Okay, you miserable pain-in-the-rear. You sure didn't amount to much as a buffalo. Turning you back to Coyote is pretty much the same process. So stand still and don't make this any harder for me than it needs to be.'

"Of course being Coyote, he jumped aside three times before he finally closed his eyes and hummed his death song, and the Big Bull Buffalo finally hit him. Well, Big Bull Buffalo was so mad by that time that he hit Coyote even harder than he had intended. In fact, he hit Coyote so hard, he is still going up.

"If you look straight up along the lip of the Big Dipper tonight, you'll see a bright star, and that star is Coyote, still going up into the sky. You see, he got hit so hard by that Big Bull Buffalo that he is still flying up into space, like an astronaut.

"But when he comes back down, my darling, he'll be Coyote again"—Cal reached over and pulled lightly at Jacinda's nose—"and he'll be glad he is."

There was a long silence while we thought over Cal's story, and then Jacinda said, "I think I have a bite." On her way over to her lines she pulled up the minnow trap, sorted out a handful of minnows from the chicken bones for her bait cup, and threw the trap back into the current. Perhaps with excessive optimism she picked up the fish basket and set off upstream a few dozen yards to where she had put the lines.

"Damned if I don't think she does have a bite," I said to Cal.

"Yeah, but she's looking for more than catfish," Cal smiled.

It took Jacinda a little longer than usual to get her line in and net the three- or four-pounder she held up for us to admire. Then instead of coming back to where we were sitting under the bridge, finishing off the Coke and root beer, she sat down with her lines, fooling around with a setline and looking at the river as if newly encouraged about the prospects of winning this unofficial fishing contest with her father.

"The Omaha tell a story a lot like that except it's about Rabbit and the Elk," I said to Cal.

"Yeah, I've heard some Omahas tell that one. But I like it better with Coyote and Buffalo."

"Me too," I said, meaning it.

About seven o'clock we ran out of refreshments and bait and the mosquitoes were getting bad, so we packed up Cal and Jacinda's fishing gear into their pickup truck. "I'll buy a round up at the tavern," I offered. "If Slick has the grill hot, I'll even spring for burgers."

"Boy, that sounds great!" she laughed. "It really gives a person an appetite, hauling in fish like that. Sometimes I wish I was more like my dad and didn't hardly catch anything at all."

"Want to be like me, do you, Coyote?" Cal put his hands alongside his head, forefingers pointing forward. He pawed the ground with his right foot. "Just stand still and . . ." He made a dash toward Jacinda, grabbed her, and hugged her as she laughed—hugged her so hard it probably hurt. Maybe it did hurt. There were tears in her eyes again anyway.

When we walked into the Town Tavern Tom Larson was sitting in his usual booth at the back of the bar. "Hey, Perfesser!" he yelled. "The Cherokees are in town! Hey, Geronimo! Hey, Pocahontas!"

Before Cal and I could so much as open our mouths Jacinda threw back her hair and laughed, "Hey, Custer!" Cal nudged me with his elbow, and I smiled back.

LaVerne's Plan

EVEN IF YOU have never lived in a small town, you can imagine what it's like. It's like living in one big family. Everyone knows everything that is going on and, for that matter, a lot that isn't. Hat says that if you sneeze in Centralia, someone in Barnston will probably say, "God bless you."

I have been up to the Town Tavern on a dozen occasions when Slick or Woodrow would lean forward to tell me something in confidence—"Next time Minnie brings over a beer, take a look at that maxi-hickey on the right side of her neck!" or "Ask Lunchbox what happened at the Barnston swimming pool last night"—and Emma Fahrquar, sitting sixty-five feet away playing cards, yelled, "Who has a hickey?" or Claire Finch would stroll over to Lunchbox before I could so much as get out of the chair, full of questions about the Barnston swimming pool.

171

Emma can't hear Farley when he loudly announces to no one in particular, "Them Fahrquar kids been filching candy bars over at the grocery again, Slick," but she can hear the whispered word "hickey" over the roar of six guys fighting with pool cues. Claire can't hardly get up the stairs anymore what with rheumatism and sciatica, but she moves like a cat when there's dirt to be dug. Amazing. But the point is, in Centralia, there are no secrets.

To make things worse, this past year there's been a lot to keep secret in Centralia. Slick and Connie broke up after twenty years of marital blitz. LaVerne dumped Lloyd five years too late. Goose has been on the road for a couple months; he says he's been in Michigan or maybe Nevada, but it really doesn't make any difference because CeCe doesn't care if he's camped down by the river, she says, just as long as he's not camped out in her front room. One of the Golddust Twins is p.g. and a team of lawyers is reviewing her diary right now with an eye toward developing a roster of candidates for prosecution.

Just yesterday someone was commenting that even though Carla no longer works at the tavern on a regular basis, Slick still smiles a lot. Lunchbox has been working extra hours on CeCe's car, the story goes, and the last time Goose came home from one of his trips he even looked under the bed; CeCe laughed at him and said that if Lunchbox ever needed to hide under her bed, she would have to set it up on concrete blocks first.

LaVerne must have something going on with Harlan, I heard one week not long ago. The reasoning goes that before the recent rash of divorces LaVerne and Lloyd, Harlan and Carla used to spend a lot of time as a foursome, but now that both couples have split up, LaVerne and Harlan are *never* seen together, and where there's smoke, there's fire. Everyone in Centralia spends time together. Therefore, if Harlan and LaVerne are *not* spending time together, then they must be up to something.

I'm sure a normal amount of personal intrigue goes on in Centralia, but if all the gossip you hear there were really true you wouldn't be able to make your way around town for all the sheets hanging out to dry. I know there used to be talk when Woodrow and his wife, Darlene, went out on double dates with Lily and me. I suppose that is because Woodrow hardly ever goes home, let alone takes Darlene out. An item in the Rising City *Clarion-Crusader*'s social column once read, "A visitor at the Woodrow Buehler home this past weekend was Woodrow Buehler." CeCe sent it in for a joke, but it was so close to the truth that no one noticed the humor of it.

Thing is, Lily was trying to get Woodrow and Darlene to double-date with us because she was sure that if they just had the chance to get to know each other, they'd really hit it off. Woodrow is gone so much, Lily figured he and Darlene just never had a chance to see how much they have in common, their three kids notwithstanding, or maybe even contributing. Darlene once told Lily that she'd leave Woodrow if she could find him, but then maybe that's just women talk because Lily says she'd leave me too if she thought for a minute that I'd notice.

Anyway, there was a lot of talk when the four of us— Woodrow and Darlene, Lily and I—would go off for an evening in Rising City to catch a movie and treat the ladies to a Swiss steak at the Hacienda Motel restaurant. Someone from Centralia saw us going into the Hacienda, I guess, and figured we were checking into the honeymoon suite with the round bed and the heart-shaped bathtub when the reality is that the closest we came to anything of the sort was the time we threw our keys in a pile and grabbed, the agreement being that if Woodrow and I got each other's keys, we could spend the night running set-lines down at the river.

So this past fall the rumor mill was grinding exceedingly fast and exceedingly coarse. While most folks in town laughed the stories off, it did get annoying. The ministers at the Baptist and Lutheran churches coordinated their sermons one Sunday, both talking on the Seventh Commandment, and the rumors were so thick that it got to be dangerous to gossip in a group of more than three other people without including one of your audience in the most recently postulated *ménage à dix*.

I came into the Town Tavern one Saturday afternoon and found LaVerne sitting at a table, mumbling to herself. I'd heard that she was seeing Slick socially, and maybe Woodrow, and even a teenager from over at Rising City. It all seemed perfectly reasonable until I also heard that she was entertaining me now and then, so I thought it might be worth listening to LaVerne's soliloquy just to hear her side of the story.

Slick was tending bar, so I had him bring a couple mugs of beer over and I sat down opposite LaVerne.

"Damn old ladies," she sputtered.

"What old ladies?" I asked.

"Not old ladies, you big dope. I mean people who gossip like old ladies. You know, the garbage diggers around here who don't have enough to do that they have time to talk about everyone else but don't seem to notice that they have enough dirt in their own houses that they could take care of if they ever decided to spend their energy doing something useful instead of prying into other people's lives and . . ."

"Oh," I interrupted since I could see that LaVerne was running short on breath. "I can understand your bad case of the snarlies, LaVerne. I heard a rumor last week that you were seeing someone over at the nursing home, which I thought was a pretty ridiculous story until I heard yesterday's gem that you and *Connie* are—well, you know."

I had started down that road thinking I might calm LaVerne down, but she seemed even madder now than she was before I bought her the beer. "Well, I'm not standing still for it anymore. I'm going to give the miserable tongue-waggers something real to chew on for a change."

"Hey, Slick, bring LaVerne another beer," I yelled. You see, the thought crossed my mind that here was LaVerne, a good-looking woman considering that she is about forty years old and considering that we are right in the middle of Bleaker County, and she's making noises like she is all set to commit some thoroughly disgusting sin just out of spite. It looked to me as if she might just be mad enough to make her move without any particular consideration of who would be her assistant in defiance, and I sure as hell wanted to be around when she started choosing sides.

She pulled me over to the dark corner booth, and for a moment I began to worry that I was about to become a George Armstrong Custer at an erotic Little Big Horn.

I've read those letters in *Bare Beauties* magazine where some middle-aged guy's twenty-year-old neighbor decides to bring a little excitement into his life and one Friday evening brings over four of her deliciously nubile and totally uninhibited airline stewardess friends and the five of them spend the weekend reducing this guy to a sticky spot on the ceiling, and here he is now, writing this letter from the Mount Bambi Hospital for the Terminally Ecstatic.

I know those letters are phony, and I know that nothing

like that is ever going to happen to me. And if it does, I'll have a head cold. Can you imagine anything worse than someone showing up at a five-stewardess orgy with a really bad head cold?

Or if an opportunity like that ever did arise, I wouldn't, if you catch my drift.

My idea of a *good* idea is to get Lily a little tipsy on a Saturday night with hopes that I might get lucky—that she'll go to sleep and leave me alone. So I was getting nervous about this booth thing with LaVerne.

Slick must have sensed my uneasiness because when he brought over the beers, he pushed into the booth on the other side of LaVerne and she told us her plan. As she revealed her plot, Slick and I both sat there with our mouths open, realizing that we had somehow fallen in with a Napoleon of social strategists.

The next Saturday evening, about 11:00 P.M., when things quieted down, Slick, CeCe, Lunchbox, Lily and me, LaVerne, Woodrow, and Carla drove our cars into town. I dropped my car off over in front of LaVerne's and drove her car across town to Slick's, parking it up on the driveway close to the back door. Slick put one of his cars in the alley behind Lunchbox's place, and Lily took his El Camino and parked it over in the park, CeCe put her car right beside it, and then they both went with me to park Lunchbox's pickup in Cindy's garage, with the door half open. Slick took Lunchbox's wife's car over to Woodrow's house.

Woodrow's service truck went over in front of Old Lady Barnston's, as we figured she wouldn't mind being in on the fun, and Carla parked her car down at our place, taking my truck back over to her place. LaVerne took all the leftover folks back to their houses, and by a little after midnight we were all back in our own beds. In town the only sound was the barking of a few confused dogs and muffled laughter from ten or twelve dark houses.

The Centralia telephone lines were completely tied up all day Sunday, what with the schemers calling each other to report who was driving slowly around town making observations and the observers making calls to report to shut-ins what was going on, right here in Centralia.

Everyone in on LaVerne's plot laid low until Sunday night about eleven, which wasn't as much of an inconvenience as you might think. I called Slick to tell him how funny it was over at our place because every time Lily and I so much as looked at each other, we would start giggling uncontrollably, just thinking about the confusion that we must have generated in town.

"Slick? Did you see the Nelsons driving . . .?" and then we both got to giggling and couldn't even continue the conversation. We were about as proud of ourselves as people can be proud of themselves.

The breakfast business was brisk at the Chew 'n' Chat Cafe Monday morning. The car shufflers were all there to see what sort of excitement they had set off among the gossipers, and the gossipers were all there . . . well, I'm not sure why they were all there. Emma, Fern, Worm Dower, Claire, Bud, Eli, and Long John just sat there looking stunned. And confused. And a trifle on the tired side.

And maybe just a *little* left out.

OSCAR

OSCAR AND I were standing out in front of his house. He was dragging around a garden hose, watering some fitzers he had planted in the narrow grassed strip between the sidewalk and street. He had salvaged the plants from the garbage pile behind Hotdog Heaven, a business not far from his place. He thought they would look good along his street. Besides, he hated to see things like that go to waste.

It was very much like Oscar that he was planting the shrubs not only along the street in front of his own house but also up and down the street in his neighbors' yards. Never mind that his neighbors might not want the evergreens planted in their yards: Oscar just did whatever he thought was right and never for a moment questioned that someone else might have another idea of how things should go.

For a moment as I watched him space the plants a hundred yards or so along the quiet neighborhood street I thought I might avoid a lot of trouble if I just went inside and watched the evening news on television because I really didn't want to be around when the neighbors came home to discover Oscar's complimentary landscaping, but, since the neighbors had lived next to him for nearly twenty years, they probably were used to such eccentricities and I only had the chance to visit with Oscar once or twice a year so I didn't want to lose a moment of his salty wit.

I helped him dig a few holes, put in the fitzers, and throw the dirt back in while he stood at the last plant we had carefully put in the neatly spaced holes. Oscar held a garden hose and was running water into the freshly turned earth. All the while we worked he talked in a slow, barely audible monotone that many attributed to a lifelong taste for Kessler whiskey but which I knew was simply Oscar's storytelling style.

"Business over at the store has been pretty good, Roger, but I think I'm getting to the age, you know, when it doesn't even matter anymore how well things are going: They just keep going. Good, bad—it doesn't really matter. You just keep plugging away."

I nodded, tucked more dirt around the fitzer currently under consideration, and started digging a hole for the next, still feeling very uneasy about digging holes in Oscar's neighbor's yard. A boy about eight years old rolled up on his bicycle and stopped at the curb where we were working and demanded, "What you guys doing?"

Oscar paid no attention to the boy and kept right on talking to me: "Of course, I like a day when the receipts are higher than usual and I hate the days when no one

comes in at all, but even the good days are just days when
you get to a certain point."

I nodded and dug. The boy said, a little louder, "Hey,
Mister, what are you doing digging in Stegmeisters' lawn
like that?"

Oscar didn't so much as look at him. I was about to
give the kid an explanation but I couldn't think of one,
and besides, Oscar talked on as if only he and I were there:
"It reminds me of the story they used to tell in Torrington,
Wyoming. You know, Roger, I had a hotel there once."

I nodded and put a fitzer in the new hole. "Hey! Mister!
I asked you what you're doing. Are you deef or sump'n?"

Oscar continued his slow, quiet story, all the while watering the fitzer I had just planted: "There were these two
little kids spent too much time in the pool hall there in
Torrington, and they knew that something was going on
over at Fifi's place that cost twenty dollars but they didn't
know what it was."

I nodded, and this time I smiled because I knew that
whatever story Oscar was about to tell me was going to
be worth hearing. The little kid at the curb was now beside
himself, "Damnit, Mister, I asked you once and I'm going
to ask again, *just what the hell do you think you're
doing?!*"

This time Oscar did glance up at the boy, but he continued his watering and his story without the slightest ripple
in his rhythm: "So these two little boys worked all summer
mowing lawns and collecting pop bottles until they had
about fourteen dollars, but that was the best they could
do and their curiosity was about to kill them."

Then, without the slightest hint of any emotion, to my
amazement and, God knows, to the obnoxious kid's,
Oscar played the stream of cold water from his garden

hose up and down the right pants leg of the boy who by now was screaming a string of insults that nearly drowned out Oscar's narrative.

I probably winced when I saw the kid's pant leg soaked like that, but I kept right on working. Oscar turned the hose back to the next fitzer in the line, and he continued his story while the boy sputtered in disbelief: "The boys took their fourteen dollars over to Fifi's and explained that they didn't really know why they were there, but they wanted whatever the big boys came there for."

"You big poop, I'm going to tell my mom you got my pants wet. Y'dumb son of a bitch!"

"Fifi asked them if they had twenty dollars and they said no, but they showed her their fourteen dollars." And as he delivered that line, Oscar also deliberately and carefully watered the obnoxious kid's *left* leg.

Now the brat on the bike was crying, but he still had the energy and composure to maintain his string of definitely unchildlike insults directed at Oscar. "You bastard! Now both my legs are all wet. And my new shoes. My dad's going to *kill* you." Profanity poured from the boy's mouth. I glanced at him in amazement, wondering where he had accumulated his advanced education in offensive linguistics, but Oscar still hadn't so much as acknowledged the lad's existence.

"She reached out and took the fourteen dollars from the boys' hands, took each one by an ear, banged their heads together three times just as hard as she possibly could, and pitched them over the railing of the porch into the dust of the street. The one little boy sat up, shook his head, and looked at the other one."

"You son of a bitch! You rotten no-good . . . my *mom's*

gonna kill you! You're gonna pay for this," spouted the soggy kid on the bicycle.

Oscar finished watering the last fitzer and then systematically ran the stream of water from his hose up and down the boy, who was now totally soaked, streams of water running down every part of his bicycle. Oscar played the gentle stream into the boy's face, over his head, and, when he turned, down his back. The kid's clothes were drenched, his hair soaked. He could hardly talk through the water running down his face. By now he was madder than any cuss words he had at his command, and so he was not doing much more than sputtering and sobbing. He had done his best, but it hadn't been enough to so much as declare his physical reality to Oscar.

Oscar concluded his story, " 'I don't know about you,' said the one little kid, 'but I don't believe I'm ready for twenty dollars' worth of that.' "

I laughed, cleaned off my shovel, and Oscar and I walked toward the house, Oscar chuckling in appreciation of his own story.

The kid on the bike pedaled soggily down the street, still shouting insults back over his shoulder in our direction: "You stupid jerk! You dip! You queer!"

"Roger," Oscar said, "did I ever tell you the one about the little boy who ran away from home?"

GYPSIES

I WAS ONCE talking with a Lakota wise man, Richard Fool Bull, wondering at his ability to sense what seemed to me to be mystic occurrences. Magic things seemed to happen to him fairly regularly. A hundred years ago they would have been called "visions" by the Indians. A thousand years ago they would have been called "miracles" even in our culture, but Mr. Fool Bull accepted them as a normal part of life.

"They *are* a normal part of life," he laughed when I expressed my amazement. "They happen all the time."

"To you maybe, Mr. Fool Bull, but not to me."

"Oh yes, to you too," he said, nodding seriously. "That is the sad thing about white culture. You see, Roger, it is not a matter of me being trained to see such things; *you* have been trained not to see them."

That's not a new idea. In anthropology classes it is a common teaching trick, for example, to tell students that

183

there are still peoples of this world who do not know the connection between sexual intercourse and pregnancy. That usually excites astonishment in the class—how can anyone not understand a cause-and-effect that obvious?

The professor lets the students throw around their obvious cultural superiority for a few minutes and then asks, "What is the result of eating asparagus?" It is rare that anyone responds with a serious response. "Your urine smells to high heaven for a couple of hours, that's what. Now, why is it you think these people are so stupid because they have not realized an association that spans nine months while you have never figured out a very obvious cause-and-effect relationship that takes place over only a few minutes?" The fact of the matter is, very obvious things, most not at all mystical, happen around us all the time and we manage to remain totally oblivious to them.

I enjoy the regular—every few months or so—articles that appear in the Omaha or Rising City newspapers that run pretty much along these lines:

The Bleaker County Savings and Loan lost an estimated $900 in an unusual fraud perpetrated against teller Judy Hockworthy last Thursday. According to Ms. Hockworthy six or seven swarthy people—probably Indians or Iranians—came in to the office at 48th and Caldwell Streets looking for change for the parking meter and a fifty-dollar bill with an L in the serial number.

Ms. Hockworthy reported that the men spoke broken English and the women were dressed in loose, colorful clothing. The men had seventeen one-hundred-dollar bills for which they wanted the change for the parking meter and the fifty-dollar bills.

After several changes of the bills, the alleged defrauders left the office and drove away in late-model pickup trucks, all with campers on the beds and all with Illinois license plates.

The police have no suspects.

I love those stories. For one thing, I think it's wonderful that these skilled con men get away with what they do in large part because they have plenty of money in their hands when they enter the bank. The thesis in our society, evidently, is, "Anyone who has lots of money is obviously to be trusted" when every indication should tell us exactly the opposite.

But there is a deeper, philosophical reason for my affection for these enduring, widespread petty bilkers. You see, I like coyotes. I don't care if coyotes take 15 percent of the lambs and calves on western ranges. To me coyotes represent something very important—that creatures under the pressure of full warfare can survive. Out here coyotes are hunted with high-power rifles, traps, exploding baits, poison, airplanes, calls, chumming, and mobs. And yet survive. They *prosper!* That prospect gives coyotes like me a lot of hope, you see.

Well, newspaper stories like that are about human coyotes, I guess. Gypsies. That's who those "Indians or Iranians" are, Gypsies. Through a thousand years of resistance, through wars and contempt and murder and expulsion, the Gypsies survive. Before Hitler murdered the Jews, he murdered the Gypsies.

And yet here they are, still with us, and so skillfully concealed that most Americans haven't the foggiest notion they are still here.

Before I forget, let me tell you what happened in Germany. The Gypsies were almost totally eradicated in Germany, and do you know what happened after the Second World War? The Gypsies *swarmed* into Germany. Where would they be safer than where they had only a few years before been pariahs? They could still be hated in England or Sweden, but not in Germany. Gypsy caravans parked illegally under Autobahn overpasses and in department-store parking lots because the gypsies knew that here, where they had been most abused, now they would be most tolerated.

I admired especially the ones camped illegally under the overpasses. Can you imagine a better place to set up camp? Families sat at picnic tables and enjoyed supper even when it was raining like crazy or when the sun was blazing, peacefully watching the traffic whiz by. Overpass railings were festooned with wet laundry, a kind of Gypsy flag of resistance.

Gypsies are still visible throughout Europe, where their distinctive clothing and wagons and a long tradition make them easily recognized by the citizens of the countries they travel. In America Gypsies are almost invisible. Americans see them not as "Gypsies" but "slightly peculiar, dark people—maybe Iranians or Indians." The average American perceives their pickup trucks with inevitable camper toppers and "For Sale" signs as something strange—but almost never as "Gypsies"!

What I love about American Gypsies is that they are seen only rarely, and then briefly, like comets. I, for one, feel graced when I have the chance to see them, even if only in passing on the highway.

Fremont, Nebraska, used to be a popular place for Gypsies to stop and for all I know may still be. It is on Highway 30, the Lincoln Highway, and that was the main artery for cross-country travel for many years. For the still nomadic Gypsies, the long, open stretches of the Lincoln Highway must have been like a hometown. And Fremont is about halfway across America, so it was a logical meeting and resting place for the eternal travelers.

As a boy I once read a newspaper report of a time when two rival Gypsy bands wound up at a Gypsy cemetery in Fremont at the same time—both paying respect, as I recall, to the hallowed memory of the same patriarch of the tribe. The result was memorable. My recollection is that something like four hundred shots were fired, and when the police finally sorted things out after the pitched battle, they amassed a huge pile of knives, clubs, guns, brass knuckles, and other weapons of choice.

Now, I am not a violent guy and you probably wonder what possible saving grace I could deduce from a violent encounter like that. Well, what I found *glorious* about it was that not a single person was hurt. It was all posturing, maneuvering, threatening, and bluster. Coyotes at play.

I've spoken with quite a few people in Fremont about the Gypsies in the old days, and there are a lot of stories. The Gypsies often asked to camp at farms and farmers would usually give them permission in order to avoid later retribution, but they made sure the chickens and children were put to bed early and the mother and father stayed up late to keep an eye on things.

Older farm women who remember when Gypsies would camp near their farmsteads tell me that the Gypsy women and children would often come to the house asking for eggs or milk and they were usually given those simple things. Later inspection revealed that the next day tools, cooking utensils, dogs, and even horses or cows showed up missing—or perhaps I should say didn't show up missing.

Today, savvy merchants close up the store the minute they hear that the Gypsies are in town. For those too slow or inexperienced to close up shop, the experience is usually that ten or twelve women with voluminous clothing sweep into the store and scatter throughout the aisles. Merchandise disappears within the ample folds of the clothing. The ensuing shouting, arguing, and linguistic confusion makes it impossible for the merchant, security, or even the police to sort out one woman from another, let alone retrieve pilfered goods, and the inventory is shot to hell for the rest of the year.

All except the new car and truck dealers. They love to see the Gypsies come to town. The Gypsies frequently buy new vehicles in Fremont, and their mode of operation is always the same. They come onto the lot, point to the vehicle they want, ask how much it is, and without any haggling whatsoever pay the price in cash.

Now, I know what's going to happen when folks read this. Latter-day Gypsies are going to say that I have slandered their people, that Gypsies never steal, that all the stories are fictions, that Gypsies actually travel around the world doing good deeds wherever they can. Well, anyone who tries to sell that sort of nonsense does the Gypsies a gross disservice. By lying about their people, they deny their heritage. I have no sympathy for people like that. Just as surely as Gypsies have leavened the cultural loaf of western civilization with their music, art, and food, they have enriched us all with their irrepressible resistance to change, their thousands of years of resistance to authority and order not their own.

There will be non-Gypsies who say I am a real jerk for

suggesting that common thievery is anything but common thievery and the Gypsies should learn to behave like Americans if they intend to live in this glorious land of the free, home of the brave. They should learn that nothing is more rewarding than money earned by the sweat of your brow—sort of like Ivan Boesky or Donald Trump or Don King, I guess. No, the Gypsies offer another alternative—survival by wit.

I don't condone cheating and thievery normally, but in the case of the Gypsies it is a cultural inheritance and its cleverness makes me glad to be a member of the same species as the Gypsies.

I used to think that one of the things I wanted to do in my life was to spend an afternoon or evening in a Gypsy camp. My fantasy was that I would spot a bunch of Gypsy pickup trucks in a small park some day, somewhere on the Plains—I know what to look for, after all. I imagined that what I would do on that occasion is walk into the camp with a couple of chickens and maybe a battered banjo I wouldn't mind losing over my shoulder. That way I could trade the chickens for something to eat—something *Gypsy*—and play my banjo in exchange for some of their legendary music.

Unfortunately, the closest I have come to realizing that fantasy is one time when some friends and I stopped for a picnic lunch in a public parking place at a large park in South Dakota. We were eating and I was eyeing ten or twelve pickup campers on the other side of the parking lot. I suspected they might be Gypsies.

As we were eating, two five- or six-year-old children approached us from the direction of the trucks. They were beautiful children—dark-skinned with enormous, black eyes. Obviously they were Gypsies. "Would you like a cookie?" I asked them.

They nodded yes.

I held out the sack, but to my surprise they backed away a couple steps. No, they explained, they would not take the cookies as a gift. They would accept them only if they could buy them from me.

Hmmm. Maybe these weren't Gypsies. Gypsies steal, I thought. They don't *buy.* I was put mentally off balance.

"How much you want for the cookies, Mister?" one of the children asked.

These were great big chocolate chip cookies, and I had a big bag of about sixty or seventy of them; they had cost me maybe eight dollars early that morning at the grocery store. "Tell you what, young man," I said. "How about a penny. Will you pay a penny for a cookie this big?"

He smiled and nodded yes, and I felt like a real prince for being such a nice guy with these kids. And I felt like a real dope for all the things I had said in the past about Gypsies being—how shall I say it?—shrewd operators.

The little boy handed me a penny, and I gave him a cookie. His little friend handed me a penny, and I gave him a cookie too. Gosh, what a pleasant little vignette, I thought.

Then suddenly, out of nowhere, I was surrounded by eighty little children, all with pennies, all wanting cookies. So we wound up selling our entire supper, all of it—cookies, sandwiches, candy bars, chips, everything, for something like eighty-five cents!

These folks were Gypsies, all right—kids and all. I had been had, but good. I had fallen for exactly the routine I had watched other people fall for for decades—my junior deceivers had confused me with their impressive wealth, they had let me believe that I was being the clever party to the exchange, they had come at me from a direction I would have never thought of looking into, and when it was all over, I still wasn't sure what had happened to me, how much I had lost, how it had ever developed, why I had been such a dope.

And I loved it. Every minute of it. I have savored the moment over and over for these twenty years now. Outwitted by the Gypsies, I was, and not just by Gypsies but by two five-year-old Gypsies.

I still keep an old banjo around the house, and a few chickens, just in case.

ROYAL CUPP

NO ONE WAS surprised when Royal Cupp died at the relatively young age of fifty-four. He was mean enough to have lived a lot longer, but even more than being mean, he was an out-and-out, flag-waving, declared white supremacist. He never missed a chance to point out when anyone of "lesser heritage," as he called it, robbed a bank, committed murder, or dropped a punt. We all knew him so well that on such occasions he usually didn't have to say anything at all; he would just look at us over his glasses and nod knowingly.

He liked to point out that Africa, Asia, and all of the Western Hemisphere except for Canada and the United States never managed to develop the atomic bomb without "Caucasian" help. He asked, rhetorically, if we hadn't noticed how ugly everyone else is. He argued that it was downright unpatriotic to be anything but a Republican because, after all, our Founding Fathers were all conservatives.

It did not help one whit to try to explain to him that the atomic bomb just might not be man's highest achievement and that beauty is a cultural decision and varies from generation to generation. Most of all, he ignored any suggestion that Washington, Jefferson, Madison, and Franklin were not only not conservatives, they were raving revolutionaries, dead set on destroying what decent people understood to be a divinely empowered aristocracy.

Just as some insist that there is a public right to know, Royal Cupp insisted that there was a public right not to know. On one occasion, typical of daily occasions, he expressed his pride that he had voted for Ronald Reagan, a man who had submitted eight balanced budgets in a row. I knew better than to argue politics with Royal, but I could not suppress my natural reaction to correct such a glaring inaccuracy.

"Royal, you idiot," I explained, "Reagan didn't submit a single balanced budget during his entire derelict two terms—not even close—and then he didn't even bother to apologize for lying."

Royal countered, "Reagan submitted eight balanced budgets in a row."

"Why, the hell he did. I'll write Congresswoman Smith—and she's a Republican just like you—and ask her about Reagan's budgets. Even she will be honest enough to admit an obvious, undeniable historical fact like that, I'll bet."

"In that case, keep your information to yourself," Royal said, clearly not amused, and he left, slamming the door of the cafe as he stormed out. When it served his fruitcake politics—and it usually did—Royal preferred ignorance. He demanded his right as a modern American not to know, not to see the obvious, not to acknowledge the undeniable, not to accept the evident, not to realize reality, not to see the truth. Royal knew that right there in the Constitution, immediately following the provision that insures our right to own hand grenades and flame throwers, there was the explicit right to remain ignorant in the face of all information to the contrary.

No one argued with Royal about anything because there wasn't any use to it. He made up facts as he needed them and discarded them when they conflicted with what he believed, no matter how obvious they might be. When the evidence was overwhelmingly against him, he would simply say in a superior way, "There you are. The exception proves the rule," and walk out, having convinced no one but himself. That was all right because no one was more important to Royal than himself, and he felt that if he had made his point with someone as intellectually superior as himself, then no one else really mattered very much. It's not easy for the ethical debater to outmaneuver a technique like that.

Another reason no one argued with Royal was because no one had the chance. Royal had a reason for not liking almost everyone. It's not as if he didn't like *anyone*; that is, he didn't hate mankind. He disliked only those who were clearly inferior to him. The problem was that in Royal's opinion that just happened to be nearly everyone he had encountered over the past ten or twenty years.

Royal had arrived at his reasons for disliking each of us individually. It wasn't prejudice; it was logic. Royal didn't hate anyone without a reason, and it just worked out that he found a reason to hate damned near everyone in Bleaker County.

What's worse, Royal simply would not abide anyone he didn't like. He could not bring himself to grace with his company anyone beneath him. So when he came into the Chew 'n' Chat Cafe he would avoid sitting at any table where there was someone he didn't like. Since he didn't like very many of us, he usually just sat down somewhere by himself.

If someone came into the cafe he didn't like, someone who made the mistake of sitting down at the table where he was already enthroned, Royal would haul up his enormous bulk with a meaningful start and make a point of looking for another place to sit.

Some mean-spirited locals would occasionally sit down beside Royal on purpose, just to see him pop up and huff around looking for another table without a pariah. More often than not, that meant he moved on to another empty table or stomped out.

Royal was somehow convinced that it actually made a difference to the rest of us when he wouldn't sit with us. He considered his company to be a prize that we must surely covet. He assumed that when he withdrew that favor, our hearts stopped, our breath quickened, our futures failed. What we did mostly was giggle.

Royal was superior, he felt, to almost every single one of us in Bleaker County, regardless of racial persuasion, but Royal reserved special contempt for those of color. That was hard on the one hand because there are only maybe three black folks here, ten or twenty Mexicans, maybe fifty Indians, and a couple dozen Southeast Asians who don't really live here but fish occasionally in the river. On the other hand, that made it a good deal easier for Royal because he didn't ever have his difficult prejudices confronted by easy truths. "Just look at 'em," he'd argue.

"They're ugly." What we usually did instead was look at Royal. There was this fat, bullet-headed parody of a human, and it was hard to imagine how he could believe his own arguments when he must have looked in a mirror at some point or another during the past couple years.

What was curious about Royal's explicit faith in the cultural, physiological, mental, spiritual, and aesthetic superiority of the white race is that he was so uncouth, fat and soft, dumb, unprincipled, and ugly himself. He would rail endlessly on how lazy "those of color" are without apparently remembering that the hardest work he ever did himself was to drive over to Rising City once a month to pick up his wife's paycheck. Royal criticized every small accomplishment of anyone in Bleaker County without ever doing anything of note himself. In contrast with the usual habit of the region, Royal never told jokes of which he was the butt, and yet no one deserved them more. In short, there couldn't have been a better argument against racial superiority than Royal Cupp.

One of Royal's finer moments was the time he was elected to the County Museum Board. Normally the board never did much but approve the annual budget and pat the director on the back, but Royal came onto the board just about the time they elected a new chairman, Tom Larson, and Tom and Royal got along just fine.

Tom Larson and Royal agreed on one thing: No one was quite as good as they were, and so they careened around the district, generally wreaking havoc and doing whatever could be done to change the mistakes of history so they better suited their understanding of the way things really should have happened. According to those two, every battle was started cruelly and without reason by the Indians and every battle—every single one—was won by the superior intellect of the U.S. military. As Slick once put it, "Those two boys are the best Indian fighters of all history. They can kill nearly a thousand redskins in one evening by just sitting around the fire and drinking enough whiskey."

An excellent example was the time an Indian tribe asked for the remains of their ancestors that the museum kept in its collection. It was a fairly obvious matter of simple decency, but for Royal and Tom it was a challenge to the very cultural foundations they believed in: Tom and Royal's ancestors had, by god, defeated the Indians and sent them packing to the Indian Territory and whatever they had had was now Tom's and Royal's, including their dead.

Some thought the whole mess was a matter of Tom and Royal hating *Indians*, but as the Museum secretary pointed out to one newspaper reporter, "Tom and Royal don't hate Indians in particular. They hate *everyone* pretty much the same."

Anyway, the Indians traveled several hundred miles several dozen times, hat in hand, asking only for the sanctity of their people's graves. Some professors from the state university came along with them, saying that the bones and burial goods really served no purpose, gathering dust on the museum shelves, but Royal was quoted in the newspaper as saying, "When I was still in the pharmacy business"—he lost his license and the store the time he went to work a little on the tipsy side and accidentally gave Widow Barnett a good dose of ipecac instead of paregoric—"I've sold aspirin and suppositories to the Iron Shell family over in Rising City for years and so I know pretty much all there is to know about Indians. I don't think these professors know anything at all. If they're so smart, why don't they own drugstores?" No one could think of a good answer, so Royal's statement stood.

Tom and Royal swung their axes wide on that occasion, refusing every polite petition from the Indians with the insufferably rude insults that are part and parcel of being superior human beings. It was clear to them that whatever hocus-pocus religion the Indians' superstitions inflicted on them would be of no consequence in the face of The True Faith, which, simply put, was "We're all that matters."

Perhaps the golden moment came when Tom was confronted by some tough questions from a reporter over at the Museum building. "These Indians are nothing but agitators. They got no reason to come here and bother us. They're not even members of the Museum Boosters," he railed, ignoring the hideous reality that the Indians had been driven from this very soil only a couple generations before, quite against their will.

It was Royal who iced the cake: "Yeah," he snarled to the reporter, "why don't they just go back to where they came from?"

That's why no one was surprised when Royal died without warning: Not even his own body would support his bigotries. It had always been evident that Royal was anything but superior intellectually, and now it was all too obvious that his body came up short too.

Actually, Royal Cupp's sudden death caused a good many more problems than his generally useless and acerbic life had dealt the community. For one thing, Royal was very fat. His pickup truck had a distinctive lean to the left. When Royal saved up enough of his wife's earnings to buy himself a new truck, the lean was only there when he was seated behind the steering wheel. Gradually, however, the tilt took on a life of its own and even when the vehicle was parked at the curb, it seemed to rest on its left elbow.

"Royal's dead and his wife wants to put him in the ground just as quick as possible before he changes his mind," Slick told us that afternoon up at the tavern. "I hope Rising City Music sold a piano today."

Without waiting for us to ask, he explained, "No undertaker this side of the Rockies is going to have a coffin big enough to hold him."

"And where in hell are we going to find eight pallbearers big enough to carry the coffin if we find one?" Lunchbox asked.

"Forget how big they are," Slick snorted. "Where are we going to find eight men who would be willing to do a favor for him?"

"Maybe we should just get the lumberyard's fork lift, and that way one man can do the job," offered Woodrow.

Slick added, "On top of that, Royal wanted a military funeral and an honor guard to fire a salute over him. Where are we going to find four veterans who we can be sure won't just fire into the coffin?"

"Now we're talking about twelve or fifteen men. I don't know of that many men in the whole damned state that Royal will put up with. He's going to see all those people, find three or four he doesn't like, and with our luck he'll get up and leave."

"Not to say anything evil of the dead, of course," Slick deadpanned. "Frankly, Royal's absence is going to make a hell of a dent in the tavern's receipts."

"Actually, your revenues should pick up because now all the people who won't come into your place when Royal's there will be able to come back and drink in peace," Lunchbox said.

"Let's have a round," said Woodrow, raising his glass. "Royal would want it that way."

"And let's all pay for our own," said Lunchbox, "Royal would want it that way too."

Royal's funeral was uneventful, considering all the interest it generated beforehand. Woodrow, Lunchbox, Slick, Goose, Myron, and I were pallbearers, and, like his ideas, there was less substance to Royal than appearances suggested. The Legion boys formed a credible honor guard, even though only two of the rifles went off for the salute.

The preacher said some nice things about Royal, which took some considerable research and effort, the information coming mostly from Tom Larson because when it came to history, he felt it important to make it say what it should say rather than what it obviously says.

The widow and Tom cried.

No one else did.

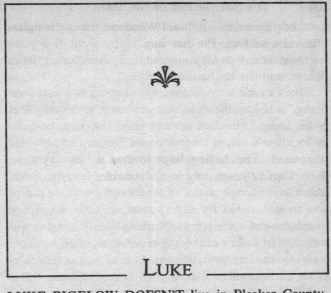

LUKE

LUKE BIGELOW DOESN'T live in Bleaker County, and there's no telling when he's going to come through for a visit. What he *says* certainly can't be taken for any sort of indication. It's to the point, in fact, that Lily and I assume the opposite of whatever seems to be his idea of the way things are going to go. If he says he'll be here next weekend, we figure we can go ahead and make other plans because he won't. All other times, when he has not announced his imminent arrival, we try to be ready for him.

He once called us and said he was in town—we lived in Lincoln at the time—and in about three hours, he said, he would be over for supper. "Great," I responded, caught unawares.

"Keep the beer cold," he called cheerily as he hung up the phone.

We waited for him until about 8:00 P.M. and finally went ahead and ate. A little after ten he called again, this

201

time from Orlando, Florida. He had run into some minor problems, he said. We saw him again about two years later, this time with his jaw wired shut, about forty pounds lighter, and not in the least subdued.

Luke's motto is "Anything worth doing is worth *over-doing*," and he adheres to that sentiment with every fiber of his body. Luke does nothing easy. One time he came by for a week, stayed for four hours. He decided he would treat us to steaks, so he went to town to the grocery store. Well, Dan Peterson, owner of the only grocery in town, didn't have enough steaks, or big enough steaks, or expensive enough steaks for Luke's taste, so Luke asked him to custom-cut some for us. Nothing Dan suggested was sufficient to Luke's exuberant appetite, so when he drove back into the farmyard, he carried out of his van this enormous package of beef, nearly a full rear quarter. "This should do it," he grinned. With a tree saw he cut three-inch-thick slabs, which I threw on the grill.

I'm pretty good at barbecuing; even monstrous hunks of beef like these were not beyond my skills, I bragged. I worked at cooking and had the steaks just about ready to bring to the table when our telephone rang. I was standing near the desk, so I picked up the telephone. A woman's voice with a heavy southern accent crooned, "Is Lukie Bigelow they-ah?"

"Just a minute," I said. "Hey, Lukie," I said winking, "it's a Miss Magnolia Blossom for you."

He took the phone. "No." He frowned. "You're kidding. Oh no. Damn. You're sure? Jeez. Oh boy. Yeah, I'll be right there."

He slammed the phone down and ran toward the door, yelling over his shoulder, "Gotta go. Gotta be in Houston before sunset tomorrow. Keep the steaks hot. I'll be back

next week." We watched his car speeding across the
bridge, engine whining, and we next saw him about
Christmas, I think. We never heard what the crisis in
Houston or who the woman with the languid drawl was.

Perhaps the most curious thing about my long friendship with Luke is that even though he is thoroughly unreliable, I nonetheless feel that I can count on him when the
chips are down. I don't know why, I just do. If I had to
guess, I'd venture that while he is utterly unreliable when
it comes to the little things in life—dinner, visits, things
like that—he is so intense about life and so utterly con-
temptuous of convention, so hungry for adventure and so
insistent on friendship that I think—I hope—that he
would be there if things were ever really desperate.

But I don't know. I can't be sure. Luke had always told
me that if I ever needed money to let him know. He has
been married two, maybe three times, but he was single
at the time and he offered his help. He had some extra
bucks, he said. Well, I was building this house we are now
living in and I found myself suddenly very much in need
of about five thousand dollars.

I called him up. "No problem, pal," he said. "The
money is on the way." A couple weeks later things got
even tighter for Lily and me and I called Luke again.
"Hey, no problem," he said again, but again there was no
money. The check never did come. Nor did Luke ever
offer an explanation for his lapse. The loan just didn't happen.

On the other hand, when I first got this farm he took
one look at the situation and said, "What you really need
on this place is a tractor," and within a week he delivered
a tractor, a 1937 Allis-Chalmers I still have and use.

"What you really need in this cabin is a good cookstove," he said on another occasion, and he delivered a cookstove. "What you need is a good heat stove," he said, and a month later there was a beautiful Buck's Hot Blast stove standing in the corner, courtesy of old Luke.

I suspect that one of the reasons I love Luke—and I might as well admit it: I love Luke—is that he is mythologic. I know two Luke Bigelows. There is the one who comes through occasionally like an earthquake and sits in my front room and either devours everything we have and leaves us with nothing for the table for the rest of the week or brings a mountain of gifts, food, and drink and leaves us buried in wealth, and there is another Luke Bigelow, one who exists primarily in legend.

"Legend" is a painfully overused word—"The Legend of John Wayne." "The Legend of Pete Rose." Well, a "legend" is a *story*. It is a narrative, a thing with a plot, a thing you can tell around a campfire. Tell me the story of John Wayne or Pete Rose. There is no story of John Wayne or Pete Rose. That use of the word "legend" means only "famous." John Wayne and Pete Rose are *famous*. Big deal. Luke Bigelow is a *legend*.

Before and after I met Luke, I heard stories about him. It amazed me that Luke would tell me about some spectacular adventure he had been through since I had last seen him, and then months later I would hear the story again, from someone who doesn't know that I know Luke. "I was camped out on the Platte last April," this person would say as if relating a fairy tale, "and some crazy damned fool comes flying down the river and does this doodad right through our camp and, so help me Willie Nelson, he put out our campfire with the backwash of his airplane. We spent all night picking up tents and equipment, and every time we heard an airplane the rest of the trip we would dive into a ditch. The next day a farmer along the river told us that the same lunatic killed two coyotes on his place, hitting them with the wheels of his airplane at a hundred and fifty miles an hour. Heard it was Luke Bigelow. He knew we were out on the river camping, and he decided to have some fun with a buddy's airplane."

Another told me, "I was there, and I saw this guy— Luke Someone—and he walks into this cowboy bar in Alkali, Nebraska. He's wearing a pony tail, for God's sake, and he just walks right into the middle of these cowboys. And the cowboys start mumbling, and this Luke—he's all alone—walks right up to them and says, 'What's troubling you, Big Ears?' and he takes this punk's hat—and you don't touch a cowboy's hat!—and he challenges the cowboys to go out on the street. One guy against seven, but then that's a cowboy's idea of a fair fight, I guess.

"Well, this Luke is in the habit of putting a big knife on the canvas awning out in front of this bar, they tell me later. Then he asks someone to go outside with him, he steps out the door, turns around, reaches up onto that awning, and pulls down the big knife. End of fight. That's his usual routine.

"But these cowboys are onto him and his knife stunt, so one of them has retrieved the knife Luke put up there when he came in. They all step out of the bar, Luke is groping around on that awning, and one of the cowboys says, 'You looking for this toad-stabber, you hippie crud?' and then they just stomp the living bejesus out of him. I hear they had to wire the guy's face together by the time the dust had settled and everyone went home."

Weeks before, Luke had come into my house, his face wired together, one of the many times he came to my place with his face wired together, and that was the story he told me too. I heard stories of Luke sewing himself up when he needed suturing because of his own accidents or someone else's intent, and then when he was helping me build my cabin, I saw him fall and get a cut that sent me running to the car, knowing that we were emergency ward bound. "It's nothing," Luke said. He pulled a suture set from his backpack and, sure enough, just like the stories I had heard, he sewed himself back together just as casually as if he had been repairing a rip in his jeans.

Maybe that's one of the reasons I like to have Luke come through. I lead a pretty quiet life here on Primrose Farm, and these little splashes of adventure are like going to an Indiana Jones movie and knowing everyone in the cast.

Luke is a good carpenter, and that's what he does when he is settling down in one place for more than a couple weeks—usually because there is a woman worth standing still for for a little while. I know he is a bounty hunter— I think they call them bondsmen—and it was fascinating listening to him compare notes with the deputy sheriff the last time he came through and we all sat in front of the fire exchanging tales. It was clear that Luke knew his way around the right side of the law just as I have always expected that he probably also knows his way around the other side. I remind myself when I am with Luke that Old West lawmen like Wyatt Earp and Doc Holliday were agile and flexible, working either side of the line as the circumstances at the time demanded. For once I didn't have much to contribute in a storytelling session.

I'm not sure what else he does to earn his way. I know that for a while he panned gold in Colorado. I'm not sure I want to know everything he does for a living.

One of the mysteries of Luke is why he looks the way

he looks. He is almost angelic. He is tall and muscular—
I heard of him before I met him, and what I heard is that
only hours before he had wagered several hundred dollars
that he could kick the tiles out of a nine-foot-high ceiling
and he had won the bet on the third and last kick, destroying a substantial amount of furniture and breaking two
ribs and an arm on his way down from the ceiling.

I've never been a good judge of the attractiveness of men
but Lily says Luke is handsome, and she ought to know.
I suppose he is, even though his nose has been broken on
innumerable occasions and his face has been slashed with
knives wielded in fury. He is eternally boyish, even though
he is now nearly forty years old. If you ask him how he
has kept his youthful looks, he usually responds with
something like "Clean living" or "Wholesome diet," almost an affirmation of the opposite.

Luke is gentle with Antonia—I have always thought he
would make a good father—but I know from direct re-
ports and a couple of terrifying personal experiences that
Luke is capable of a concentrated fury that must be the
sort of whirlwind the Vikings spoke of when they desig-
nated their most peculiar and ferocious warriors as "Ber-
serkers."

Luke is one of the few men on earth whose presence
makes me uneasy about Lily's inclinations. Lily is the best
woman—the best person—I've ever known, and I trust
her. Luke is a good friend, and I trust him. But Lily is
beautiful, and so is Luke, I guess. It may not be possible
for women to resist Luke. Women are drawn to Luke in
a way I don't understand. He is dangerous, crazy, irresponsible, sexist to an embarrassing, unembarrassed degree, and yet women disregard all of those obvious faults
and gravitate to him as if hypnotized. I have seen him with

perhaps fifty attractive women over the past two decades—not always one at a time. I have seen him walk into a tavern and within ten minutes have a companion for the duration of his stay, be that two hours or two weeks. "Wife for a night," he calls them, sometimes while they stand there smiling at him.

I know that sounds impossibly sexist. It sounds as if I am suggesting that women are not in control of their own passions, that they are irrational, that they are stupid when it comes to romance. It is sexist, but it is also true. You see, I too know these things about Luke, and yet I am also attracted to him. I cannot find many reasons for wasting much time on inconsiderate grasshoppers like Luke. I'm busy and I have many things to do, but Luke . . . ? Well, Luke is Luke and Luke is different.

Luke once called and said that he would be coming through during the next week, and I said that that would be great because I was cutting wood and sure could use some help. Luke said that he needed the exercise and we would just take care of a couple years' worth of firewood needs in no time at all. He would even bring his own saw.

Great. I got my saws ready, and the tractor, and the chains, and the wedges. Luke showed up, for a change, precisely when he said he would. We went up to the Town Tavern to have some supper, drink a little beer, and organize our plans for the weekend's efforts. We had no more than sat down when a young woman walked into the tavern who was not so much attractive as she was confident. Everything about her suggested that she knew exactly what she was about. Luke pushed back his chair, and I knew from the way he put his hands on the table and smiled that I would be cutting wood alone that week.

Monday I was bringing in the last trailer load of wood

and spotted Luke's van coming full-tilt down the gravel road toward me. He slid to a stop—he never starts or stops without throwing gravel even if he isn't in a hurry. He yelled a couple of regrets to me, promised to be back soon—he still hasn't been back—made some off-color evaluations of the young woman he had driven off with three days before, and he was gone again. That's the way he operates.

When Lily and I got married nine years ago, to my amazement Luke showed up with his bride of a few months. I was amazed because of the gifts he brought to the ceremony—two thirty-six-inch buzz-saw blades embossed HIS and HERS—and because it just didn't seem like Luke to show up in accordance with any sort of previously planned formality like a wedding invitation.

Luke added a lot to the ambience of the evening of our wedding. He broke his wife Pearl's arm, but only after she broke his eardrums, but those were the only injuries inflicted on anyone during the wedding and so Lily and I felt that we got off pretty easy, considering.

I was *not* surprised, therefore, when Luke called up one day a year or so later and said that he and Pearl had broken up. But I was touched that he seemed fairly despondent about the situation, and I sympathized with him—not at all because I thought he might be blameless but because he is a friend and he was obviously unhappy.

We talked about how the breakup had come to pass. He said that he had come home from a soccer game in Eagle, about twelve miles from where he and Pearl were living, and there were all his possessions out on the lawn— furniture, books, clothes, everything. She had just tossed everything out over the porch railing.

He said he had thought things had been going fairly

smoothly in their marriage the past few months in spite of earlier problems. He had spent a lot of time puttering around the place, staying home more than usual, doing little carpentry tasks, doing his best to make the place a cozy little home, and generally being a lot more domestic than was his custom.

"Gee, Luke, that sounds pretty good to me. Sounds like you were trying harder than usual. I'm surprised Pearl was unhappy. Are you sure she didn't have something to complain about? You haven't been fooling around again, have you?"

"Hell no, Rog," he said tentatively. There was a pause. "Well, at least no more than natural. Honest!" For Luke that was an astonishing declaration of restraint.

I tried to console him, we talked about this and about that, but we kept coming back to Pearl's breaking point and irrational behavior, and still something didn't seem right. "Luke," I asked, "after all the trouble you and Pearl have had, after that terrible fight you two had at our wedding and all, what was it that finally pushed her over the edge?"

"I cannot for the life of me imagine," Luke said, and I could tell from the way he said it that he couldn't. "Like I said, I went to Eagle to play soccer, and when I left the house everything was fine. Pearl was cooking a late supper, and we even kissed good-bye at the door.

"When I came home, there was all my possessions out on the lawn. She wouldn't even let me in the house. I tried to reason with her, but you know women. She just told me to pick up my stuff and get out of there or she'd call the cops."

"Jeez, Luke, Pearl's pretty easygoing. What do you suppose could have set her off?"

"Beats me, Rog. Sure, I was late getting home but . . ."

"I don't get it," I puzzled. "After everything you two have been through, it just doesn't make sense that she would blow up and break up the marriage just because you were late coming back from a soccer game. Just how late were you, Luke?"

"Oh, about twelve days," he admitted.

I'll bet Luke still doesn't understand what had set Pearl off. But I hear he's engaged again, and so he'll probably have another chance to figure it out.

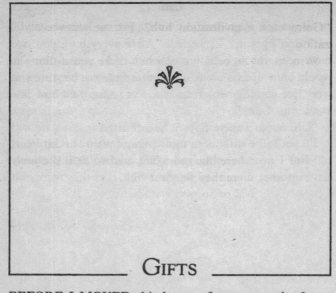

GIFTS

BEFORE I MOVED this house of ours onto the farm, I had a log cabin down by the river. The place was only a retreat from the city and my job, not at all a place to live. There was no electricity, no telephone, no plumbing, and yet it has always been the most comfortable place of my life. If I had the good sense to cut some wood during the fall, the cabin was warm through the winter. If I trimmed the wicks and brought down kerosene from up in town, I would have plenty of light during the long winter evenings. If I saw to it that the leathers in my pump were in good shape and that I had priming water, then I had plenty of water for cooking and washing. If I did my part, the cabin did its part and life there was by and large about as easy as can be imagined.

I used to laugh when my friends here in Bleaker County would see me packing up to go back to the city and say,

"Going back to civilization, huh?" For me, *this* was civilization.

Winter was especially nice when there was nothing at the farm but the cabin. The snow made everything so quiet. At night all you could hear were the owls and coyotes. One night Lily and I were lying in bed upstairs reading and we could hear a pack of coyotes making its way downstream, not more than a quarter mile from the cabin. Their screams were like those of a madwoman. We could actually tell where they were moving, that they were only a hundred yards or so north of the cabin.

Then they moved past the trees where they could see the light from our window, and they were silent. They began howling again moments later, now another hundred yards away from the cabin. As they approached the highway a quarter of a mile away, they stopped their cacophony until they had crossed, and finally we again heard their trills disappearing to the east.

About that time, after a full fifteen minutes of this operatic treat, our dog, Slump, who had been sleeping on an old couch on the front porch, finally growled as if to let us know that hey, he wasn't the least bit frightened of that lunatic pack that just whisked by the house, and as a matter of fact, he had just this second noticed the racket! "And don't you come back, you yodeling crazies," he postured.

Slump, originally a city dog, has learned a lot of lessons since we moved out here onto this land, and so have I. My Indian friends tell me that it's not so much that they have learned how to read the Mysteries of life as we whites have learned how *not* to read the Mysteries of life. Even though I believe that absolutely, I never suspected that the Mysteries were so blunt. The Mysteries may be hard to understand, but they are not hard to see.

One winter before Lily and I were married I was spending my Christmas holidays at the cabin. I loved doing that. I could grade papers without interruption. I could read for days if I wanted to. I slept whenever I felt like it, ate when I was hungry. If I felt like a whiskey, I drank a whiskey. If I felt like bacon and eggs, it was bacon and eggs. Every couple of days I would walk up into town, buy some groceries, buy a newspaper, have a few drinks with friends, pick up my mail, and walk back.

One day I put on snowshoes and walked across the hills to town, doing all of the regular chores, the most important of which was the mail. Among the letters in my box was one from an old friend, Bernie. His letter was mostly friendly gossip, but there was one paragraph that shook me. He shared my attraction to Indian culture—in fact, that's how we became friends. Although his association had been with the Cheyenne-Arapaho and mine with the Omaha and Lakota, Bernie shared my appreciation for the Mysteries that the Indians understand and appreciate.

In his letter he told me that he didn't quite understand why he had done it, but he had given away a precious eagle feather he had owned for almost a generation. Now, you need to understand that an eagle feather is a rare and potent gift in Indian culture and is perhaps even weightier for us non-Indians because it is illegal for us to possess any part of an eagle. Many years before, my friend had been given this very special eagle feather by a very special Indian friend and he had cherished this treasure carefully. But now, for reasons he could not quite understand himself, he had given it away.

"How," he asked me in his letter, "do we get back something as utterly unique as that eagle feather once we have given it away?"

I read his question over and over. It was a problem I had dealt with, in a way, many times before. I have worked extensively among the Omaha and Sioux Indians of the Plains, where gift giving is a part of every social occasion. I understand the Indians' system of gift giving as an anthropological paradigm, but I have a very hard time acting within that paradigm.

I know that among the Omaha Indians to give truly is better than to receive. I have given something special— say, a handmade shirt—to an Omaha friend, only to see him turn around on the spot and give it to someone else. But, I wanted to say, I meant that gift for *you.* My wife made that for *you.* I want *you* to have it, and you just gave it away to somebody I don't even know!

Within the Omaha system, I have to instruct myself, this is a splendid compliment. My friend is in effect saying, "This is such a fine gift you have given me, that I am proud to give it away too. It is a gift good enough to merit being given yet again."

It's not easy for us non-Indians to deal with that. I know too, for example, that Indians never "exchange" gifts as we in non-Indian culture do as a matter of course. When an Omaha gives me a gift, on the contrary, I have to exercise some caution *not to give that person a gift* for a period of time commensurate with the value of that gift—the more valuable the gift, the longer the period of caution— to see to it that I do *not* give a gift to my benefactor. It is important to avoid even the appearance of an exchange. My Indian friends argue that exchanging gifts is like going to the store: You give them money, and they give you merchandise. How is that different from the you-give-me-a-present-and-I'll-give-you-a-present system of the white world? they wonder. And I have no explanations to offer them.

But that's not quite the same as my friend's question: Once you give away a possession as precious and unusual as that eagle feather, he was asking me, how do you ever get something as powerful back in return? Is that gift forever lost? Is the power gone?

I read my friend's letter and thought about it a good part of that afternoon. That day I did some cooking, I cut some wood. I read a little from a book. My friend's question would not leave my mind.

So I bundled up and walked out into the snow. It was so cold the hairs in my nose crackled as I breathed. I walked down to the river, thinking all the while about the question of the gifted gift. The river was frozen solid, but its life was still obvious because I could hear the ice rumble and pop as the water beneath it still moved. I walked to the edge of the bank where I could see as much of the river as possible.

I looked down the bank to the edge of the ice four or five feet beneath my feet, and there, so help me God, was an eagle feather. If you have ever seen an eagle feather, you know that one does not mistake a bluejay feather, or turkey feather, or pheasant feather, or kestrel feather for an eagle feather. And there one was. I picked it up with my left hand, as befits the handling of eagle feathers.

Eagles pass by my land and spend time in my trees, feeding on fish and birds that die in the winter ice. But in the forty-five years of my life I had never before found an eagle feather and have not found another in the seven years since that day. Yet here was a fine, big feather, on this of all days.

I went back to the cabin and wrote a letter to my friend:

How does one get back a treasure as powerful as an eagle feather once one gives it away? Here is the answer, I wrote my friend, and enclosed the fine feather I had just found at the river.

Just as surely as spring lies under the iron-hard winter ground of the Plains, just as surely as the water runs beneath the ice, such gifts are never gone, even when they are given away. The way we keep such gifts of love, it turns out, is to give them away.

ABOUT THE AUTHOR

Formerly an English and Anthropology professor at the University of Nebraska, Roger Welsch lived most of his life in Lincoln. A few years ago he and his family left the city to live on a small tree farm. Welsch hosts the popular *Postcards From Nebraska* on *Sunday Morning With Charles Kuralt* on CBS.

Maryellen

1954

The One and Only

by Valerie Tripp

★ American Girl®

Greetings from FLORIDA Tropical Wonderland

My teacher

My school picture

I like school, even though I'm not so good at cursive!

The beach is just a short walk from my house.

Florida

DAYTONA BEACH
F L O R I D A

Roller Skating

My house looks just like the others in our neighborhood—except for the door!

Beautiful
FLORIDA

Maryellen's Family & Friends

My parents

Joan, 17, and her boyfriend, Jerry

Carolyn is 14, Beverly is 6

Tom is 4 and Mikey is almost 2

Davy lives next door. The boy with the beanie is Wayne the Pain!

The Karens and Angela

TABLE *of* CONTENTS

A Peek into Maryellen's World

The Room Switcheroo

* Chapter 1 *

Maryellen Larkin liked to make up episodes of her favorite TV shows and imagine herself in them. This morning, for example, Maryellen was walking down the hot, sunny sidewalk with her dog, Scooter. Really, she was mailing a letter to her grandparents. But she was *pretending* that she was in an episode of the exciting Western *The Lone Ranger*. Her only companion was her trusty horse, Thunderbolt. (That was Scooter's part.) Maryellen leaned forward as if she were battling her way through a blinding blizzard. If she didn't deliver the medicine she was carrying, hundreds of people would die.

Maryellen never gave herself superpowers in any of her imagined shows. She didn't fly or do magic. The difference was that in her TV shows, everyone listened to her great ideas. They followed her advice, and—*ta-da!*—everything turned out just right.

Maryellen put her letter in the mailbox, imagining that she was handing medicine to a kindly old doctor in a snowy town in the Old West.

"Thank you, Miss Larkin, ma'am," the imaginary

doctor said. "We desperately needed this medicine. You have saved hundreds of lives today."

Maryellen smiled modestly and shrugged as if to say, "It was nothing." Then she turned to go. "Come on, Thunderbolt," she said to Scooter. "Our work is done."

Scooter, a stout dachshund, had *just* flopped down and made himself comfortable in the shade of the mailbox. Maryellen whispered, "Come on, Scooter. Get up, old boy." So Scooter rose with a good-natured sigh and waddled behind Maryellen, who pretended to trudge through drifts of snow while grateful townspeople called after her, "Thank you, Miss Larkin! You're our hero!"

"Hey, Ellie," said a real voice, calling her by her nickname. The voice belonged to her friend Davy Fenstermacher, who lived next door in a house that looked exactly like the Larkins' house. Maryellen and Davy had been friends forever.

"Howdy, pardner," Maryellen drawled.

"I'll race you to the swing!" said Davy. "On your mark, get set, *go!*"

Maryellen and Davy ran to the Larkins' backyard, with Scooter loping along behind them. Maryellen got to the swing first, jumped on, and began to pump. "I win!" she called down to Davy. "You be the Lone Ranger, stuck in quicksand, and I'll jump down and rescue you."

"Okay," said Davy agreeably. Of course, they both knew that cowboys didn't usually jump off swings. But the tree swing in Maryellen's backyard was so much fun that they used it in lots of the TV shows they made up.

Maryellen swung high and then jumped off, landing on the grass with a soft thud. "Come on, Thunderbolt!" she called to Scooter. "We've got to save the Lone Ranger!"

Scooter, already asleep in the shade, snored.

"Better wake him up first, Ellie," said Davy.

But before Maryellen could rouse Scooter, her six-year-old sister, Beverly, came clomping out of the house in an old pair of Mrs. Larkin's high heels. Beverly wore one of Dad's baseball caps turned inside out so that it looked like a crown. Right behind Beverly came Tom and Mikey, Maryellen's younger brothers. They were four and not-quite-two years old.

"What are you doing?" Beverly asked.

"Nothing," said Maryellen, wishing that Beverly and the boys would go back inside, but knowing that they wouldn't. Maryellen, Beverly, Tom, and Mikey shared a bedroom, and even though the little kids were cute and sweet and goofy, they drove Maryellen crazy. Now that it was summer, Beverly, Tom, and Mikey stuck to her like glue.

They couldn't bear to be left out of anything fun that
Maryellen might be doing.

Sure enough, Beverly said, "I want to play with you
and Davy!"

"Me too!" said Tom.

"Me!" said Mikey.

Davy shot Maryellen a sympathetic look. He had years
of experience dealing with Beverly, Tom, and Mikey.

Thinking quickly, Maryellen suggested to Davy,
"What if the little kids are in the quicksand, too, and
I rescue all of you?"

"Good idea," said Davy.

"Pretend I'm a queen that you're rescuing," said
Beverly.

"Oh, brother," Maryellen muttered. That was another
problem with Beverly. She liked to pretend, but she
always pretended the same thing: that she was a queen.
Dad called her Queen Beverly. "I don't think they had
queens in the Wild West," Maryellen said. "I've never
seen one on a TV show, anyway. Have you, Davy?"

"Nope," said Davy firmly.

Maryellen smiled. Good old Davy always backed
her up.

Queen Beverly looked stubborn. Maryellen was just
about to give in to Her Majesty when their mother called

out the back door, "Ellie, honey, come in for a minute. I need you."

"Okay," called Maryellen, feeling pleased. Mom needed *her*!

Maryellen's pride wilted just a bit when Mom added, "Beverly, Tom, and Mikey, you come, too." She wished Mom wouldn't always lump her together with Beverly, Tom, and Mikey as if they were one big bumpy creature with four heads, eight arms, and eight legs. Mom certainly treated Maryellen's older sisters, Joan and Carolyn, as separate, serious people.

I'm tired of being one of the "little kids," grumped Maryellen to herself, for the millionth time. *I guess I'm stuck with Beverly, but I'm much too grown-up to share a room with Tom and Mikey. Somehow, I have to convince Mom that I should share a bedroom with Joan and Carolyn so that she'll think of me as one of the "big girls" and take me—and my ideas—more seriously.*

"What do you need us for, Mom?" asked Maryellen.

"Just a quick family meeting," said Mom.

"Oh," said Maryellen without enthusiasm. She knew from experience that it was hard to get a word in edgewise during family meetings. They were not at all like one of her pretend TV shows where she was the hero and everyone hung on her every word. Maryellen sighed and said to Davy, "See you later, alligator."

"In a while, crocodile," said Davy. "I'll wait here."

Maryellen walked into the kitchen and slid onto the bench in the breakfast nook next to Joan, her eldest sister. Joan, who was seventeen and therefore nearly all grown-up, looked sideways at Maryellen's grass-stained shorts and inched away, closer to Carolyn. It was crowded on the bench, but Maryellen wanted Mom to see her next to Joan and Carolyn, on their side of the table, so that Mom would think of the three of them as a group.

Maryellen could tell that this family meeting would be like all the others: frustrating. The kitchen was already noisy. Dad had left on a three-day business trip earlier that morning, but Mom and Carolyn, Maryellen's next-oldest sister, were talking a mile a minute. Tom was wailing like a siren as he rode his toy fire truck around the kitchen. Mikey was banging a spoon on the tray connected to his high chair. Mrs. Larkin took Mikey's spoon away from him and gave him a piece of toast, which was quieter to bang, and then said, "Kids!"

Everyone quieted down.

"I have an important announcement," said Mrs. Larkin. "My friends Betty and Florence are coming to spend the night."

"Who're Fletty and Borence?" asked Beverly.

"*B*etty and *Fl*orence," said Mrs. Larkin. "You kids have never met them. We worked together at the factory. They live in New York City now. We're going to a reunion luncheon at the factory tomorrow."

Maryellen knew that Mom was referring to the aircraft factory where she had worked during World War Two. Her mind sped ahead. Lots of TV quiz shows were filmed in New York City. Maybe Mom's friends could get her a spot on one of them! She'd be the youngest contestant *ever*—

Joan interrupted Maryellen's daydream with a practical question. "Where will Betty and Florence sleep?"

Maryellen's mind sped ahead again. This could be the moment she had been waiting for! "I have an idea," she announced.

But Mom didn't hear Maryellen. No one did. Mom was saying, "I guess they'll have to sleep on the sofa bed in the living room, though that doesn't seem very welcoming."

"I've got an idea," Maryellen said again. She tugged on her mother's sleeve. "Listen!"

But Mrs. Larkin just patted Maryellen's hand and gave her a wink and a smile while everyone else kept talking as much and as loudly as ever.

Maryellen grabbed Mikey's spoon and pounded it on the table the way she'd seen judges pound gavels in TV courtroom drama shows. "HEY!" she shouted. "Order in the court!"

Mom winced and held her hands over her ears. "Ellie, sweetie pie, settle down," she scolded gently. "Please don't shout and bang the table like Mikey. It's childish."

"Sorry, Mom," said Maryellen, red in the face. The last thing she wanted was for Mom to think that she was childish. "But listen—I have a great idea!"

"Tell us," said Mom. "You have our attention."

"I think Mom's guests should sleep in Joan and Carolyn's room."

"*My* room?" said Joan. "That's impossible! Carolyn and I hardly fit in there together as it is."

"We're squooshed!" Carolyn agreed. She and Joan shared a set of bunk beds in a tiny bedroom.

"I have it all figured out," said Maryellen. "Joan, you and Carolyn will give your room to Betty and Florence. You'll sleep in the big bedroom with Beverly and me, in Tom and Mikey's bunk beds, and the boys will sleep in Mom and Dad's room." Maryellen smiled at Tom. "You *like* sleeping on the floor, don't you?"

"Yes!" said Tom. He looked happy. But then, Tom just

about always looked happy. With spiky yellow hair sticking straight out all over his head, he looked like a cheerful dandelion.

Joan frowned. She started to say, "I don't—"

But Mom interrupted, "Why, Maryellen Larkin! I do believe you've hit upon a solution to our problem."

Maryellen beamed, although she wished that Mom hadn't sounded quite so surprised that she had had a good idea. Flushed with her success, she rattled on eagerly. "After Betty and Florence leave," she said, "Tom and Mikey can move into the little room, and the big room will be the All-Girls Room." Maryellen was sure that sharing a room with Joan and Carolyn would change everything for her, and change the way everyone thought of her and treated her, too. They'd see that she was mature. After all, she was nearly ten. She was going to be in the fourth grade!

"But—but," Joan sputtered, "that means *four* of us will share *one* closet and—"

"Whoa!" said Mrs. Larkin, holding up both hands. "Hold it, everyone." She turned to Maryellen and said, "Ellie, dear, you're getting carried away, as usual. We'll give Betty and Florence the little room tonight. But let's do one thing at a time, okay?"

"Sure, Mom," said Maryellen.

"All right then," said Mrs. Larkin. "Meeting adjourned."

Mom lifted Mikey out of his high chair, and he toddled behind Beverly and Tom to go watch cartoons on TV. But as Maryellen, Carolyn, and Mom started to leave, Joan stopped them.

"Just for the record," said Joan, "I'm not crazy about this whole room switcheroo."

"Why not?" asked Maryellen.

"Well," said Joan. "For starters, you're sloppy."

Maryellen could see that her sweaty hair and grimy hands were a sharp contrast to Joan's crisp, clean appearance. "Well, maybe I'm a little messy right *now*," she said honestly. She smoothed her rumpled T-shirt, which was a faded and stained hand-me-down from Carolyn. "I was playing outdoors."

"I know," said Joan. "You were goofing around with Davy like a wild tomboy, as usual. *That'll* have to stop soon anyway, because you can't be friends with a boy in fourth grade."

Maryellen frowned. "Why not?"

"It just doesn't work. You wait and see," Joan went on. "But it's not only your appearance that's grubby. Your bed, your drawers, your closet—*all* your things are messy. Last night, you flooded the bathroom, and before that, you stepped in the popcorn bowl and overturned it. Face it, Ellie—you create a disaster area wherever you go."

"Hey!" said Carolyn, sticking up for Maryellen. "Just because Ellie's not persnickety like you doesn't mean she's a hopeless mess."

"Right!" said Maryellen indignantly. "And I don't create disasters. Do I, Mom?"

"Well," said Mrs. Larkin, "I think what Joan means is that you're not very tidy or organized, honey."

"See?" said Joan. "I don't think it's fair that I should have to share a room with such a messy little kid."

"A messy little kid?" Maryellen repeated, horrified. Granted, she was not a finicky fussbudget like Joan. But a *messy little kid*? One who was childish, wild, untidy, tomboyish, disorganized, and grubby? A messy little kid who created disasters wherever she went? Was that how Joan and—Maryellen gulped—*Mom* thought of her?

The All-Girls Room
* Chapter 2 *

L et's say this," said Mrs. Larkin. "We'll give the All-Girls Room a try tonight. Sharing a room with your big sisters will be a test for you, Ellie. If you show that you can be tidy and responsible, we'll consider making the All-Girls Room permanent. Do we have a deal, ladies?"

"I suppose so," said Joan with a shrug.

"It's fine with me," said Carolyn.

"Yes," said Maryellen. She understood that if she failed this test, she'd lose her chance for the All-Girls Room. But there was something even more important than that at stake. If she failed the test, she'd lose her chance to improve Mom's opinion of her.

"That's settled, then," said Mom. "Joan and Carolyn, come with me and I'll give you fresh bedsheets. And you'd better move your pajamas and whatever else you'll need for tonight into Ellie's room. Ellie, if I were you, I'd start a Cleanup Campaign right away."

"I will, Mom," said Maryellen.

While the others headed to the linen closet, Maryellen

dashed outside to speak to Davy. "Looks like I'll be inside for a while," she said. "I've got to clean up my room."

"How come?" asked Davy. He was sitting on the swing, spinning to make himself dizzy.

Maryellen explained about the room switcheroo. "Joan didn't want to do it, because she thinks I'm messy. Mom said that she had to, but that it'll be a test for me."

"A test of what?" asked Davy.

"Neatness, mostly," Maryellen said, "and being careful of what I do."

Davy grinned. "Or what you *don't* do," he said. "Just *don't* make a mess."

"Right!" said Maryellen, cheered up by Davy as always. "That'll be easy!"

✳ ✳ ✳

Usually, when Mom asked Maryellen to clean up her room, she gave it a lick and a wish, shoving her clothes into drawers, tossing her shoes into the closet, and yanking the bed covers up. But now, Maryellen folded her clothes neatly, lined up her shoes in the closet, and pulled her covers taut so that not one lump or wrinkle could be seen. Then she dusted the top of the bureau in case Joan and Carolyn wanted to put their brushes and combs there.

"Look, Mom," she said. "*Ta-da!* I made everything tidy and beautiful."

Mrs. Larkin gave Maryellen's work a quick glance. "Good," she said as she tucked a sheet under the mattress of the upper bunk.

Mom didn't seem overly impressed by her efforts, so Maryellen looked around to see what else she could do. She collected Tom's trucks and Mikey's blocks in a box and slid the box under the bed just as Joan and Carolyn appeared, their arms full. Maryellen was delighted to see that in addition to her pajamas, Joan was bringing her tennis dress, bobby pins, cold cream, and several books and magazines. Carolyn was bringing some clothes, some rock 'n' roll records, and her portable record player.

Now that's more like it! thought Maryellen. *Instead of babyish toy trucks and blocks, the All-Girls Room will be full of grown-up things like books, rock 'n' roll records, and movie-star magazines.*

"You need all that for *one night*?" asked Mom, shaking her head at Joan and Carolyn.

"Not all of it is for me," said Carolyn. "I thought while I was at it, I might as well move these dresses I've outgrown into Ellie's closet." Carolyn showed Maryellen a plaid dress. "I wore this dress to the first day of fourth grade," she said, "so I thought you'd like to, too." Carolyn hung the dress in the closet, and then scrambled up onto the top bunk.

"Uh, thanks," said Maryellen, polite but not thrilled.

"Hey," said Joan, "I remember that dress. I wore it in fourth grade, too. I used to think it was so cute."

After Joan and Carolyn left, Maryellen held the plaid dress up in front of herself as she looked in the mirror. She sighed. "Mom," she said, "don't you think this hand-me-down dress is sort of old and worn-out? I sure would love a brand-new outfit to wear for the first day of fourth grade." Maryellen imagined herself in a chic, fashionable outfit like the ones girls wore on TV shows. The perfect back-to-school dress would guarantee the perfect start to school and a perfect year in fourth grade! She said eagerly, "Mom, you and I should go shopping and—"

"Maryellen!" Mrs. Larkin interrupted in a no-nonsense voice. "Carolyn's plaid dress is perfectly fine for your first day of school. You don't need anything new, except maybe some socks and underwear. But right now, I can't even *think* about a shopping trip. I've got my hands full getting ready for Betty and Florence. Now come and help me gather up these sheets for the laundry."

"Okay, Mom," said Maryellen. She was disappointed, but even new underwear was better than nothing. And Mom sounded unusually harried. As one of six children, Maryellen had long ago learned the sad but true lesson that parents had only a certain amount of patience and energy and attention to give, and you couldn't use more than your share or your parents got mad. So she quietly helped Mom with the sheets. She'd save the shopping conversation for later.

✳ ✳ ✳

After lunch, Mrs. Larkin said, "Kids, I've got to scrub the kitchen floor. I need you out of my hair and out of the house for a while. So why don't you all go to the beach?" She turned to Davy, who had come over for lunch, and said, "Davy, ask your mom if you may go, too, if you like."

The girls hurried off to put on their swimsuits. The

Larkins lived in Daytona Beach, Florida, just a few blocks from the ocean. Maryellen felt lucky that on hot days like this one, she could go to the beach to swim and cool off.

Maryellen was ready in a flash, so she went back to the kitchen, where Mom was helping Mikey put on his bathing trunks. Maryellen saw an old photo that she'd never seen before on the kitchen table. The photo was of Mom and two smiling ladies standing in front of a factory. Maryellen immediately figured out that the two ladies were Betty and Florence. "Hey, Mom," she asked as she looked at the photo, "what did you and Betty and Florence do at the factory?"

"Well, they worked on the assembly line, and I was the line manager," said Mrs. Larkin.

"The manager?" repeated Maryellen. "You mean you were the boss of the whole assembly line?"

"I sure was," said Mom, tying Mikey's shoelaces.

Maryellen was stunned. She had never realized that Mom had had such an important job! And now Mom just stayed home and made life organized and smooth and pleasant for their family. "What do Betty and Florence do now?" Maryellen asked.

"They're secretaries at an airline company in New York," said Mom.

"Oh," said Maryellen. Mom's friends' jobs sounded

swank and fancy. She asked, "Are you sorry you're not working now, Mom?"

"Ellie, my dear," said Mom in a jokey way as she pulled a T-shirt down over Mikey's head, "managing you kids is harder work than managing the assembly line was."

By now, everyone was ready to go. Mom handed some beach towels to Joan and said, "Okay, troops! Off you go to the beach. Be back by two, no later. Joan, keep an eye on the little ones. Vamoose!"

"Okay, Mom," everyone said. "Bye!"

Davy joined the parade of Larkins walking to the beach, falling in step with Scooter and Maryellen. "What's up, Doc?" Davy asked, pretending to be Bugs Bunny.

"I'm thinking about Mom," said Maryellen, "and what her life was like when she had a job during the war. Guess what? It turns out that Mom was important! She was a line boss at the factory."

"Wow!" said Davy. "Why'd she quit?"

"Lots of women quit working after the war," said Carolyn, "so the returning soldiers could have jobs."

"Mom shouldn't have quit. She was famous," Beverly sighed, "like a movie star."

"Well, she wasn't exactly a movie star, but she was the star of the factory back when Betty and Florence worked with her," said Maryellen. "And now Mom's life is about as exciting and glamorous as . . . as . . ."

"Scooter's," Davy finished for her.

"Yes," sighed Maryellen. Her heart swelled with love and sympathy for Mom. Probably Mom felt sort of taken for granted. Maryellen knew how *that* felt. Surely Mom missed standing out and being admired, as she had been when she was an important boss at the factory. Maryellen made up her mind right then: *I'm going to think of a way for Mom to impress her friends.* Her next thought made her so excited, her heart skipped a little skip: *And then Mom will be impressed with me.*

✳ ✳ ✳

Maryellen loved the ocean: its roar, its salty tang, and the huge blueness of it stretching all the way to the sky. "Last one in is a rotten egg!" she challenged Carolyn and Davy.

Legs pumping, arms waving, the three kids raced across the scorching sand. Maryellen plunged headfirst into an incoming wave. *Swoosh!* She had timed it just right, so that the wave lifted her up into the bright summery air.

"Ya*hoo!*" Maryellen hooted exuberantly.

In a second, Carolyn popped up next to Maryellen in the water. "All right," she said. "You win."

Davy popped up next. "I guess I'm the rotten egg," he said. "But watch out—*someday* I'll be faster than you."

Maryellen doubted it. Davy was a pretty good runner, but Maryellen was fiercely determined when it came to running. She had had a sickness called polio when she was younger, and one leg was a little bit weaker than the other. Sometimes Maryellen worried that Mom babied her because of her leg. But Maryellen never let her leg slow her down. She still remembered two years ago when she was sick. The local swimming pool had closed that year to avoid spreading polio. Ever since then, Dad had put the kibosh on going to the community pool. It was forbidden.

Although it was fun to be at the beach with Davy and her brothers and sisters, Maryellen missed Dad. He always rode the waves with her. She floated in the water and looked back at the shore. Queen Beverly was building a sand castle. Tom and Mikey kept knocking her castle down, so after a little while, Davy got out of the water to help her by distracting them. "Hey, boys!" Davy shouted as he walked up the beach. "Let's dig a hole to China."

Joan was lying on a beach towel, reading as usual. Scooter snoozed next to her.

"Say, Joan," Carolyn called. "Come on in—the water's fine."

Joan didn't even take her eyes off her book. "No thanks," she called back.

"I bet she doesn't want to get her hair wet," Carolyn said to Maryellen. "She has a tennis date with Jerry later."

"Oooh, a date!" said Maryellen, instantly interested. Jerry was Joan's boyfriend. He went to college and had a car. Maryellen thought Jerry was a dreamboat because he was so handsome. Even though she was still mad at Joan for the crabby, critical things she'd said that morning, Maryellen had to admit that pretty Joan and handsome Jerry were the perfect couple.

A brilliant thought came to her. If Joan married Jerry, she'd move out and go to live with him. Then she'd stop picking on Maryellen all the time—and Maryellen would have only Mom to win over about the All-Girls Room.

Maryellen turned to Carolyn, who knew all about love and marriage because she was in high school, and asked, "Do you think Joan and Jerry will get married?"

"Well," said Carolyn, "millions of girls get married after high school. And Joan and Jerry are already going steady. The next step is for Jerry to give Joan his fraternity pin. That means they're engaged to be engaged. Then he gives her an engagement ring, and *then* comes the wedding."

"Gee," said Maryellen. "I didn't realize there were so many steps. I was sort of hoping they'd get married *soon*."

"Me too," said Carolyn. "I love weddings! I wonder if Joan would let us be bridesmaids."

"Maybe you and I could *encourage* Joan and Jerry," said Maryellen.

"How?" asked Carolyn.

"Well, first of all, we could give Jerry a little nudge," said Maryellen, "and tell him to hurry up and propose to Joan."

"Yikes," said Carolyn. "I'm too chicken to do *that*."

"I'm not," said Maryellen. "Jerry's not scary."

"It's not Jerry I'm scared of," said Carolyn. "It's Joan. She'd skin us alive if she found out."

"She doesn't need to know," said Maryellen. "We'll just talk to Jerry sometime when Joan's not around."

Carolyn began to say, "Joan won't—" But right then, Davy came splashing back into the water.

"Come on," he said. "Let's do underwater somersaults."

"Okay!" said Maryellen and Carolyn, putting the topic of marriage aside.

Extraordinary, Not Extra Ordinary

✳ Chapter 3 ✳

I n a little while, Joan stood up and called out, "Okay, kids! Time to go home."

Normally, everyone would beg to stay longer at the beach. But today, Maryellen, Davy, and Carolyn ran up to the umbrella and toweled off and put their shoes on, and Beverly and the little boys picked up their sand pails and shovels and got ready to walk home without a murmur. Today Betty and Florence were coming!

Maryellen rushed to help Joan shake the sand off her beach towel and fold it neatly. Joan said nothing, but she raised her eyebrows at Maryellen's unusual eagerness to be neat. Then Joan tucked her towel and book under her arm, put Mikey in his stroller, and took Tom by the hand. Carolyn, Maryellen, and Beverly hoisted the beach umbrella onto their shoulders and carried it, all in a row, with Maryellen in the middle. Davy brought up the rear, herding sluggish Scooter homeward.

Maryellen knew just about everyone who lived in the houses on her street. She waved at the neighbors who were out in their yards, washing the car, mowing the lawn, or sitting and sipping lemonade. She had always liked how safe and familiar her neighborhood was, and how homey the pretty little matching houses were, all lined up in rows, facing one another cheerfully across the street. Each house had a driveway, a carport, a small lawn, and a palm tree. But suddenly, today, the sameness felt flat. Today, it occurred to Maryellen that the neighborhood might look dull to Betty and Florence. They lived in New York City, for heaven's sake! Maryellen had never been to New York, but she knew that it was an exciting, bustling big city full of action and variety. And she could tell that Mom wanted to impress Betty and Florence. How could their home be impressive if it was just like all the other houses on the street?

"You can hardly tell these houses apart," Maryellen said aloud. "We should do something to make *our* house stand out."

"Like what?" asked Carolyn.

"I don't know yet," said Maryellen. "But I'll think of *some*thing."

As they walked up the driveway, Maryellen thought hard about what she could do to make their house look *extraordinary* instead of *extra ordinary*. Davy waved good-bye and went next door to his own house. Mom met them at the kitchen door, standing in the shade of the carport.

She was wearing a dress and a hat and high-heeled sandals, and the car keys jingled in her hand. "I'm on my way to the airport to pick up Betty and Florence," Mom said.

"Wow, Mom, you look beautiful," said Maryellen. "You look just like a mother on TV." That was Maryellen's highest compliment. It worried her a little bit that most of the time, Mom distinctly did not look like one of the mothers on TV who vacuumed their spotless houses wearing high heels and pearls and always had a chocolate cake on hand. Instead, Mrs. Larkin usually wore sneakers, pedal pushers, and one of Dad's old shirts. But today, Maryellen saw that Mom's fingernails and toenails had fire-engine-red polish on them. They were as red and shiny and eye-popping as Mom's red lipstick. Now Maryellen was absolutely positive: Mom *really* wanted to impress Betty and Florence. Oh, she ached to help Mom do just that!

That's when Maryellen had a great idea about how to snazz up their house. She thought of a surefire way that she could make their house stand out from every other house on the street. She couldn't *wait* to make it happen.

Meanwhile, Mrs. Larkin was saying, "Thank you, darling. Everything is spick-and-span and perfect for Betty and Florence, and I want it to stay that way. So everyone, please hose off your feet before you go inside. I don't want you tracking sand all over my clean kitchen floor."

"Okay, Mom," said everybody.

"What smells so good?" asked Carolyn.

"Oh, I'm glad you reminded me," said Mom. "There are brownies in the oven. Take them out when the timer dings, okay? But don't eat any."

"Okay, Mom," said everybody again, but Maryellen was so excited about her idea that she wasn't really paying much attention.

"Well, all right. I'd better go," said Mrs. Larkin. As she drove away in the car, she waved and called out the window, "Be good!"

"Okay, Mom," said everybody one more time.

Hurray, thought Maryellen, happy and excited. *Mom's finally gone. Now I can work on my surprise.*

✳ ✳ ✳

The hose was right next to the kitchen door. Tom, who always liked to pretend that he was a fireman, held the hose while Joan washed the sand off Mikey's feet. Then

Tom squirted Scooter, who sat agreeably and let him do it.

Maryellen hurriedly changed out of her bathing suit, went to the carport, and began rummaging around on Dad's workbench for red paint and a paintbrush. She was going to paint the front door of their house red, *really* red: bright, shiny, eye-catching, fingernail-polish, lipstick-y red. No one else in the neighborhood had a red front door! Betty and Florence would be so impressed. They'd say to Mom, "My goodness, Kay! Your house really stands out from the rest. It's extraordinary! It's the only one with a bright red door!" And Mom would smile proudly and say, "Maryellen painted our door red. It was her idea. She always has great ideas!" And *then*, when Betty and Florence talked to Maryellen for the first time, they wouldn't say what people *usually* said, which was, "You're Maryellen? Which one are you, the second, third, or fourth sister?" Instead, they would say, "You're *Maryellen*? Oh! You're the one with all the great ideas!"

Maryellen was so intent on imagining Mom's pride and Betty's and Florence's admiration, and so focused on her search for paint, that she jumped when Beverly's squeaky voice asked, "What are you doing?"

Maryellen turned to see Beverly, Tom, Mikey, and Scooter standing in a row behind her, watching her. Beverly was wearing her baseball-cap crown. Except for

Scooter, they were all eating orange Popsicles, so their mouths were wreathed in orange stickiness.

"What are you doing?" asked Beverly again.

"Nothing," Maryellen answered. "Go find Carolyn."

"She left for her piano lesson," said Beverly. "She said to tell you to take the brownies out."

"What about Joan?" said Maryellen.

"She's getting ready for Jerry," said Beverly. "She gave us Popsicles and told us to come find you."

Maryellen sighed. She could see that she was stuck with Beverly, Tom, Mikey, and Scooter as an audience for her project whether she liked it or not. "All right," she said briskly. "I'm going to paint the front door red, like Mom's fingernail polish. You can watch. But don't get in the way."

Maryellen found a can of red paint and a paintbrush left over from when Dad had touched up Tom's fire truck. The paint was sort of lumpy and smelly, and the brush had dried so that it was stiffened into a hard curve. Maryellen knew that before starting her project, she should clean the brush with turpentine, but she didn't have time to fuss. She had to finish her surprise before Mom and Betty and Florence came home. To make herself faster and taller, Maryellen put on her roller skates. She pictured herself gliding smoothly as she painted, like the waitresses on roller skates at a drive-up restaurant.

"I want to paint, too," said Beverly. She and Mikey trailed along behind Maryellen as she roller-skated to the front door. Scooter, who had an unerring instinct about where he'd be most in the way, plunked himself down right behind Maryellen.

"I want to paint, too," echoed Tom, pedaling his fire engine along behind them.

"Paint!" said Mikey.

"No," said Maryellen.

"Why?" asked Beverly.

"Because there's only one brush."

"Can I have a turn with it?" asked Beverly.

"Me, too?" asked Tom.

"Paint!" said Mikey.

"No," said Maryellen shortly.

"Why not?" asked Beverly.

"Because it was my idea and I'm doing it," said Maryellen. She sounded crosser than she meant to. The truth was that she was cross at *herself*, because only now that she looked at the front door did she realize that it might have been a good idea to wash the door first. The old white paint was pretty dirty. But there really wasn't time. And besides, once the door was covered with a nice fresh coat of red paint, nobody would be able to see the dirt.

So Maryellen plunged ahead. *It's just a door. How hard can it be?* she thought to herself. She remembered seeing a TV commercial in which a lady painted her whole living room all by herself, and there was nothing to it! Maryellen pretended to be in that TV commercial. She held the can of paint in one hand, dipped the brush into it, and boldly swiped a stroke of red on the middle slat of the white front door.

"Uh-oh," said Beverly.

"Uh-oh what?" asked Maryellen, even though she had spotted a problem, too.

"It's all bumpy," said Beverly.

"Oh, no one will see," said Maryellen airily, even though it was easy to see that she'd painted over dead bugs, and their bodies were now permanently attached to the door, like raised polka dots. She was glad when Joan's boyfriend, Jerry, drove up in his convertible hot rod. He would be a great distraction for her pesky audience.

"Hi, Jerry!" Maryellen, Beverly, and Tom called. Maryellen turned and waved her paintbrush.

"Hi, kids," said Jerry as he got out of his car and came up the front walk. Maryellen thought he looked very handsome in his white tennis outfit. "What's with the paint, Ellie?"

"Paint!" said Mikey.

"I'm painting our door red," Maryellen explained. "It's a surprise for Mom."

"She'll be surprised, all right," said Jerry. "I guess I'd better knock on the kitchen door to let Joan know I'm here for our date."

Maryellen seized the opportunity, even though she knew she was risking Joan's wrath. "Speaking of dates," she said to Jerry, "have you ever thought about *setting* a date? To marry Joan, I mean."

"To—to what?" Jerry sputtered. He looked surprised.

"Marry Joan," Maryellen plowed on doggedly. "She's almost eighteen, you know. She'll graduate from high school next June. And millions of girls get married right after they graduate."

Jerry looked stunned, as if someone had bonked him on the noggin. He was speechless.

Maryellen pressed on. "You had better ask her soon," she advised Jerry. "She's awfully pretty, and very popular, and—" But Maryellen didn't have a chance to finish her sentence, because just then, everything happened at once.

Beverly had finished her Popsicle and was now dipping the stick into the paint can and painting her fingernails red. Suddenly she stopped and looked up. "Ellie," she asked, "what's that smell?"

Maryellen turned and saw smoke billowing out of

the kitchen door just as Carolyn came running up the
driveway waving her piano music and shouting, "Ellie!
The brownies—they're burning!"

Joan, rushing out to see what the fuss was, flung open
the front door. Maryellen gasped and began to wobble
on her roller skates. As her feet flew out from under her
and she landed bottom-first in a bush, red paint went
flying—all over her, all over the front step, and all over
Jerry's white tennis shorts and shirt.

"Hey!" exclaimed Jerry.

"Oh *no!*" shrieked Joan.

Tom, making siren noises and clanging the bell on his fire truck, pedaled to the kitchen door and turned on the hose. He squirted water through the kitchen screen door, trying to put out the fire in the oven like a fireman. Beverly held up her hands, which were covered in red paint, and wailed. Mikey, unperturbed, picked up the paintbrush and began painting red stripes on Scooter, who didn't seem to mind.

And it was at that exact moment that Mrs. Larkin's car pulled into the driveway, horn honking *"Honk, honk!"* to announce its happy arrival.

Taking Responsibility
* Chapter 4 *

OM!" yelled Joan, Carolyn, Maryellen, Beverly, and Tom at the top of their lungs.

"Fire!" yelled Jerry.

"Paint!" yelled Mikey.

"*Ar-oooo!*" howled Scooter.

The car screeched to a stop, and Mrs. Larkin, Betty, and Florence jumped out.

"What's going on?" Mrs. Larkin shouted, over and above all the noise. "Oh, my stars—look at this mess! How on earth did this happen?"

Suddenly, everyone was quiet. None of them had ever seen Mom this mad before.

Maryellen stepped forward. "Mom," she began. Her voice sounded as wobbly as her knees felt. "I was only trying to paint the door. I didn't mean to make a mess. I'm sorry."

"*Sorry?*" Joan repeated. "You've ruined Jerry's tennis clothes. You've ruined our date. You've ruined the front of our house. And all you can say is *sorry*?" Joan put her hands on her hips and leaned toward Maryellen. "This is just the kind of disaster I was talking about earlier. When are you going to grow up?" She stormed off with Jerry, holding him by the arm, but gingerly, so that she wouldn't get red paint on her tennis dress.

"Oh, Ellie," moaned Mom. She closed her eyes and pressed her red fingertips to her forehead. Then she opened her eyes and said, "Ellie, I will speak to you about this privately. Carolyn, please help Betty and Florence get settled, and then give them a glass of iced tea on the back patio."

"Sure, Mom," said Carolyn. Everyone skedaddled, and Jerry and Joan drove away. Mom and Maryellen were alone.

Maryellen picked up the paintbrush and the paint can and tried to explain. "I only wanted to—"

But Mom interrupted. "No explanations right now, please. And just leave the mess," she said flatly. "We'll deal with it later, after Betty and Florence have left. Honey, I am disappointed in you. It is childish to get so carried away that you don't stop to think. I understand that in a big family like ours, it's hard to get your fair share of attention. But there are better ways of getting attention than showing off and slathering red paint all over. Didn't you promise me just this morning that you'd act more responsibly?"

Maryellen nodded. She was too close to tears to speak. She was sorry to have upset Mom, and she was even sorrier that her surefire way of pleasing Mom had completely backfired. What a flop! What a failure! What a *disaster*.

She sure had failed Mom's test. Now Joan and Mom would *never* agree to the All-Girls Room. Worse than that, instead of thinking that she was more grown-up, Mom and Joan now thought of her as even more messy and irresponsible than before.

The full moon shone so brightly into the bedroom that Maryellen could not sleep. Lying on her upper bunk, she tossed and turned and couldn't stop thinking of the red paint disaster.

"Jeez Louise, Ellie," Joan said sleepily. "Stop spinning around. What are you doing—practicing your underwater somersaults? Go to sleep, why don't you?"

"Sorry," said Maryellen. She flinched, expecting Joan to jump all over her again the way she had earlier when Maryellen had used the inadequate word *sorry*.

But Joan didn't. In fact, her voice was kind when she said, "Listen, Ellie-jelly, don't be so hard on yourself. You're upset because your red paint idea didn't work out. But everybody makes a mistake once in a while. Your mistake today just happened to be a lulu."

"*All* my ideas seem to be mistakes," said Maryellen. "They're *all* lulus."

"Oh, I don't know about that," said Joan. "You had one good idea today."

"I did?" asked Maryellen. She could hardly believe her ears. "What was it?"

Joan giggled a little. "You told Jerry to, uh, get on the ball," she said.

Maryellen gulped. "You're not mad about that?" she asked.

"Well, no," said Joan. "In fact, I'm glad you said something."

Maryellen was flabbergasted. "Glad?" she repeated.

"Mm-hmm," said Joan. "Thanks to you, Jerry finally gave me his fraternity pin."

"He did?" squeaked Maryellen.

"Yep," said Joan. "I was hoping that he would pin me before he went back to college in the fall, but of course I couldn't ask him. *Girls* don't propose to *boys*."

"So that means you're engaged to be engaged, right?" Maryellen asked. "And does *that* mean you'll be getting married soon?" Now that Joan was being so nice, Maryellen wasn't sure she wanted her to leave—not right away, at least.

"No, we won't be getting married for a while yet," said

Joan. "So don't say anything to Mom and Dad. Jerry and I want to talk to them together, because it's a pretty big deal. Getting pinned *does* mean there's a wedding in our future."

"Oh boy!" said Maryellen. "A wedding! Can I help you plan it?"

"You bet," said Joan. "So, see? Not all of your ideas are bombs. Even this All-Girls Room isn't as bad as I thought it would be. I have more space in here, and you organized your stuff pretty well. After Betty and Florence leave, I think I'll tell Mom it's all right with me to make the move permanent."

"Really?" asked Maryellen, her heart lifting.

"Really," said Joan. She yawned, and then she said, "You still have to get Mom to agree, though. Now if you could just come up with another one of your Great Ideas to undo the mess you made with the red paint out front, you'd be all set. Meanwhile, go to sleep, okay?"

"I'll try," said Maryellen. Full of gratitude for Joan's forgiveness, she closed her eyes and tried to go to sleep. But her brain kept going over and over what Joan had said. *Undo the mess, undo the mess . . . How,* Maryellen thought, *can I undo the mess?*

❋ ❋ ❋

Maryellen slid out of bed and quietly tiptoed outside

into the balmy Florida night. She skittered over the grass in her bare feet and slipped through the hedge that divided her yard from Davy's.

*Tap, tappety, tap, tap. Tap, **tap**.* Maryellen used her fingernail to beat their secret signal on Davy's bedroom window.

After a moment, Davy appeared. He took one look at Maryellen and climbed out his window. "What's up, Doc?" he whispered.

Maryellen held one finger to her lips to signal *quiet*. With the other hand, she gestured to Davy to follow her as she led the way to the garage and to Dad's workbench. She handed Davy the can of red paint and the paintbrush, and gathered up rags, a scrub brush, and the tin of turpentine. Then she led Davy to the front of the house.

"Holy cow," breathed Davy when he saw the paint mess. "What happened here?"

"It's a long story," Maryellen sighed sadly. "Anyway, would you finish painting the door while I scrub the step?"

"Sure," said Davy without hesitation. Just then, Scooter ambled into view. "Holy *cow!*" Davy exclaimed softly. "Get a load of Scooter's stripes. He looks like a pudgy tiger, for Pete's sake!"

"Hi, old boy," Maryellen said to Scooter. "I'm afraid

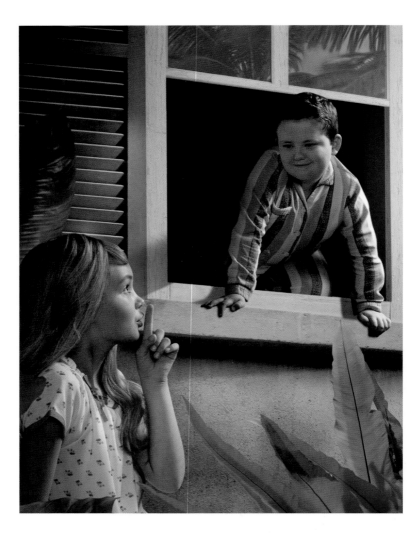

Davy took one look at Maryellen and climbed out his
window. "What's up, Doc?" he whispered.

your shampoo will have to wait."

The front of the house was bathed in moonlight. As Davy started on the front door, Maryellen soaked her rags in turpentine and scrubbed and *scrubbed* to remove the red paint from the front step. How had it splattered so far and wide? The turpentine had a sharp smell that made her eyes sting and nose run. But Maryellen did not give up.

Davy seemed to enjoy painting. "Hey, let's pretend we're in an episode of a TV show about pirates," he suggested.

"Or how about if we're explorers," said Maryellen, perking up, "and we were sailing the seven seas when we were *captured* by the pirates? They make us work day and night! You're painting the mast, and I'm swabbing the decks of the pirate ship. But pretty soon, with our brave companion, Sea Wolf—that's Scooter—we'll jump overboard and swim away."

"Good idea," said Davy. "Ahoy there, Sea Wolf!"

Scooter thumped his tail to show that he was in on the game.

Pretending helped the time go faster, but it still felt to Maryellen as though she was scrubbing for hours. Her knees hurt, her arm was sore, and her hands felt rubbed raw.

At last, most of the splattered red paint was gone.

Maryellen thought the step looked a bit pinkish, but perhaps it was just a trick of the moonlight. Davy finished painting the door, and then he and Maryellen wiped their hands on the turpentine rags and washed them with the hose.

Davy saluted and said quietly, "Anchors aweigh, matey."

Maryellen saluted back. She sure hoped Joan was wrong about not being friends with a boy in fourth grade. Davy was such a good pal. "Anchors aweigh," she said. "And Davy, thank you."

Davy grinned. "Any time," he said and then zipped home.

Maryellen sneaked back to bed, tired and smelling of turpentine.

✳ ✳ ✳

The next morning, Mom woke Maryellen with a kiss. She opened her eyes to see Mom smiling at her. "Hey, Ellie," Mom said softly. "Are you the magic fairy who scrubbed away the red paint?"

Maryellen nodded. "And Davy painted the door," she said.

"That was a big job," said Mom. "And that's what I call taking responsibility. You're forgiven for yesterday. You know, I rather like having a red door and a pink step out

front. And I bet Dad will like them, too! Come on, let's
have breakfast. Betty is making pancakes."

"Yes, *ma'am*," said Maryellen. She hugged Mom hard
for a moment and then bounced out of bed. She was so
happy and relieved that she practically flew into the
kitchen.

After breakfast, Mom and Betty and Florence got all
dolled up. As soon as they left for their reunion, the house
felt dull and empty. Maryellen was glad to see Mom when
she got home that afternoon, after having dropped Betty
and Florence off at the airport.

"Was the reunion luncheon fun?" Maryellen asked
Mom. She wondered if seeing her old coworkers made
Mom wish she were still the star of the factory.

"Yes, it was," said Mom as she kicked off her high
heels and took off her hat. "It was lovely to see everyone
again. But do you know, Betty and Florence said that
they had more fun here at our house. They said it was
far more entertaining than the reunion." Mom winked
at Maryellen, who blushed. "Betty and Florence got a
big kick out of you kids. They told me that Dad and I are
lucky to have such a lively, rowdy family." Mom hugged
Mikey and tousled Tom's hair. "And I think they're exactly right."

"Well," said Joan. "*Most* of the time."

And everyone—even Maryellen—laughed.

✳ ✳ ✳

The very next day, Maryellen was in her bedroom sketching hairdos when Mom popped her head in and said, "I checked, and just as I suspected, you *do* need new socks and underwear. How would you like to go shopping today?"

"Sure," said Maryellen.

"All right then," said Mom. "Let's go!"

So, just like *that*, Maryellen found herself skipping happily through the shopping center parking lot next to Mom, trying to keep up with her mother's long strides. She was excited and delighted to be on a shopping trip, even if it *was* only for underwear and *not* for a new dress to wear on the first day of school instead of Carolyn's plaid hand-me-down. That didn't matter. The important thing was that today, for a few hours at least, Maryellen had Mom *all to herself.*

The Poodle Skirt
* Chapter 5 *

aryellen and Mom walked into the cool air-
conditioning of O'Neal's, the nicest department
store at the shopping center, and rode the stately silver
escalator up to the Girls' Department on the second floor.
As Maryellen stepped off the escalator, she came to a
sudden stop. There on a mannequin, right before her very
eyes, was the most wonderful outfit she had ever seen. It
was a pink blouse, a black patent leather belt, and a very,
very full black felt skirt with a pink poodle appliqué on it.

"Oh, Mom, *look*," said Maryellen exuberantly. "A poodle
skirt!" She touched the poodle's shiny black button eyes
and traced the loops of its leash. "Isn't this the cutest outfit
in the world?"

"It's cute," said Mom briskly. "But we're here for
underwear."

"Yes, of course," said Maryellen. Dutifully, she followed Mom to the underwear section.

"While we're here, let's get underwear for Tom and
Dad, too," said Mom.

Maryellen swallowed a groan. Underwear for boys

and men was even more boring than underwear for girls. But she was patient as Mom chose underpants for Tom and boxer shorts for Dad. And she was patient while she and Mom waited in line to pay for their purchases at the checkout counter, though she couldn't help looking longingly over her shoulder at the poodle skirt in the Girls' Department. A small, sad sigh escaped her.

Mom heard the sigh, and saw what Maryellen was gazing at. "Ellie, sweetie," Mom said with a note of warning in her voice, "we're not shopping for skirts today, remember? You already have a perfectly fine back-to-school dress—the plaid one from Carolyn. Didn't we agree on that?"

"Yes," said Maryellen. Mom was right: The plaid dress was perfectly fine. It was just so very *ordinary*. She knew that she should not bug Mom about the fabulous poodle skirt, but . . . She gathered her courage, and asked, "Mom, what if I just zipped over there and tried on the skirt while you're waiting here in line?"

"Well, all right," said Mrs. Larkin. "But I won't be long, so don't dillydally."

"I won't," Maryellen promised. She grabbed a skirt in her size off the rack, rushed to a dressing room, and tried the skirt on. The poodle skirt looked even *more* wonderful than she'd expected. She twirled around in

front of the three panels of
the dressing-room mirror to
make the skirt swing out in
a perfect circle, and she was
delighted to see hundreds of
twirling Maryellens reflected
around her in a swirling *swoosh*.

Mom poked her head in around
the dressing-room curtain. "Ready to go?" she asked.
Maryellen nodded.

Mom looked at Maryellen and raised an eyebrow.
"My, but the poodle on that skirt is *pink*," she said dryly.
"And pink is a color that I should think you'd like to avoid
today. Your hands are still a bit pink from scrubbing away
all that red paint."

"Oh, Mom," Maryellen burst out. "You were right—
I *did* paint the front door red to show off and get attention.
But I also painted it for you. I thought that if our house
looked special, your friends would be impressed. They'd
see how special *you* are."

"Oh," said Mom. She stepped into the dressing room
and sat down hard on the little stool next to the mirror.
"Really?" she asked.

Maryellen nodded. "Yes!" she said fervently. "I didn't
want our house to look boring and ordinary, because

I didn't want Betty and Florence to think that we were boring and ordinary—especially not *you*."

"I see," said Mom. "You were feeling overlooked and underappreciated, and you thought I was, too. So you wanted to make a big splash for both of us."

Maryellen winced at the word *splash*, but said, "Yes."

"I see," said Mom again. "I'm glad I understand better now. It was sweet of you to think of me and how I might be feeling. And it was good of you to scrub off the red paint, too. I know that was hard work. You made a mess, but you took responsibility for cleaning it up."

"It was actually Joan who sort of gave me the idea," said Maryellen.

"Did she?" said Mom. "It sounds like she's forgiven you for splattering red paint on Jerry."

Maryellen smiled and shrugged. She knew the reason why Joan had forgiven her, but Joan had asked her not to tell Mom about being pinned, so she kept quiet.

"Anyway, you seem to be back in Joan's good graces," Mom went on. "If she gives her approval to the All-Girls Room, then as far as I'm concerned, it's a done deal. You can help Joan and Carolyn move in permanently when we get home."

"Really, Mom?" Maryellen asked. "I'm pretty sure Joan likes it. At least, she told me she did."

Mom stood up, crossed her arms, tilted her head, and observed Maryellen from head to toe. "All of a sudden, you're looking more mature to me, Miss Maryellen Larkin," she said. "And I don't think it's just because of that very chic poodle skirt you're wearing, either."

Maryellen beamed.

"In fact, the more I look at it, the more I think that skirt suits you," said Mom. "It's quite grown-up, and you are, too. Ellie-girl, I think you've found yourself a very glamorous back-to-school skirt, don't you? Let's buy it."

Maryellen gasped. She threw herself at Mom and said, "Oh, thank you, Mom! Thank you, thank you, *thank* you. I love it!"

Maryellen was thrilled. The poodle skirt would be one of the first *new* things, and certainly one of the most *beautiful* things, she'd ever owned in her life! It was fun and fancy and fashionable. She was absolutely sure that the poodle skirt guaranteed she'd have not only a great first day of school but also a great *year* in fourth grade.

Even better, the poodle skirt was a perfect reminder that Mom didn't think of her as a little kid anymore, but as someone more grown-up, whose ideas should be taken seriously. After all, even if *some* of her great ideas did not work out as perfectly as they did in her imaginary TV shows, *some*how *some*times *some* things still ended happily, just as they had today.

The thought of happy endings reminded Maryellen of her Jerry-and-Joan Wedding Project. "Say, Mom," she asked casually, "on our way out of the store, may we swing through the Bridal Shop?"

"Sure!" said Mom. "That's a great idea. It'll be fun."

Oh boy! thought Maryellen. *A poodle skirt, the All-Girls Room, fourth grade . . . and a wedding to look forward to!* The months to come were sure to be *extra* extraordinary!

✳ ✳ ✳

Maryellen often thought she was the luckiest girl in the world, because she had *three* best friends. There was Davy right next door, of course, and then she also had two best girlfriends. If that wasn't fun enough, both girls were named Karen! One was Karen Stohlman and one was Karen King. Maryellen mostly saw the Karens at school, because they lived in a different neighborhood. When summer vacation ended and school started again, she and her three best friends were going to be in fourth grade together.

One afternoon shortly before the first day of school, Karen Stohlman's mother drove the two Karens over to Maryellen's house to play. Mr. Larkin had painted permanent hopscotch squares on the driveway, so the girls were having a hopscotch marathon.

Maryellen tossed her marker, which was an old Popsicle stick, and hopped to the square it landed on, talking at the same time. "I hope Mrs. (hop) Humphrey (hop) is nice (hop, hop, hop)," she said. "Joan and Carolyn had her as their teacher when they were in fourth grade, and they liked her a lot."

Karen Stohlman, who took ballet, rose up on tiptoe and twirled. "I'm so glad the three of us are all in the same class," she said.

"And Davy's in our class, too," Maryellen reminded her, "so this is going to be our best school year ever. I just know it."

"Yes!" said Karen King. Her round, freckly face looked cheerful. "Plus this year we finally get to be Girl Scouts."

"Hurray!" cheered Maryellen, and Karen Stohlman twirled again. Maryellen, Karen, and Karen had liked being Brownies well enough, but they'd been looking forward to being Girl Scouts for years.

"We'll be the *most outstanding* Girl Scouts ever," said Maryellen. "We'll earn *more* badges than anyone else, and sell the *most* Girl Scout cookies, and have the *most* fun on the hikes."

"Do you two have your uniforms yet?" asked Karen Stohlman.

"Yes," said Maryellen and Karen King.

"Me too," said Karen Stohlman. "Mine was a little too long, so my mom's hemming it." She didn't say so, but Maryellen knew that Karen Stohlman's Girl Scout uniform was brand-new. She had only an older brother, so all her clothes were new. "You know what's going to be great?" Karen continued. "When we all wear our uniforms, we'll look exactly alike. We'll be triplets!"

"Uh, not exactly," said Maryellen. "My uniform is a hand-me-down. First Joan wore it, then Carolyn. It's so old that it's different from the new ones. It has long sleeves."

"Oh," said Karen Stohlman, sounding disappointed. She always liked the girls to be the *same*.

"My uniform is a hand-me-down, too," sighed Karen King, "from my sister Kathy. She's really hard on her clothes. They look like they've been through a hurricane by the time I get them."

"I know what you mean," said Maryellen. "My clothes go through both Joan and Carolyn before they come to me." Maryellen thought with a *zing* of excitement, not *all* of her clothes were previously worn. The Karens did not know about the wonderful new skirt with a pink French poodle that she was going to wear on the first day of fourth grade. Maryellen had been planning to keep her skirt a secret and to surprise Karen and Karen with it on the first day of school, but she was so excited about it that she thought she might pop.

"Guess what?" Maryellen said to the Karens. "Mom and I went shopping at O'Neal's, and now I have something brand-new to wear on the first day of school!"

"You went to O'Neal's?" gasped Karen King. "You lucky duck!"

"What did you get?" asked Karen Stohlman.

"Well, it's a . . ." Maryellen stopped. The poodle skirt was simply too wonderful to describe in mere words. To be fully appreciated, it had to be seen in all its pink-poodle glory. "Come on inside," she said impulsively, "so you can see it."

The three girls dropped their hopscotch markers and stampeded inside. Maryellen led her friends to her room. There, carefully displayed on a chair, was her poodle skirt. Both Karens gasped in appreciation.

"Isn't it the cutest skirt you've ever seen?" asked Maryellen.

"Yes!" said Karen Stohlman. "I wish I had one, too!"

"On the first day of school, I'm going to wear a pink blouse that Carolyn gave me," said Maryellen, "and I'm going to borrow Carolyn's crinoline, to make the skirt stick out."

"Goll-lee," sighed Karen King. "Ellie Larkin, you'll be the

most fashionable girl in the fourth grade. Everybody will be impressed. You'll look like a movie star." Karen pointed to a photo of Maryellen's favorite movie star, Debbie Reynolds, which Maryellen had taped to her mirror. "If you cut your bangs shorter, you'd look just like Debbie Reynolds."

Maryellen beamed. She held the poodle skirt to her waist and twirled around, saying, "I can't wait to wear it on the first day of school."

"If I had one, I'd wear it *every* day," said Karen Stohlman.

"Put it on so we can see how it fits," said Karen King.

But just then, Tom stuck his head in the door. "Mrs. Stohlman's here," he said.

"Oh, no, we've got to go," said Karen King, turning to leave. "Well, see you on the first day of school."

"Yes!" said Maryellen. "Davy and I will ride our bikes like always, and I'll meet you on the playground. See you later, alligator!"

"See you soon, raccoon," said the Karens. "Bye!"

After the girls left, Maryellen practically danced in to dinner, filled with happy anticipation. This was going to be the best school year ever.

Tickled Pink

O n the first day of school, Maryellen woke up very early. *This is it!* she thought with a shiver of nervousness. Silently, Maryellen sat up in bed. She could see her gorgeous poodle skirt waiting for her, draped neatly on the chair. Yesterday, the last day of summer vacation, Carolyn had very nicely ironed her hand-me-down pink blouse, and Maryellen had polished a pair of oxfords she had inherited from Carolyn, so they looked shiny and ready to go.

Finally, Maryellen couldn't wait a moment longer. She anchored her feet between the mattress and the wall and dangled her head and arms off the top bunk so that she could tug on Carolyn's pillow.

"Carolyn!" she whispered. "Are you awake?"

"Yes," said Carolyn right away.

"Let's get up and get dressed," said Maryellen.

"Okay," said Carolyn. "But be quiet. Don't wake up Joan." Maryellen, Carolyn, and even Queen Beverly had learned the hard way that Joan was very cross and snappish if she was awakened one minute too early.

"Thanks for letting me borrow your crinoline," Maryellen said softly as Carolyn helped her slip it on over her head. The crinoline would go under the skirt to make it puff out a bit more.

"You're welcome," said Carolyn, who seemed almost as excited about the poodle skirt as Maryellen was. Carolyn was quite a bit taller than Maryellen, so they had to pull the crinoline up to Maryellen's armpits to keep it from hanging below the hem of the poodle skirt.

"I'm like a bride," joked Maryellen. "I've got something old—my shoes—and something new—my skirt—and something borrowed—your crinoline. All I need is something blue."

"Well, what color's your underwear?" asked Carolyn.

This made both Maryellen and Carolyn dissolve into giggles. They clamped their hands over their mouths to stifle their laughter, which of course only made them giggle harder.

"Oh, honestly!" moaned Joan, rising from her pillow, looking cranky. "You two are about as quiet as cackling hens." She propped herself up on her elbow and scrutinized Maryellen. "Pretty good, Ellie-deli," she said. "But your hair should be in a ponytail. And the shoes are all wrong. Poodle skirts go with sneakers or saddle shoes, not oxfords." Then she yawned and sank back into her pillow.

Maryellen and Carolyn stared down at the clunky brown oxfords on Maryellen's feet. They both knew that Joan was right. Without saying a word, Maryellen slipped off the oxfords. Her summer sneakers had grass stains and holes in the toes, so she put on her saddle shoes from last year. The saddle shoes felt a bit tight, but they looked, as Carolyn said softly, "Perfect."

Then Maryellen and Carolyn wrangled Maryellen's hair into a ponytail tied with a scarf.

Carolyn went off to the bathroom, and Maryellen checked herself against the photos of Debbie Reynolds. She spotted a problem. Karen Stohlman was right: Debbie Reynolds's bangs were much shorter than hers. In fact, all the movie stars and models who wore poodle skirts had short bangs. Even Mamie Eisenhower, President Eisenhower's wife, wore short bangs.

Well, how hard could it be to cut my bangs? It looks easy when Mom does it, Maryellen thought. She got scissors out of the desk, and *snip, snip, snip,* cut her bangs in a line across her forehead.

Hmm, thought Maryellen as she looked in the mirror. For some reason, her shortened bangs did not go straight across her forehead, like Debbie Reynolds's and Mamie Eisenhower's. Instead, her bangs slanted diagonally, longer on one side and shorter on the other. Maryellen immediately cut the longer side to make it match, and then looked in the mirror again. Now her bangs looked sort of zigzaggy.

She was trimming the ends to even them up when Carolyn returned from the bathroom and gasped, "STOP!"

Joan sat bolt upright in bed. "Oh, my gosh, Ellie. You look like you got chopped by hedge clippers!"

"I do *not*," said Maryellen huffily. She didn't want to let on that, now that she really looked at her bangs, she was surprised—*horrified*, actually—by what she had done. It had happened so fast! Just *snip, snip, snip,* and now . . . DISASTER! The short, spiky bangs stuck straight out from her forehead. *I look like I have toothbrush bristles attached to my head,* thought Maryellen miserably. Oh, how she wished she could tape her hair back on!

Maryellen put the scissors down and gathered up the snippets of hair from the floor. Her voice was only a little bit wavery when she said, "I think they look okay."

"They're much too short," said Joan, stating the obvious.

"Never mind," said Carolyn kindly. "Your bangs will grow fast."

"Wait till Mom sees you," said Joan. "She'll have a fit."

"Joan, will you cut it out?" said Carolyn. "You're making Ellie feel bad. How would you like to start the first day of school with a terrible haircut?"

Now Maryellen was upset *and* worried. She tugged at her bangs as if she could make them longer by pulling on them. She smoothed them and pushed them down to make them lie flat, but it was no use. As soon as she took her hand off them, her bangs sprang up and stuck straight out over her forehead like a sailor's salute.

"Girls!" Mom called from the kitchen. "Time for breakfast."

Maryellen took a deep, shuddery breath. *What is Mom going to say?* she wondered, full of dread. She was grateful when Carolyn grabbed her hand as they walked together to the kitchen.

When Mom saw Maryellen, her eyebrows shot up. "Ellie," Mom gasped. "What on earth have you done?"

"I, well, I . . . " Maryellen faltered.

Mom held up her hand. "You don't need to tell me," she said. "I can see for myself. You cut your own bangs."

Tom, whose hair stuck straight out all over his head, said, "I *like* your new bangs, Ellie."

"Bang!" yelled Mikey, banging his fist on his high-chair tray. "Bang, bang, bang!"

"I'm sorry, Mom," said Maryellen. "Are you mad?"

"Well," said Mom. "I'm . . . *surprised*. But what's done is done and can't be undone. Besides, you're the one who has to wear the bangs, not me. But Ellie, honey, please talk to me first before you do any more do-it-yourself barbering."

"Oh, *Mom*," wailed Maryellen. She ran to Mom and threw her arms around her and hid her face against her. "Now I don't want to go to school at all!"

"I understand how you feel," Mom said, hugging her. "But you're just going to have to face school, short bangs and all."

"And hey, your new skirt looks nice," said Dad cheerfully, looking up from his coffee. "It's a doozy!"

"That's right. Just concentrate on your snazzy new skirt," Mom advised. "There's no question that, outfit-wise, you are going to be *the most* fashionable girl in the fourth grade. Right?"

Maryellen managed a watery grin. "I guess so."

Mom kissed Maryellen's exposed forehead. "Eat your cereal. Soon it'll be time to go."

Maryellen sat at the table, one hand pressed against her bangs, and the other holding a spoon, with which she only pretended to eat. Her stomach was tied in knots.

The knots tightened when the doorbell rang and Joan, who was wafting by the front door, called out, "Ellie, it's

Davy, and he's got some other little boy with him."

"It's that mean boy, Wayne," Beverly hissed.

"Oh no!" Maryellen whispered. "*Wayne?*" Maryellen and Davy had planned to ride their bikes to school together, as they always did, but Davy hadn't said anything about including *Wayne*, of all people.

"I can't face them!" Maryellen said in a panic. "Please, somebody, tell them I'm not ready! Tell them I'm sick! Tell them I left already!"

Mom shook her head. "You're going to have to face people sooner or later," she said. "You might as well get it over with."

"I can't," Maryellen wailed. "Wayne is sure to say something smart-alecky."

"This is what happens when girls try to be friends with boys in fourth grade," said Joan. "It never works."

"*I'll* handle the boys," said Carolyn heroically. Maryellen cowered in the breakfast nook while Carolyn went straight to the front door and flung it open. "Boys, Ellie told me to tell you that she doesn't want to bike to school with you," Carolyn said firmly. "She's afraid she'll get too sweaty, and she doesn't want to ruin her outfit."

Maryellen heard Wayne snort and mutter, "Typical girl!"

Davy just said, "Oh." He sounded disappointed and confused. Maryellen didn't blame him, because Carolyn's

excuse did not ring true; Davy knew that Maryellen was
the kind of girl who *never* worried about getting messy.

"You'd better get going, boys," Carolyn said in a no-
nonsense voice. Then, before she had completely shut the
door, Carolyn turned toward the kitchen and called out,
"The coast is clear, Ellie. I got rid of the boys like you told
me to!"

Maryellen groaned. Now Davy was probably mad at
her, because Carolyn had made it sound like Maryellen
wanted him to get lost. So far, this sure wasn't the wonderful start to a wonderful year in fourth grade that she
had imagined. Maryellen wondered, *Could this morning
get any worse?*

As she rode her bike to school, Maryellen tried to
forget about her hair and concentrate on her skirt. If
anything could salvage this day, the black-and-pink poodle
skirt could. Maybe everyone would be so dazzled by her
skirt that they wouldn't notice her hair.

When she got to the school playground, where the
students were milling around before lining up to go
into the school building, Maryellen parked her bike and
looked for Davy so that she could apologize to him. Her
heart sank when she saw that Davy was shooting baskets
with Wayne. Nevertheless, she squared her shoulders and

made herself march toward the boys.

"Hey, Ellie!" a voice shouted. "We're over here!"

Maryellen turned and saw Karen King waving wildly amid the throng of students. She waved back and ran to join Karen and Karen, thinking that really, it would be better to apologize to Davy later, when he was alone. Halfway to the Karens, Maryellen stopped short. She blinked. *Karen Stohlman was wearing a black-and-pink poodle skirt exactly like hers!*

"SURPRISE!" the Karens sang out. Karen Stohlman twirled, lifting her arms over her head like a ballerina. She was wearing a pink blouse and saddle shoes, too.

"Look!" gushed Karen King. "Yesterday, Karen went out and got a poodle skirt just like yours."

"We're twins, Ellie," Karen Stohlman said gaily. "My mother and I went shopping at O'Neal's yesterday, and . . ." She stopped. "Gosh, Ellie—you cut your bangs!"

"Whoa! I'll say!" said Karen King. "Aren't they kind of too short?"

"Yes," said Maryellen sharply. She turned to Karen Stohlman, eager to get off the subject. "So you got your skirt yesterday?"

"Yes!" said Karen Stohlman. "To match yours. Isn't this the best surprise ever?"

"Mm-hmm," said Maryellen. She smiled, because she

knew the Karens expected her to smile. They expected her to be delighted—to be tickled pink!—and she herself thought she should be. But her smile was crooked and forced. She couldn't help noticing that Karen's ponytail was longer than hers, and of course, Karen didn't have ridiculous bristle bangs like her unfortunate ones.

In her heart of hearts, Maryellen had wanted to be unique. She had wanted to stand out as the one-and-only girl in the fourth grade who looked like a movie star. Now she couldn't. In fact, Karen looked more stylish and movie-star-ish than she did. *Karen Stohlman has stolen my idea,* Maryellen thought. *She's a copycat!*

"Patty Zender has the same skirt, too," said Karen King.

"You're kidding!" said Maryellen. For some reason, it made her feel a lot better to know about Patty Zender. *So I wouldn't have been unique even if Karen Stohlman hadn't copied me.*

The idea of three matching poodle skirts on the playground cheered Maryellen up. *Well, we might as well make the best of it,* she thought as she waved Patty over to join them. "Come on, Karen," she said. "The three of us can pretend we're the McDoogal Sisters."

Maryellen held her hand up to her mouth as if it was a microphone and she was on TV. "Ladies and gentlemen," she announced. "We're everyone's favorite trio, the McDoogal Sisters, and we're going to sing for you our big hit of 1954, 'Time to Go.'"

Karen Stohlman and Patty giggled, but they sang along with Maryellen, "Time to go, oh, it's time to go . . ." They copied Maryellen and put their hands on their hips and swayed from side to side. When Karen King sang the "doot-dootle-doot-doots" in the background, they twirled around and made their skirts flare out. At the end of the song, they sank down in curtsies, all at the same time.

It turned out to be quite fun to be part of the poodle-skirt trio. Singing and dancing helped Maryellen forget about her terrible bangs and the misunderstanding with Davy. She tucked her disappointment and her annoyance at Karen Stohlman away, deep down in a hidden corner of her heart, and sang—almost—as if she truly *were* tickled pink.

Hand-Me-Down Teacher
* Chapter 7 *

P retty soon, the school bell clanged and it really was "time to go," or at least time to line up, boys in one line, girls in another. The two Karens, Patty, and Maryellen went upstairs to Mrs. Humphrey's fourth-grade classroom together, feeling grown-up and superior to the third-graders, who were still on the first floor with the other lower grades.

Maryellen's saddle shoes squeezed her toes uncomfortably and went *tsk-tsk-tsk* as she climbed the stairs. It was as if they were scolding her for making the mistake of wearing them even though they were definitely too small.

"Welcome, fourth-graders!" said Mrs. Humphrey as the students entered the room. "Please be seated. Take any desk."

Maryellen sank gratefully into a seat and banged her heels softly on the floor to make space for her toes inside her shoes. The felt poodle skirt was too hot for this sunny September morning, and Carolyn's crinoline itched under her armpits. She wriggled and scratched as inconspicuously as she could.

"Fleas, pardner?" Davy asked sympathetically, from his temporary seat behind her. "On loan from Scooter?"

Maryellen knew that Davy was only joking with her in a friendly way. Even so, she felt a tiny prick of annoyance.

And then Wayne, next to Davy, began to chirrup, "Ooh, ooh! Ah, ah!" as he scratched his head and his armpits, pretending to be a monkey scratching its fleas. Suddenly, he stopped and stared. "Yikes! What happened to *you*, Baldy?"

"Holy cow," breathed Davy, his eyes wide at the sight of Maryellen's sticky-out bangs.

"Hmph!" snorted Maryellen, turning away to hide how hurt she was. She had expected teasing from Wayne, but not from *Davy*. Up till now, Davy had always made her feel better about things, not worse. She decided that she wasn't going to apologize to him for what Carolyn had done. So there!

Maryellen turned her attention to Mrs. Humphrey, who smiled and nodded at the students as they entered. After everyone was seated, Mrs. Humphrey said, "Now I'll call the roll and assign permanent seats alphabetically."

As she waited for her name to be called, Maryellen looked around the fourth-grade classroom. She was glad to see lots of maps, rolled up like window shades above the blackboard, because she loved thinking about other countries and different languages. She was not so glad to see, above the blackboard, green placards with models of uppercase and lowercase letters swooping along in white script. Handwriting was not her best subject. She recognized all the kids except one new girl, who had long, dark braids and, Maryellen saw with amazement, *pierced ears!*

"Larkin, Maryellen?" Mrs. Humphrey called.

"Present," said Maryellen.

Mrs. Humphrey beamed at Maryellen as she pointed to the desk she wanted her to take. "I could have guessed that you were a Larkin," she said. "You and your sisters Joan and Carolyn are as alike as three peas in a pod. I'd recognize that Larkin nose anywhere. I had your sister Carolyn in my class a few years ago and Joan a few years before that. They were excellent students."

"Yes, Mrs. Humphrey," said Maryellen, thinking, *I'm off to a good start. Mrs. Humphrey likes me already!* She slid into the chair at her assigned desk, which was behind Jimmy Lansing, as usual. After three years behind Jimmy Lansing, she was getting to know the spindly back of *his* neck very well.

"I'll bet you're as tidy and organized as Carolyn and

Joan were, too," said Mrs. Humphrey.

Maryellen's smile faded a bit. *Uh-oh,* she thought. Mrs. Humphrey would soon figure out that she was not tidy or organized. Then again, Mrs. Humphrey would also soon figure out that she wasn't Carolyn or Joan.

The funny thing was, Mrs. Humphrey *didn't* seem to figure that out. As the morning went on, pretty soon everyone in the class knew that when Mrs. Humphrey said "Carolyn," she meant "Maryellen." It was confusing. During math class, whenever Mrs. Humphrey said, "Tell us how to divide these numbers, Care—" Karen King, Karen Stohlman, and Carol Turner all looked up, expecting to be called on. After a while, Maryellen looked up, too, because often Mrs. Humphrey was looking straight at her and calling her Carolyn. If that happened and Maryellen didn't look up, Wayne took it upon himself to lean across the aisle and poke her hard in the ribs and hiss, "She means *you.*"

To add to the confusion, when Mrs. Humphrey said "Joan," everyone, including Maryellen, naturally thought that the teacher was calling on Joan Martin, who sat right behind Maryellen. But sometimes Mrs. Humphrey was looking at Maryellen and calling *her* Joan. When that happened, both Maryellen and Joan Martin would answer Mrs. Humphrey at the same time.

Maryellen couldn't help noticing that Mrs. Humphrey was starting to get flustered and look annoyed every time she called her by the wrong name, whether Maryellen responded or not. It was almost as if Mrs. Humphrey suspected Maryellen of trying to trick her deliberately.

This is what happens, thought Maryellen, *when even your teacher is a hand-me-down from your sisters.*

✳ ✳ ✳

At lunch that day, Karen King said to Maryellen, "Mrs. Humphrey seems to think that your name is 'Carolyn-Joan-I-mean-Maryellen.'"

Maryellen grinned. Quickly, she drew a sketch on her napkin of a frowning Mrs. Humphrey saying, "Carolyn! Joan! Maryellen! Whoever!" and pointing her finger like Uncle Sam in an army recruitment poster. Under the drawing, she wrote in capital letters: THIS MEANS YOU!

All the girls giggled. Davy, who was passing their table, asked, "What's so funny?"

Wayne, who was right behind Davy, snatched the napkin out of Maryellen's hands. "Get a load of this," he crowed. "A cartoon of Mrs. Humphrey!"

"Give it back!" Maryellen demanded, twisting in her seat.

But Wayne waved the napkin over

THIS MEANS YOU!

Maryellen's head, just out of her reach. "You can't make me," he taunted.

"Got it!" shouted Davy, snatching the napkin out of Wayne's hands.

Just then, someone took the napkin out of Davy's hand. "Hey!" he began to protest, until he saw that it was Mrs. Humphrey.

"Uh-oh," breathed Karen King.

"I am disappointed in you children," said Mrs. Humphrey. "Fighting over a napkin! Is this the proper way for fourth-graders to behave in the lunchroom?"

"No, Mrs. Humphrey," said Davy, Maryellen, and the two Karens. Wayne had somehow disappeared, slithering away in the lunchroom crowd like a snake.

Maryellen got very red in the face while Mrs. Humphrey looked at the drawing on the napkin. "I'm sorry, Mrs. Humphrey," she began.

"Why, I'm surprised at you, Care-Jo-no-oh! Miss Larkin," interrupted Mrs. Humphrey. She held the napkin with the very tips of her fingers as if it were radioactive, tore the napkin in half, dropped the two pieces in the trash, and left.

"Davy! Look what you did," said Maryellen crossly.

"What do you mean?" asked Davy. "I took the napkin away from Wayne to give it back to you."

"Well, if you hadn't been yelling and waving it around, Mrs. Humphrey wouldn't have noticed it," said Maryellen. "You got me into trouble."

"You got yourself into trouble," said Davy, "by drawing the cartoon in the first place."

"I—" Maryellen started to say.

"Never mind!" said Davy. "I'll get lost. That's what you want me to do, right? Just like this morning." He turned on his heel and stormed off.

"Yikes," said Karen King softly. "He's mad."

"Well, I'm mad, too," said Maryellen. "Now Mrs. Humphrey doesn't like me, and it's Davy's fault."

"I think it's Wayne's fault," said Karen King.

"Why does Davy put up with Wayne the Pain, anyway?" said Maryellen crossly. "I don't like him."

"And I don't think Mrs. Humphrey liked your cartoon," said Karen King, who prided herself on telling the truth no matter how unpleasant it might be.

"I never meant for her to see it," said Maryellen miserably. "She may not be sure who I am, but now she *is* sure that she doesn't like me."

"Well, we still like you, Care-Jo-no-oh! Miss Larkin," said Karen King kindly.

"Thanks," said Maryellen. Her smile was weak but grateful. What would she ever do without the Karens, her two best, best friends, especially *now*, when for the first time ever, she and Davy were on the outs?

✳ ✳ ✳

That afternoon, when Maryellen was back at home changing into her play clothes, Joan asked, "So how was the first day of fourth grade?"

"Fine," sighed Maryellen, sounding as if she meant the opposite.

"Mrs. Humphrey is nice, isn't she?" said Carolyn.

"I guess so," said Maryellen gloomily.

"You don't sound very enthusiastic," said Joan. "What happened?"

"Mrs. Humphrey kept calling me Joan or Carolyn," Maryellen grumbled, "and I, well, I drew a cartoon about it and she saw it."

"Uh-oh," said Carolyn.

"I didn't mean to be disrespectful," said Maryellen. "Really I didn't. I was just sort of making a joke about how she didn't seem to know that I was me."

"Did you tell Mrs. Humphrey that you were sorry?" asked Joan.

"Yes," said Maryellen. "And I really am sorry."

"Mrs. Humphrey will forgive you," said Joan. "She knows that it's what you do *after* you've made a mistake that matters. Anyway, *everyone* makes mistakes."

"Yes!" Carolyn interjected brightly. "Like your bangs!"

"Ohh," moaned Maryellen, not at all cheered up. "Mrs. Humphrey never would have seen the cartoon if Wayne hadn't snatched it and Davy hadn't waved it around."

"What did I tell you?" said Joan. "You cannot be friends with boys in the fourth grade. They're okay again in high school." Maryellen knew that, of course, Joan was thinking of dreamy Jerry, to whom she was practically engaged. "But right now, Ellie-mellie, if you're smart, you'll concentrate on your friendship with the Karens."

"Right," said Carolyn. "Girls won't let you down."

Maryellen hoped that Carolyn was right—and that Joan was wrong. She really didn't want to have to wait until high school to be friends with Davy again. Deep down, she was sorry about their fight, and she already missed him.

✳ ✳ ✳

The next morning, Maryellen put on the plaid school dress and the brown oxfords that she had inherited from Carolyn. She waited, but Davy did not stop by to bike to school with her, so she rode to school by herself.

It was amazing, thought Maryellen as Mrs. Humphrey explained long division, how much better her brain worked when her feet weren't squashed and she didn't have to worry all the time about Carolyn's crinoline falling down.

When the math lesson was finished, Mrs. Humphrey pulled down the map of the world.

Good, thought Maryellen. She liked geography. She always helped Dad plot their route and read the map when they went on car trips, and she liked to doodle the shapes of different states and countries just for fun.

"Boys and girls," said Mrs. Humphrey, "in fourth grade, we study history, social studies, and current events. To understand any of those subjects, we need to know geography. In fact, geography is so important that we're going to have a class Geography Bee at the end of every month, and the winners will get prizes."

The class murmured with excitement. Maryellen and the Karens exchanged delighted glances, and Maryellen saw Wayne playfully punch Davy in the arm. Everybody loved bees and prizes!

Mrs. Humphrey covered the name of one of the countries on the map of Europe. "Now," she said, "who can tell me the name of this country?"

Maryellen shot her hand up. She knew that the country was Italy, because she knew that Italy was shaped like a boot.

Mrs. Humphrey glanced at Maryellen, but she called

on the new girl with the long braids and earrings, even though the girl had not raised her hand. "Angela?" Mrs. Humphrey said.

The new girl smiled, and her whole face lit up as if the sun was shining on it. "*Italia,*" she said.

"Yes, good," said Mrs. Humphrey. "This is the country your family came from. In English, we call it *Italy.*"

The class murmured again. Everyone stared at the new girl, who stopped smiling and looked down at her desk.

Oh, so the new girl is **Italian,** thought Maryellen. *How different and interesting!*

The Lunch Bunch
✳ Chapter 8 ✳

Mrs. Humphrey covered the name of another country on the map. She had not even asked for its name before almost every hand in the room went up.

"That's East Germany," Davy called out. "Everybody knows that, because the Germans were our enemies in World War Two."

"Japan and Italy were against us, too," added Karen Stohlman with a sideways glance at the new girl. Maryellen hoped Angela did not understand enough English to be offended. Karen Stohlman went on, "My uncle fought in Italy. He was a hero, but the Italians—"

"Yes, well, the war ended in 1945, nearly ten years ago," Mrs. Humphrey interrupted briskly. "The Germans, Italians, and Japanese are not our enemies anymore. Let's move right along, now. Who can tell me the name of the capital of East Germany?"

This time only Maryellen's hand went up.

"Uh, yes?" said Mrs. Humphrey, who seemed to have decided not to call Maryellen by any name at all, much to the relief of everyone in the class.

"The capital of East Germany is Berlin," said Maryellen. She knew all about Berlin because Joan had written a report about it last year, and Maryellen had drawn the maps for her since she was good at sketching. "After the war, Germany was divided up. The Russians have one part, and now their part is behind the Iron Curtain."

"The Russians have a curtain made of *iron*?" asked Wayne, sounding skeptical.

"It isn't real," said Maryellen. "But the Russians won't let people come and go freely and they keep things secret on their side, so it's as if they've closed a curtain. America doesn't like the way the Russians are treating people, so now the Russians are sort of our enemies and we're in a Cold War with them."

"What's a cold war?" Patty Zender asked.

"It means that each side tries to have more bombs than the other side, even though they don't use them," said Maryellen. "We're not fighting battles against the Russians, but we don't trust them and we're not friendly with them, either."

Mrs. Humphrey smiled at Maryellen. "Good explanation," she said. "Splendid."

Maryellen beamed. Maybe Mrs. Humphrey would forgive her for the napkin cartoon and like her again. She was sorry when geography was over and Mrs. Humphrey passed out handwriting workbooks.

Last year, in third grade, all her classmates had been excited about learning to write in script instead of printing. But Maryellen had discovered that because she was left-handed, her letters seemed to lean in the wrong direction, tilting and wobbling so badly that no one could read them. Finally, Maryellen had solved the problem by inventing a sort of fake script for herself, which she made by smooshing printed letters together. She tried hard to make her loopy letters look nice and neat. But no matter how careful she was, she smudged the words she had written when her left hand passed over them.

Mrs. Humphrey came by and looked at Maryellen's work over her shoulder. She didn't say anything, but Maryellen knew that her workbook page looked messy.

When it was time to line up for lunch, Mrs. Humphrey announced, "Boys and girls, I sometimes invite students to join what I call my 'Lunch Bunch' and meet me here in the classroom after lunch instead of going out for recess. Today, I'm inviting Angela, Davy, and, uh . . ." Mrs. Humphrey paused to be sure she got the name right, then said, "*Maryellen* to join me."

Karen King rolled her eyes at Maryellen. Mrs. Humphrey had made her announcement in a cheery tone of voice, as if joining the Lunch Bunch was a privilege. But everyone knew perfectly well that it wasn't.

"It isn't much of a 'bunch' anyway," Karen Stohlman said while the girls ate their sandwiches in the cafeteria. "It's just you, that new Italian girl who doesn't speak any English, and Davy, who needs help with multiplication."

"Gosh, Ellie," said Karen King. "Do you think Mrs. Humphrey is punishing you because of that cartoon?"

"No," sighed Maryellen. "I think I'm in the Lunch Bunch because Mrs. Humphrey doesn't like my script handwriting."

Maryellen's Lunch Bunch hunch turned out to be right.

When she went back to the classroom, Davy didn't even look up from his math book.

Mrs. Humphrey said, "Now, Care—uh, Maryellen, let's talk about your handwriting. I see that you're not really writing in cursive. You're just running your printed letters together. Is that what your teacher showed you how to do in third grade?"

"No," admitted Maryellen. "I kind of invented my handwriting all by myself."

"I see," said Mrs. Humphrey. "Well, you are in the

fourth grade now, and I think that your script should look like everyone else's. With practice, I am sure that your script can look like those beautiful letters on the placards there, above the blackboard. Will you try?"

"Yes," promised Maryellen earnestly.

"Good!" said Mrs. Humphrey. "I've thought of a way that you can practice your handwriting and help Angela learn English at the same time." Mrs. Humphrey handed Maryellen a composition book. "Now, we both know that you are quite good at simple line drawings, like *cartoons*, don't we?" said Mrs. Humphrey.

Maryellen looked up sharply. Was Mrs. Humphrey still mad about the napkin cartoon?

But Mrs. Humphrey had a twinkle in her eye. "So, I was thinking that you could draw objects and write their names in English for Angela. Use your best handwriting, because you will be making a dictionary for Angela. You can begin with objects in the classroom."

"Yes, ma'am!" said Maryellen, feeling hopeful that she was forgiven. Mrs. Humphrey's plan sounded sort of fun. Well, except for the handwriting part.

For the rest of the week, the Lunch Bunch met every day after lunch in the classroom. Davy did not speak to Maryellen, and she did not speak to him. It made her sad, because by now, she had fully admitted to herself that Davy was right; she had gotten herself into trouble by drawing the cartoon. She also admitted to herself that she had gotten mad at Davy because she resented how he seemed to prefer being with Wayne. But even when he wasn't working on his multiplication tables with Mrs. Humphrey, Davy ignored her.

It was fun to work with Angela, though. The two girls went around the classroom, and Angela would point to an object, such as a window.

"Window," Maryellen would say in English.

"Window," Angela would repeat. Then Maryellen would sketch the window in the composition book and label it in painstaking cursive, and Angela would read the name aloud.

Pretty soon, Angela began to teach Maryellen the names of the objects in Italian. Maryellen loved the Italian words because they sounded so pretty, and they were fun to pronounce because they were tickly and delicious in her mouth. Window was *finestra*, desk was *banco*, and book was *libro*. She felt almost as if she were singing when she pronounced the Italian words that Angela taught her.

Mrs. Humphrey let Maryellen and Angela pull down the maps, and they taught each other the names of the seven continents, which were easy, and then the names of the big countries like India and China, and then the names of the tricky little countries that made up Europe. Maryellen could never stump Angela at any of the European countries. Even when she just sketched their outlines in the composition book, Angela could name them quick as a wink in both English and Italian.

When the girls ran out of objects in the classroom to name, Maryellen drew a person waving and saying hi. Then she waved to Angela and said, "Hi!"

"Hi!" repeated Angela. "In Italian, *ciao.*"

"*Chow,*" repeated Maryellen. "Thanks!"

"In Italian, *grazie,*" said Angela. She pointed to herself

and then to Maryellen and said, "In Italian, *amiche*. In English, I think, *friends*?"

"Oh, yes," said Maryellen. "Friends."

"Good!" said Angela, smiling her sunshiny smile.

After that, Maryellen taught Angela how to count to one hundred in English and Angela taught her how to count to *cento* in Italian. It was all unexpectedly fun. The only slightly worrisome thing was that her handwriting was not really improving. Angela never complained, but Maryellen could see that Angela had a hard time reading her cursive unless she went back to her old looped-and-linked style.

One day at lunchtime, Angela gave Maryellen a gift. It was a pretty plastic headband.

"Thanks, Angela!" said Maryellen. "It's pretty."

"Come," said Angela. She led Maryellen to the mirror by the classroom sink, and showed her how to use the headband to push her bangs back from her forehead and sort of hide them under the headband.

"Oh!" said Maryellen, delighted. "*Grazie*, Angela! *Grazie* very much!" Impulsively, she gave Angela a hug. "You're the first person who has actually come up with a helpful solution to the problem of my bangs!"

Angela smiled and hugged Maryellen back.

Another day Karen King was absent and Karen

Stohlman had ballet, so Maryellen walked her bike home with Angela, who lived near the school.

"Come in?" Angela asked.

Maryellen felt a little bit shy at first, but the minute they walked in the door, Angela's dog trotted up to welcome them and wagged his tail hello.

"Oh!" Maryellen exclaimed, kneeling to pet the dog. "What's his name?"

"Amerigo," said Angela.

"Oh, he's so cute!" said Maryellen. "My dog is named Scooter. Hi, Amerigo! I mean, *ciao*."

Angela's mother and father were at work, but her grandmother, whom Angela introduced as "Nonna," was in the kitchen making meatballs. Maryellen had never seen anyone making meatballs before. At her house, spaghetti and meatballs came straight out of the Chef Boy-Ar-Dee can. After the girls washed their hands, Nonna let them make meatballs, too.

"This is fun," said Maryellen, rolling the meat in her palms.

Nonna let Angela give a meatball to Amerigo, and he leapt up into the air to take it from her hand. Maryellen clapped and cheered. "I'd love to teach Scooter to do that," she said.

Maryellen was sorry when it was time to go. As she was leaving, Nonna said something to her in rapid Italian. Angela laughed and translated it. "Nonna says, next time, stay for dinner, have meatballs. But no jumping for meatballs like Amerigo!"

"*Grazie*, Nonna!" said Maryellen. She grinned and hopped a little hop, to show Nonna that she understood.

✳ ✳ ✳

At the end of that week, on Friday, Maryellen wore her poodle skirt to school again. Her bangs weren't bothering her anymore, thanks to the headband from Angela, and she did love the skirt, even if she was not the one-and-only girl who had one. Later that day, as she and the Karens were leaving school to walk home, Karen Stohlman said, "Next time you're going to wear your poodle skirt, call me first and I'll wear mine, too, so we can be twins."

Maryellen winced an invisible wince, but she said, "We can call Patty, too, and be the McDoogal Sisters on the playground again."

"Except you're never *on* the playground anymore," said Karen King. "Not after lunch, anyway. How long are you going to be in that Lunch Bunch? All year?"

"I don't know," said Maryellen. "I don't mind it, really. It's sort of fun. Like today, Angela pointed to my skirt and taught me to say *barboncino francese*, which is 'French poodle' in Italian. Don't you love that? Angela loves dogs. She has one—not a poodle, but a spaniel, named Amerigo—and he's adorable! Angela says—"

"Wait," Karen Stohlman interrupted sharply. "You've met Angela's dog?"

"Yes," said Maryellen, "when I went to her house."

"You went to Angela's house?" asked Karen King.

"Yes," said Maryellen, "but what I'm trying to say is that Angela told me that in Italian, dogs go *arf arf* instead of *woof woof* like they do in English. Isn't that funny?"

"Angela this and Angela that," said Karen Stohlman. Her voice sounded a little brittle. "You've met her dog and you've been to her house. You're getting awfully chummy with her."

"She's nice," said Maryellen. "You'd like her, too, if you got to know her."

The two Karens exchanged a look.

"I don't think so," said Karen King.

"What do you mean?" asked Maryellen.

"She's so different," said Karen Stohlman. "She has those long braids, and *pierced ears*. She stands out like a sore thumb."

"I think the ways she's different make her interesting," said Maryellen. "And what's wrong with standing out, anyway?"

Maryellen's Cold War
✴ *Chapter 9* ✴

ell," said Karen King, as if she were stating the obvious, "no one wants to stand out for a weird reason."

"Right," said Karen Stohlman. "I mean, do you like standing out and being different because of your polio?" Maryellen was speechless. It had never occurred to her before that her friends thought her polio made her *weird*. When she recovered from her shock and hurt, she said curtly, "I *did* want to stand out by being the only girl who had a poodle skirt, but you copied me."

Now Karen Stohlman was surprised. "I thought you would like it if we matched!" she exclaimed. "I didn't realize you were so set on being 'different' and 'interesting.' No wonder you like Angela so much; she's different all right. For Pete's sake, she's *Italian*."

"What's wrong with that?" asked Maryellen. "So what?"

"So, Italy was friends with Germany and Japan during the war," said Karen King. "The Italians were our *enemies*."

"But that was nearly ten years ago!" said Maryellen. "Remember how Mrs. Humphrey said that we're not enemies anymore? And anyway, Angela is just Angela. She's not responsible for Italy during the war. She wasn't even born yet."

"Fine," said Karen Stohlman with a shrug. "Go ahead and be disloyal if that's what you want to do."

"Disloyal?" said Maryellen.

"Yes," said Karen Stohlman tartly. "You seem to have forgotten, Ellie, but Italians killed my uncle during the war. I could never be friends with an Italian."

"But—" Maryellen sputtered.

Karen Stohlman talked over her. "And I could never be friends with anyone who was *friends* with an Italian."

"Me neither," said Karen King.

Maryellen felt as if she had been walloped in the stomach. Her two best friends—the only old friends she had *left* now without Davy—seemed to be saying that they would not be friends with her anymore if she was friends with Angela. For a moment, she felt flummoxed, unsure what to do. Then an unexpected feeling surprised her, a spurt of red-hot anger. *How dare they tell me how to act?*

"Well," Maryellen said quietly. "I can't be friends with anyone who couldn't be friends with someone who was friends with an Italian."

"Then I guess—I guess that means we can't be friends anymore?" squeaked Karen Stohlman.

"Yeah, I guess it does," said Maryellen.

"Come on, Karen," said Karen Stohlman. "Let's go."

Maryellen watched the two Karens walk away. She felt very lonely standing there on the sidewalk all by herself.

Then Karen Stohlman turned around and called, "And *I* don't have any Italian *bar-bon-chee-noh fran-cheh-seh* on *my* skirt. I have a regular American French poodle!"

The two Karens ran away, so Maryellen wasn't sure whether Karen Stohlman heard her shout, "You wouldn't have any poodle *at all* if you weren't a copycat!"

✳ ✳ ✳

Make new friends
But kee-eep thee-ee old;
One is silver
And the other's gold.

It was Wednesday, two weeks later, and Maryellen's Girl Scout troop was meeting in the cafeteria after school for the first time.

Maryellen sighed. She thought about how she and the two Karens had really looked forward to being Girl Scouts together, and how just before school began, they'd talked about earning badges, selling cookies, and going on overnight camping trips. Now, as they sang "Make New Friends," Maryellen couldn't even look the two Karens in the eye. The three of them sure had not "kept the old," friendship-wise. The Karens obviously didn't think that *she* was gold.

When Mrs. Nichols, their troop leader, told the girls to choose groups of four to share tents on their first overnight campout, which was to take place in October, the two Karens rushed to invite Patty Zender and Carol Turner to share the tent with them. That meant that Maryellen would have to be in the leftovers tent with Mrs. Nichols and her daughter Debbie, who wasn't even *in* the troop because she was too young.

Maryellen sighed again as she watched the Karens, Patty, and Carol giggling over the Kaper Chart. They had all signed up for KP, which was kitchen patrol and the most fun job on the Kaper Chart because you were in charge of finding sticks for roasting hot dogs and for toasting marshmallows for s'mores. Later, during the meeting, Maryellen saw that the Karens had used matching material to make their sit-upons. *And I just know they'll sit upon their sit-upons far away from me,* she thought.

It had been this way for two weeks now, ever since the conversation about Angela.

"It's as if the three of us are having our own little

private Cold War," Maryellen said to Carolyn that night as they got ready for bed. "We don't fight. They just snub Angela and me, and they try to get other kids to ignore us, too. Of course, Davy *already* acts as if I don't exist."

"It's like you're blacklisted," said Carolyn, stepping over Scooter, who was in the way as usual. "We learned about blacklisting in social studies. It means that you're excluded because people don't like something you did or something you believe."

"Exactly!" said Maryellen. "The Karens don't talk to Angela and me on the playground before school. They won't sit at a lunch table with Angela and me or walk home after school with us. It's like the Karens and I are on different sides of the Iron Curtain—as if we're enemies, when we used to be friends and allies."

"But do you *want* to be friends with them after what they said about Angela?" asked Carolyn.

"Oh, I don't know," said Maryellen. "They hurt my feelings, and I think they're completely wrong about Angela. The Karens would like her if they got to know her. Still," she admitted, "I miss Karen and Karen, just like I miss Davy. And remember what Joan said about how it's what you do *after* a mistake that matters? The Karens are making a mistake about Angela, but if they stopped their mistake, I'd be glad to be friends again."

"The Karens *have* been your friends for a long time," Carolyn agreed. "But you're doing the right thing, sticking up for Angela, even though it's hard. I know that's probably cold comfort."

"Well," sighed Maryellen, "maybe cold comfort is all you get in a Cold War."

The One and Only Maryellen

* Chapter 10 *

Fourth-graders!" said Mrs. Humphrey in her most listen-because-this-is-important voice. "Today is the day for our Geography Bee."

"Hurray!" the class cheered.

"Count off by twos," said Mrs. Humphrey. "Then all of you on Team One stand by the windows, and all of you on Team Two stand by the door."

In a jiffy, the class was divided into two teams. Maryellen was glad to see that Angela was on her team, Team Two. She was not as pleased to see that both Karens were also on Team Two, as was Davy.

Everyone was fizzy with excitement. Mrs. Humphrey clapped her hands. "I'd like your full attention, please," she said. "I will ask each one of you a geography question, and you must answer with the name of a country. If you answer incorrectly, you must take your seat. The team with the last person standing wins the Geography Bee."

"Can we help each other?" asked Patty Zender.

"Yes," said Mrs. Humphrey. "Even after you're sitting down, you can help a teammate. You may not tell your teammate the answer to any question, but you may act out a clue silently, as if you are playing the game charades. All right, let's begin," said Mrs. Humphrey. "Ready?"

"Yes!" cheered the class.

Maryellen's heart rose when she saw that her teacher had made maps just like the ones that she had made for Angela. Mrs. Humphrey had drawn the outlines of different countries but had not labeled them. Both Team One and Team Two had no trouble naming the continents like Africa and Australia. They did well naming the really big countries. But when Mrs. Humphrey started to ask for the names of the smaller countries in Europe and South America, both Ones and Twos started dropping like flies. Pretty soon, there were three students left on Team One: Joan Martin, Carol Turner, and Jimmy Lansing. The only Team Twos left were Karen Stohlman, Angela, and Maryellen. Then Maryellen said Argentina by mistake when she should have said Chile, so she had to sit down. Joan Martin missed Chile, too, but Angela got it. Jimmy Lansing missed on Bolivia, and so did Angela, but Carol Turner got it.

"All right, girls," said Mrs. Humphrey to Carol and Karen Stohlman. "It is down to the two of you." She held up the outline of a country. "Carol?" she asked.

"Spain?" said Carol.

"No, I'm sorry," said Mrs. Humphrey. She turned to Karen Stohlman. "Karen, if you can name this country correctly, your team, Team Two, will win the Geography Bee. If you cannot name it correctly, then you and Carol will keep going until one of you can name a country that the other one cannot name."

France, it's France! Maryellen wanted to shout out to Karen Stohlman, who was biting her lip and looking as if she wasn't sure of the correct answer. *Oh, how can I help her?* Maryellen fretted. Then she had a brilliant idea. She waved to Karen Stohlman to get her attention. Karen looked at her with an expression that was wary but desperate. Maryellen stood up and made the shape of a full skirt around herself. She made Patty Zender stand up, and pointed to the skirt of her dress. Then she pointed to the skirt of Karen's dress, too.

Karen looked befuddled.

Suddenly, Davy jumped up. He put his hands on his hips and swayed from side to side, singing silently. The class howled with laughter.

Karen looked even more at a loss than before.

Then Angela held her fists by her chin like paws and mimed barking like a dog.

"Skirts and singing and a dog?" said Karen, frowning. "Oh!" she exclaimed, rising up on her toes. "I get it! You mean our *poodle* skirts."

Angela nodded vigorously. Davy pretended to collapse in relief. Maryellen put one hand in front of the other, making the sign from charades that meant *the word that goes* **before.**

"Oh!" Karen exclaimed again. "They're French poodles. So—" She turned to Mrs. Humphrey. "That country must be France!"

"Yes!" said Mrs. Humphrey. "Team Two wins the Geography Bee. Congratulations!"

"HURRAY!" shouted the students on Team Two, jumping out of their seats. Karen Stohlman ran over and hugged Maryellen, who was already hugging Angela. The three of them bounced up and down with excitement, their arms all tangled up together.

Maryellen turned to say thank you to Davy, but Wayne was raising one of Davy's hands in the air, as if he had won a prizefight.

"I had no idea what Ellie and Davy were doing," said Karen Stohlman to Angela. "I never would have gotten France if it weren't for *your* clue. Thank you so much!"

"You mean *grazie*. That's how you say 'thank you' in Italian," Maryellen told Karen.

Karen hesitated, and then she grinned. "*Grazie*, Angela," she said. "And *grazie*, Ellie, too. Have you two been secretly studying geography?"

"No, but during Lunch Bunch we sometimes drew countries and wrote their names so that Angela could learn English and I could practice my handwriting," Maryellen explained.

"Well, you two seem to know the whole world!" said Karen King.

"Except for Chile and Bolivia," Angela said softly, and everyone laughed.

Then Karen Stohlman asked Maryellen and Angela shyly, "Want to sit together at lunch?"

"Okay," said Angela.

"Sure!" said Maryellen. Her heart flooded with forgiveness for the Karens. They hadn't come right out and said that they were sorry, but they were showing that they wanted to be her friend again—and Angela's friend, too.

"Angela, you've certainly learned a lot of English," said Karen King.

"Ellie taught me," said Angela. "She made it fun."

Maryellen grinned at Angela. Then she sighed and said, "I just wish my handwriting had improved as much as Angela's English. Mrs. Humphrey probably wishes that, too. I mean, that's the whole reason I was in the Lunch Bunch."

✳ ✳ ✳

Maryellen and Angela arrived early for Lunch Bunch that day. Neither Davy nor Mrs. Humphrey was there yet.

The girls decided to work on sentences.

"If something happened in the past, you use *was*," said Maryellen. "Like, 'The Geography Bee *was* fun.' But if the thing is happening now, you use *is*. Like, 'Angela *is* smart.' Now you try."

"Okay," said Angela. "How about: 'Davy is your friend.'"

Maryellen smiled sadly, and gently corrected Angela. "Davy *was* my friend," she said.

Angela shook her head firmly. "No," she said. "He *is*."

"Well," Maryellen sighed. "Let's just say that I hope that maybe someday, he *will be* my friend again. *Will be* is what you say when you're talking about the future, and the things you hope for."

When Mrs. Humphrey and Davy arrived, Mrs. Humphrey told Davy and Angela that they could go to recess, and then she called Maryellen to her desk.

"Maryellen," Mrs. Humphrey said, without any Care, Jo, no, or ohs!, as if she knew *exactly* who Maryellen was without any doubt now. "You and Angela have had a good time helping each other, haven't you?"

"Oh, yes!" said Maryellen. "We're good friends."

"Splendid," said Mrs. Humphrey. She hesitated, and then she went on, "It was kind of you to befriend Angela, and it was brave, too. I saw how your old friends disapproved. It's not easy to take a stand when you have to stand apart."

Maryellen nodded, pleased that her teacher had noticed what was going on. "I think we're all friends now, though."

"Good," said Mrs. Humphrey. She began leafing through the composition book with Maryellen's sketches and labels in it. "I know that you have been trying for quite some time to change your handwriting, and I appreciate your effort. But I think that loopy style you invented for yourself actually looks better than your attempts at normal cursive. Just keep doing what you're doing. You've got your own way of doing things, so I guess it makes sense that your handwriting is unique, too." She handed the book back to Maryellen with a smile.

"Thanks!" said Maryellen, hugging the book to her chest. *That's me,* she thought, *I'm the one-and-only Maryellen Larkin, and there's no one else quite like me in the whole wide world.*

✳ A Sneak Peek at ✳

Taking Off

If Maryellen's going to become famous, invent a flying machine, and get her sister's wedding off the ground, she'll need all the help she can get!

✳·✳·✳✳✳·✳·✳

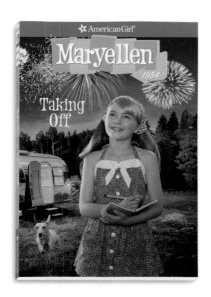

To celebrate the last day of school, Mom had cut up a chilled watermelon and set up the sprinkler in the front yard. Within minutes of getting home from school, Maryellen and Beverly were in their bathing suits running through the deliciously cold sprinkler water. Tom and Mikey danced from foot to foot just at the edge of the spray, and whenever the cold water rained down on them gently, they squealed with delight. Scooter, lying with his head on his paws, watched from the shade.

Suddenly Beverly said, with wide eyes, "Look!"

Dad was turning in to their driveway, and attached to his car was a huge silver trailer. Dad honked the car horn, and Mom, Joan, and Carolyn came dashing out of the house. As Dad got out of the car, Tom and Mikey ran to greet him.

"What on earth is *that*?" asked Mom when everyone had settled down a bit.

"Isn't it a beauty?" said Dad, patting the trailer with pride. "It's the 1955 Airstream. And it's all ours. We are going to see the U.S.A. this summer, kids, and this will be our home away from home."

"Hurray!" cheered everyone but Mom.

"We're taking a family road trip," said Dad. "It'll be a chance for some real togetherness. I thought we'd head out west, to Yellowstone National Park."

"I love the idea of heading west!" Maryellen gushed.
"Just about all my favorite TV shows are Westerns!"
Maryellen pictured herself riding a galloping horse across
the sagebrush prairie, sleeping out under the stars, and
crossing raging rivers like the pioneers. "Please can we
go to the Alamo, Dad?" she begged. "Davy Crockett was
there." Maryellen and the little kids sang the song from
the TV show:

> *Davy, Davy Crockett!*
> *King of the wild frontier!*

"Davy Crockett?" sniffed Joan. "I can't believe you
idolize a guy who walked around with a dead raccoon on
his head. I think all those Westerns you love so much are
ridiculous."

"They are not," Maryellen protested. "You—"

But Mom held up both hands to stop them. She looked
harried. "I've got Joan and Jerry's wedding breathing
down my neck," she said to Dad. "There's still so much to
do. The painters are coming next week to get the house
ready for the wedding. Who'll supervise them—Scooter?"

"Scooter will come with us," said Dad. "And don't you
think you'd like a vacation from all the wedding worries?"

"I'm not sure that it *will* be a vacation for *me*," said Mom. "Staying in a trailer in a campground just means that I'll be doing all my usual work of cooking and laundering and cleaning under tougher-than-usual conditions."

Everyone was quiet, thinking about what Mom had said. Maryellen could see that Mom had several valid points.

"Mom," said Maryellen, "what if Grandmom and Grandpop came here? That way, we could see them, and they could take care of the house while we're gone and be sure the painters are doing everything right. They could stay for a while after our trip, too, so that we could have a nice long visit together."

Mom considered her suggestion. "That might work," she said, nodding and smiling a little.

"That's a great idea, Ellie," said Dad, beaming.

Maryellen turned eagerly to Mom. "And I'll take care of Scooter on the trip, I promise." Truthfully, she didn't think that being responsible for lazy, sleepy Scooter would be very hard. She added, "And I'll help with other chores, too."

"I'll help, too," said Carolyn. "It'll be fun to keep the Airstream neat and tidy and shipshape!"

"You needn't worry about cooking much, sweetheart,"

said Dad to Mom. "We'll mostly be eating the fish I catch. I'll fry 'em up over a campfire."

"We'll have s'mores for dessert," added Maryellen. "And you can teach Joan to cook in the little Airstream kitchen, and then she can make dinner for us, too."

"All right," said Mom. She shrugged in surrender. "Westward ho, I guess."

Inside Maryellen's World

The 1950s were years of peace, prosperity, promise, and exuberant growth in the United States. World War Two was over, and the economy was booming. Families were booming, too, and big families like Maryellen's were not unusual. In fact, so many children were born during this era that it became known as the *baby boom*. Millions of young families and retired people moved to the

During the baby boom, maternity wards were filled to bursting with new arrivals!

New homes for growing families sprang up in the suburbs. Houses could be built more quickly if they were all the same, as in Maryellen's neighborhood.

Advertisers encouraged people who couldn't move to the sunbelt to vacation there instead.

Sun Belt—southern states like Florida that had much warmer weather than the *Snow Belt* states up north.

Jobs were plentiful as industries switched from making wartime products to making goods for families to buy. Advertisers and companies encouraged Americans to "keep up with the Joneses" by having homes, cars, and appliances that were as nice as their neighbors', so that people would buy lots of new products. Homeowners like the Larkins were proud of their new appliances and modern conveniences. Neighbors would often gather to admire big new purchases such as

Chevy puts the <u>purr</u> in performance!

Completely New! General Electric's "Push-button" Range...with Two Complete Ovens!

GENERAL ⓖ ELECTRIC

Advertisements for household goods boasted about their great new technology and convenience.

televisions and cars! In Maryellen's time, television shows were in black and white, and networks broadcast only a few hours each day. Whole families would gather to watch popular comedies such as *I Love Lucy,* Westerns such as *The Lone Ranger,* and variety shows such as *The Ed Sullivan Show.* Only a few channels were available, so most people watched the same news shows, programs, and advertisements.

This gave newscasters and advertisers great power to shape the public's view of life, yet TV didn't always depict life accurately. For example, women were usually shown as homemakers even though millions of women worked outside the home. And except for a few Native Americans in Westerns, almost everyone on TV was white. Americans whose lives didn't match the television version of life sometimes felt ignored or as if they didn't belong.

Even the government encouraged *conformity,* or agreement and sameness. Although the United States was not officially at war with the Soviet Union, the two countries were deeply suspicious of each other and had an unfriendly relationship known as the *Cold War.* People who admired the Soviet Union's communist form of government were known as *Reds.* People who were suspected of being "Red," or of having friendly feelings toward the Soviet Union, could be *blacklisted,* which meant they might be fired from their jobs and questioned by the government. When this happened, sometimes their former friends shunned them, too. Maryellen feels this pressure to conform when she makes friends with Angela, the Italian girl.

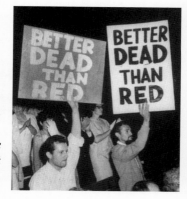

Many Americans were hostile to anyone who admired communism or communist countries like the Soviet Union.

The Soviet Union (U.S.S.R.) covered a large part of Europe.
It was led by Russia and included many smaller countries.

Still, many Americans look back on the 1950s as fun and happy years full of optimism. Middle-class children like Maryellen had comfortable lives, with more opportunities for education and entertainment than any previous generation of children. Television encouraged conformity,

*Some people wanted American Communists to be **registered**, or a list kept of their names, to make it easier to blacklist them. This bumper sticker promotes that idea. Political bumper stickers first appeared in the 1950s.*

but it also broadened people's views by showing how other people lived and by bringing the whole world right into peoples' living rooms. Just like Maryellen, many Americans felt energized, inspired, and challenged to find a balance between being what people wanted or expected them to be and being unique or "one and only."

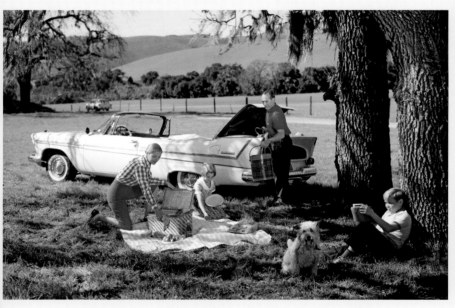

A middle-class family in the 1950s enjoying a Sunday drive in their convertible, followed by a picnic in the country